LA FOLIE
BAUDELAIRE

LA FOLIE
BAUDELAIRE

·

ROBERTO CALASSO

TRANSLATED FROM THE ITALIAN
BY ALASTAIR McEWEN

FARRAR, STRAUS AND GIROUX
NEW YORK

Farrar, Straus and Giroux
18 West 18th Street, New York 10011

Distributed in Canada by D&M Publishers, Inc.
Printed in the United States of America
Originally published in 2008 by Adelphi Edizioni, Italy
Published in the United States by Farrar, Straus and Giroux
First American edition, 2012

Library of Congress Cataloging-in-Publication Data
Calasso, Roberto.
    [Folie Baudelaire. English]
    La folie Baudelaire / Roberto Calasso ; translated from the Italian by
Alastair McEwen. — 1st American ed.
        p.   cm.
    Includes bibliographical references and index.
    ISBN 978-0-374-18334-9 (alk. paper)
    1. Baudelaire, Charles, 1821–1867—Criticism and interpretation.
2. Art, French—19th century.   3. Art criticism—France—History—
19th century.   4. Aesthetics, Modern—19th century.   5. Paris (France)—
Intellectual life—19th century.   I. McEwen, Alastair.   II. Title.

PQ2191.Z5 C23613 2012
841'.8—dc23
                                                                    2011047013

Designed by Jonathan D. Lippincott

www.fsgbooks.com

1   3   5   7   9   10   8   6   4   2

"I ask every thinking man to show me what remains of life."

—Charles Baudelaire

CONTENTS

I

THE NATURAL
OBSCURITY OF THINGS

Baudelaire used to suggest to his mother, Caroline, that they meet surreptitiously at the Louvre: "There isn't a place in Paris where you can have a better chat; it's heated, you can wait for someone without getting bored, and what's more it's the most respectable meeting place for a woman." The fear of the cold, the terror of boredom, the mother treated like a lover, surreptitiousness and decency conjoined in the place of art: only Baudelaire could combine these elements almost without noticing, as if it were fully natural. It is an irresistible invitation, extended to anyone who reads it. And anyone can respond to it by roaming through Baudelaire as in one of the Salons he wrote about—or even in a Universal Exposition: finding all kinds of things, the memorable and the ephemeral, the sublime and trash; and moving constantly from one room to another. But then the unifying fluid was the impure air of the time. Now it is an opiate cloud, in which to conceal and fortify oneself before going back into the open, in the vast, lethal, and teeming expanses of the twenty-first century.

"All that is not immediate is nothing" (as Cioran once said). While making no concessions to the cult of the untamed expression, like very few others, Baudelaire had the gift of immediacy, the capacity to let words instantly run through the mental circulation of those who encounter them and in whom they remain, sometimes in a latent state, until one day they ring out intact, painful, and enchanted. "In a low voice, now he converses with each of us," wrote Gide in his introduction to *Les Fleurs du mal* of 1917. A phrase that must have struck Walter Benjamin, for we find it isolated in the material for his book on the *passages*. There is something in Baudelaire (as there is in Nietzsche) so intimate as to conceal itself in the forest that is the psyche of any individual, without emerging from it again. It is a voice "muffled like the sound of carriages in the night [heard] from the quiet of *boudoirs*," says Maurice Barrès, following the words of a concealed prompter, who is Baudelaire himself: "You hear nothing else but the sound of some belated and decrepit hackney cab." It is a tone that surprises "like a word said in one's ear when one is not expecting it," according to Jacques Rivière. In the years around the First World War, that word seemed to have become an indispensable guest. It tolled in a feverish brain, as Proust wrote in his essay on Baudelaire, reeling off quotations from memory as if they were nursery rhymes.

For those who are enveloped in and almost numbed by desolation and weariness, it's hard to do better than to open a page of Baudelaire. Prose, poetry, prose poems, letters, fragments: it's all fine. But, if possible, prose, and preferably his writings on painters. Sometimes they are painters unknown today, of whom all that remains is the name and the few words Baudelaire spent on them. We observe him in his *flânerie*, mingling with a teeming crowd—and we get the impression that a new nervous system is being superimposed over our own, subjecting it to frequent, minimal shocks and spasms. In this way, a lethargic and barren sensorium is forced to reawaken.

There is a *Baudelaire wave* that rolls across all things. It originated before him and swept over all obstacles. Between the crests and the troughs of that wave we recognize Chateaubriand, Stendhal, Ingres, Delacroix, Sainte-Beuve, Nietzsche, Flaubert, Manet, Degas, Rimbaud, Lautréamont, Mallarmé, Laforgue, Proust, and others, as if that wave swept over them and submerged them for a few moments. Or as if they ran into it. Surges that meet, diverge, and go their separate ways. Eddies, sudden whirlpools. Then the flow resumes. The wave rolls on, always heading for the "depths of the Unknown" from which it came.

We experience a feeling of gratitude and exultation on reading these lines of Baudelaire on Millet: "Style sits poorly with him. His country folk are pedants who have too high an opinion of themselves. They show a kind of bleak and deadly brutishness that makes me feel like hating them. Whether they are harvesting or sowing, grazing cattle or shearing animals, they always look as if they're saying: 'But it is us, the poor have-nots of this world, who make it fruitful! We are carrying out a mission, we practice a priesthood!' "

Visitors moved through the Salons with a booklet that showed the subject of the individual paintings. Judging a painting consisted in assessing the appropriateness of the visual representation in relation to the topic illustrated, which was generally historical (or mythological). Otherwise, landscapes, portraits, or genre paintings. The nude made its way in through the exploitation of any opportunity offered by mythological, historical, or biblical episodes (such as Chassériau's Esther, the regal archetype of all pinups). Or, alternatively, it was shielded by the label of the Orientalist genre. One day Baudelaire observed two soldiers who were visiting the Salon. They were in "puzzled contemplation of a view of a kitchen: 'So where's Napoleon?' said one (the catalog contained an error, and the kitchen was listed under the number that ought to have corresponded to a famous battle). 'Idiot!' said the other, 'can't you see that they're making the soup for his return?' And off they went, pleased with the painter and pleased with themselves."

Diderot's *Salons* mark the beginning of all roving, capricious, intolerant, and temperamental criticism, which refers to paintings as if they were so many persons. Wandering curiously among landscapes and figures, this kind of criticism uses the images as springboards and pretexts for exercises in metamorphosis to which it gives itself over with the same readiness as it later rids itself of them. *To write a Salon* can also be the equivalent of letting a sequence of images run before the eyes, images that represent, in orderly ranks, the most disparate moments in life: from the inaccessible muteness of the still life to solemn biblical episodes and the ceremonial pomp of History. For a man such as Diderot, with a mercurial mind open to almost everything, the Salon became the most suitable occasion on which to reveal that turbulent and perennially active workshop whose premises were in his head.

Properly speaking, Diderot did not have *one* way of thinking, but the capacity to make thought gush forth. It sufficed to give him one sentence, one question. From there, if he yielded to his fascinating automatism, Diderot could arrive anywhere. And discover many things on the way. But he did not stop. He was almost unaware of what he was discovering, because it was only a transition, one link among many. Diderot was the opposite of Kant, who had to justify every phrase. For Diderot every sentence was groundless per se, but acceptable if it spurred him to go farther. His ideal was perpetual motion, a constant vibration that did not admit of remembering the point of departure and left it to chance to decide where to stop. This is why Diderot said of the *Salons*: "None of my works resemble me so much." Because the *Salons* are pure movement: not only do you pass ceaselessly from one painting to the next, but you also enter the paintings, come out of them—and sometimes you get lost in them: "A rather good way to describe the paintings, especially rural landscapes, is to enter the scene from the right or the left and, as you follow the lower border, to describe the objects as they gradually present themselves." Diderot's stroll through the Salon, with his lopsided, discontinuous, turbulent gait, subject to constant distractions, digressions, and asides, heralds the very pace that was to be adopted not just by thought, but by the experience in general. By now, faced with the world, one cannot say more than this: "I have given the impression the time to arrive and to enter."

The first time Baudelaire saw his name (then Baudelaire-Dufaÿs) on the cover of a slim volume—the *Salon of 1845*—he immediately hoped that someone would notice the affinity between those pages and Diderot. He sent this note to Champfleury: "If you wish to write a *light* article, please do so, just don't hurt me too much.

"But *if you wish to please me*, write a few serious lines, and TALK of *Diderot's Salons*.

"The TWO THINGS together *would perhaps be better.*"

Champfleury respected his friend's wishes, and the *Corsaire-Satan* of a few days later ran an unsigned article that read, "M. Baudelaire-Dufaÿs is bold as Diderot, but without the paradox."

What was it about Diderot that attracted Baudelaire? Certainly not "the cult of Nature," the "great religion" that united Diderot and d'Holbach but was wholly alien to Baudelaire. Rather, the attraction was due to a certain pace of thought, a certain capacity for psychical oscillation, where—as Baudelaire wrote of one of Diderot's theatrical characters—"sensibility is united with irony and the most bizarre cynicism." And then: Should this perhaps be ascribed to the fateful coincidence that Diderot was one of the first Frenchmen to use the word *spleen*? In a letter to Sophie Volland dated October 28, 1760, he wrote, "Don't you know what *spline* or the English vapors is? I didn't know either." But his Scottish friend Hoop had explained that new scourge to him.

In all his aspects, Diderot was congenial ground for Baudelaire, who in the end could not refrain from showing his hand in a paragraph from the *Salon of 1846*: "I recommend those who must have been occasionally scandalized by my pious fits of wrath to read Diderot's *Salons*. In the midst of other examples of the right kind of charity, they will find therein that the great philosopher, with regard to a painter who had been recommended to him because he had a family to support, said that it was necessary either to do away with the paintings or the family." Attempts to find the corresponding passage in Diderot's *Salons* have proved vain. But this was certainly what Baudelaire wished that Diderot had written.

In the chain of insolence, effrontery, and immediacy that connects Diderot's *Salons* to those of Baudelaire there is an intermediate link: Stendhal's *Histoire de la peinture en Italie*. Printed in 1817 for an almost nonexistent public, this book must have struck the young Baudelaire as a precious source of encouragement. Not so much for the understanding of the painters, which was never Stendhal's forte, but for his impertinent, cursory, breezy manner, like that of someone prepared to do anything except get bored as he writes. Stendhal had plundered Lanzi to spare himself certain laborious tasks (descriptions, dates, details) in writing the book. For his part, Baudelaire appropriated two passages from Stendhal's book, out of devotion, according to the rule whereby the true writer does not borrow but steals. And he did this in the most delicate part of his *Salon of 1846*, the point where he talks about Ingres. The entire history of literature—a secret history that no one will ever be able to write except in part, because authors are too skilful at obscuring themselves—can be seen as a sinuous garland of plagiarism. By this I do not mean functional plagiarism, due to haste and laziness, such as Stendhal's plundering of Lanzi; but the other kind, based on admiration and a process of physiological assimilation that is one of the best protected mysteries of literature. The two passages that Baudelaire took from Stendhal are perfectly in tune with his prose and come at a crucial point of his argument. Writing, like eros, is what makes the bulkheads of the ego sway and become porous. And every style is formed by successive campaigns— with squads of raiders or entire armies—in the territory of others. Anyone wishing to give an example of the unmistakable timbre of Baudelaire the critic might choose some of the lines that originally belonged to Stendhal: "M. Ingres draws admirably, and he draws swiftly. In his sketches he naturally touches the ideal; his drawing, often not very intense, contains few strokes; but each one depicts an important outline. Compare them to the drawings of all these workmen of painting, often his pupils: first of all they render the details, and this is why they enchant the common man, whose eye—in all genres—opens only for that which is small."

Then there is another case: *"the Beautiful is none other than the promise of happiness."* Baudelaire must have set great store by these words, which are a variation on Stendhal, for he quoted them three times in his writings. He had found them in *De l'amour,* a book that until then had circulated among only a small number of the happy few. Stendhal was not referring to art, but to female beauty. That he wrote his celebrated definition of beauty without introducing metaphysical implications can be deduced from one of his notes in *Rome, Naples et Florence.* It is five in the morning and, still enchanted, Stendhal leaves a ball held by the storekeepers' association of Milan. He notes, "In all my life I have never seen an assembly of such beautiful women; their beauty makes you lower your eyes. For a Frenchman, it has a noble and somber character that makes one think of the happiness of the passions far more than the passing pleasures of lively and gay gallantry. Beauty is never, it seems to me, any more than a *promise of happiness."* One immediately notices Stendhal's childish brio, his *presto.* On the basis of his words, Baudelaire was to follow another path. Stendhal thinks of life—and contents himself with that. Baudelaire cannot resist grafting a thought onto this, making a decisive shift: he redirects Stendhal's words toward art, and instead of "beauty," he talks of the "Beautiful." Now it is no longer a matter of female beauty, but a Platonic category. And this marks the collision with *happiness,* which aesthetic speculation—even in Kant—had not yet managed to link to the Beautiful. Not only this, but with this slight and overwhelming twist in the discourse, the "promise" develops an eschatological aura. Whatever can be the nature of the happiness heralded by the Beautiful? Certainly not that happiness petulantly celebrated during the Enlightenment. Constitutionally, Baudelaire never felt tempted to follow that path. But what other happiness can we be dealing with? It is as if now that *promesse du bonheur* refers to a perfect life. To something that goes beyond aesthetics and absorbs it into the life itself. In Baudelaire far more than Stendhal, this is the utopian light in which the *promesse du bonheur* was to reemerge almost a century later: in Adorno's *Minima moralia*.

With the advent of photography—when the world was about to reproduce itself an indeterminate number of times more than usual—waiting to greet it was a *concupiscentia oculorum* in which some persons identified themselves with the immediate complicity of the perverse. "This sin is our sin," Gautier pointed out. And Baudelaire's voice blended with his: "very young indeed, my eyes brimming with painted or etched images had never been sated, and I believe worlds could end, *impavidum ferient*, before I become an iconoclast." Instead, a small tribe of iconolaters had come into being, who explored the meanders of the great cities, immersing themselves in the "delights of chaos and immensity," overflowing with simulacra.

The greediness of the eye, nourished by the countless art objects sifted and scrutinized, was a potent stimulus for Baudelaire's prose. He trained his pen to "struggle against plastic representations." And this was a *hypnerotomachia*, a "struggle of love in dream," rather than a war. Baudelaire was not enthusiastic about inventing from scratch. He always needed to work on preexisting material, some phantasm glimpsed in a gallery or a book or on the streets, as if writing were above all a task involving the transposition of forms from one register to another. This led to the birth of some of his perfect turns of phrase, which allow themselves to be contemplated at length, and soon have you forgetting that they could well be the description of a watercolor: "At a brisk trot, the carriage bears away, along an avenue zebraed with light and shade, beauties lying back as if in a small boat, indolent, vaguely listening to the compliments that fall into their ears and giving themselves over idly to the breeze of the ride." Those who do not participate to some extent in Baudelaire's unique devotion to images will grasp very little of him. If one of his confessions is to be understood literally, and in all its consequences, it is the one he makes in *My Heart Laid Bare*: "To glorify the cult of images (my great, my only, my earliest passion)."

The writing of a book gets under way when the writer discovers that he is magnetized in a certain direction, toward a certain arc of the circumference, which is sometimes minimal, delimitable within a few degrees. Then everything he comes across—even a poster or a sign or a newspaper headline or words heard by chance in a café or in a dream—is deposited in a protected area like material waiting to be elaborated. This was the effect of the Salons on Baudelaire. Every time, they were a pretext for making the unmistakable chords of his prose in formation ring out—and of his poetry, too. Let's observe him as he moves around: Baudelaire is reviewing the works at the Salon of 1859 and he has come to the paintings of military subjects. A vast and depressing zone. Because "this kind of painting, if we think it over well, demands falsity or insignificance." But the reporter has his duty and he proceeds, finding something to admire, too: a painting by Tabar where the uniforms stand out like poppies against "an immense verdant ocean." It is a scene from the Crimean War.

Here, suddenly, like a skittish horse, Baudelaire shies from his obligatory trail and launches into a few definitive lines on the imaginative process: "because imagination is all the more dangerous the more it is easy and open; dangerous as prose poetry, as the novel, it resembles the love inspired by a prostitute and falls speedily into puerility or baseness; dangerous as all absolute freedom. But the imagination is as vast as the universe multiplied by all the thinking beings who inhabit it. It is the first come among all things, interpreted by the first to come; and, if this last has not the soul that sheds a magical and supernatural light on the natural obscurity of things, then the imagination is a horribly useless thing; it is the first come contaminated by the first to come. Here, therefore there is no longer analogy, if not by chance; but on the contrary murkiness and contrast, a multicolored field through the absence of a regular culture." These are lines that, suddenly, hurtle off very far away. They are a blend of autobiography, literary history, and metaphysics, the like of which no one had dared to write until then. And that plausibly no one had noticed in the chronicle of a Salon similar to the many that came before it, and would follow it later. But it is precisely here, as with Tabar's poppy uniforms, that "a magical and supernatural light" stands out against "the natural obscurity of things." In these last words there rings out one of those chords that *are* Baudelaire. It would be vain to seek them in Hugo or Gautier. The "natural obscurity of things" is the commonest perception, the one that everybody knows. But we had to wait for Baudelaire before it was named. And Baudelaire had to conceal those words in a comment on a painting among the many others portraying military subjects. Something similar happens in the way Baudelaire allows himself to be perceived. Often through scraps of verses, fragments of phrases dispersed in the prose. But this suffices. Baudelaire acts like Chopin (the first to bring the two names together was Gide, in a note to an article of 1910). He penetrates parts where others cannot reach, like an irrepressible whisper, because the source of the sound is indefinite and too close. Chopin and Baudelaire are recognizable above all for the timbre, which can appear in flurries from a piano hidden behind half-open shutters or detach itself from the dust of memory. And in any case, it wounds.

What did Baudelaire mean when he wrote, "Here therefore there is no longer analogy, if not by chance"? It is a blunt, decisive allusion. The implication? If there is no analogy, there is no thought, no way to tackle, to elaborate, the "natural obscurity of things." *Analogy*—this word held in disrepute by the philosophers of the Enlightenment for its lack of rigor and reliability—ensconced, like metaphor, in the vast territory of that which is improper, now revealed itself to be, for Baudelaire, the only key with which to access that knowledge "which sheds a magical and supernatural light on the natural obscurity of things." And are there perhaps other forms of knowledge? Certainly, but not the sort to attract Baudelaire. For him analogy was a science. Perhaps even the supreme science, if the imagination is the "queen of faculties." In fact, as Baudelaire was to explain in a memorable letter to Alphonse Toussenel, "the *imagination* is the most *scientific* of the faculties, because it is the only one to understand the *universal analogy*, or that which a mystical religion calls *correspondence.*" Hence the sense of unease, repulsion, and rejection when someone uses a *false analogy.* It's like witnessing a calculation based on an evident error, which affects everything but is tolerated because most people think that analogy is something ornamental and not binding. In those lines of an occasional letter to an anti-Semitic Fourierist and votary of a fantastic zoology Baudelaire had taken the chance to call up his Muse, whose name was Analogy.

How did *analogy* emerge in Baudelaire? It was a concept he could have found in Ficino or Bruno, in Paracelsus or Böhme, in Kircher or Fludd. Or even, in more recent years, in Baader or Goethe. But Baudelaire could encounter it, initially, from even closer, in someone who swung between visionary inspiration and foolishness: Fourier. The works of this incurable buttonholer are full of references to the *universal analogy,* seen as an answer to every question. It is pointless to probe its speculative foundations, always inconsistent in Fourier. Baudelaire, however, did once mention, en passant but confidently, the reasons for this fleeting youthful inclination of his: "One day Fourier came, too pompously, to reveal the mysteries of *analogy* to us. I do not deny the value of some of his meticulous discoveries, even though I think that his mind was too much a lover of material exactitude not to make mistakes and suddenly attain the moral certainty of perception." And behind Fourier we immediately glimpse the shadow of another eccentric, whose affinity with Baudelaire was far greater: Swedenborg. "On the other hand, Swedenborg, who possessed a far greater soul, had already taught us that *the sky is a very big man*; that everything, form, movement, number, color, scent, be it in the *spiritual* or the *natural* sphere, is meaningful, reciprocal, converted, and *corresponding.*" This last is a revealing word. *Analogy* and *correspondences* are, for Baudelaire, equivalent terms. ("Fourier and Swedenborg, one with his *analogies*, the other with his *correspondences*, are embodied in the vegetable and the animal that your gaze falls upon and, instead of teaching through the voice, they indoctrinate you with form and color.") Writing about Wagner, Baudelaire has recourse to a singular expedient. To reinforce his argument—and as if appealing to an anonymous authority—he quotes the first two quatrains of the sonnet "Correspondances," which stands on the threshold of *Les Fleurs du mal* as the psychopomp of the place. And the phrase that precedes and introduces those verses yet again states the way in which correspondences and analogy are indis-

solubly interwoven: "since things are always expressed through reciprocal analogy, starting from the day in which God proffered the world as
a complex and indivisible totality."

In other periods—and for the last time in the pansophist seven-
teenth century—similar axioms were used as the basis for the construction of Mesopotamian architectures with rotating tables of *signaturae*
meant to link up in a meticulous accounting all the strata of the cosmos. But in Baudelaire's day? With harassing creditors and *Le Siècle*
daily proclaiming the splendors of progress, this "dark lamp" that "casts
shadows on all the objects of knowledge"? In Baudelaire's time, thinkers
were obliged to commit an "infinite sin"—that which according to
Hölderlin had its origin in Oedipus: to *interpret infinitely*, without a *primum*
and without an end, in unceasing, sudden, shattered, and recursive motion. The real *modernity* that takes shape in Baudelaire is this hunt for
images, without beginning or end, goaded by the "demon of analogy."
If correspondences are to be collocated in their correct *locus* we need a
canon to refer to. But already in Baudelaire's day it was obvious that
every canon had foundered. And subsequently this condition would become normality itself. There was no longer any orthodoxy of interpretation, which did exist in ancient China, where *etiquette* made it possible
to transmit, in the due forms, a preexisting thought, based on a web of
correspondences. By then, while certain canons sought to establish themselves, it was obligatory to get rid of them, because they were definitely
insufficient (hence Baudelaire's intolerance of any kind of system). So
there was nothing else to do but proceed through a multiplicity of levels,
signs, images, without any guarantee either of the starting point, always
arbitrary, or the end point, which, in the absence of a canon, one was
never sure had been reached. This was going to become the condition
of anyone alive—at least from Hölderlin's time onward. And perhaps
never as in Baudelaire, in the graphs of his nervous reactions, was that
situation so manifest. Intensifying, sharpening. This may also help to
explain Baudelaire's intact totemic power in the face of that which appears, of that which is new, elusive. One hundred and fifty years have
not sufficed to weaken that power. And no other writer of the time is still
able to exercise it. It is not something that concerns the power or the
perfection of form. It concerns sensibility, in the precise sense that Baudelaire gave to the word. ("Hold no one's sensibility in contempt. The

sensibility of each person is his genius.") Once the straitjacket that is any system had been slipped off, what would have happened? Baudelaire described this, beginning in an ironical vein and ending with the maximum gravity: "Condemned constantly to the humiliation of a new conversion, I have made a great decision. To flee from the horror of these philosophical apostasies, I have proudly resigned myself to modesty: I have contented myself with feeling; I have returned to seek shelter in impeccable naivety." Seldom had Baudelaire revealed so much about himself. "I have contented myself with feeling": it could be his motto— and also the explanation for that sense of indubitableness that often issues from his words.

When Baudelaire entered the landscape of French poetry, the cardinal points were called Hugo, Lamartine, Musset, and Vigny. All positions could be defined in relation to them. Wherever one looked, the space was already occupied, as Sainte-Beuve observed. But only horizontally. Baudelaire opted for the vertical. It was necessary to inject a drop of metaphysics into the language, something that had been missing until then. And Baudelaire secreted this within himself, well before encountering Poe and Joseph de Maistre, who taught him to think, as he himself acknowledged. Like John Donne, Baudelaire was a naturally metaphysical poet. Not because he frequented philosophers very much (all in all, he knew little about them). Nor because he was inclined to construct bold speculations, if not in fits and starts, which burned up in a few lines, and mostly in journalistic writings. Baudelaire possessed something that was lacking in his Parisian contemporaries—and was lacking even in Chateaubriand: a metaphysical antenna. When Nietzsche wrote that Baudelaire was "already wholly German, apart from a certain hypererotic morbidity, which smacks of Paris," this is what he meant. The others around him might also possess prodigious inventive gifts, such as Hugo. But Baudelaire had the stunning capacity to perceive that which is. Like John Donne, whatever he wrote about he made peal out in his verse, and in his prose, a vibration that overran every corner—and soon vanished. Prior to all thought, what is metaphysical in Baudelaire is the sensation, the pure comprehension of the moment, the congenital tendency to surprise himself in certain occasions in which life, as if unrolling a long carpet, reveals the indefinite profundity of its plans: "I have contented myself with feeling"—words of false modesty that say everything about the immensity of his gamble.

Universal analogy: it suffices to utter this formula to call up, like some vast submerged architecture, the esotericism of Europe starting from the early fifteenth century. The forms it assumed were numerous—from the mild Platonism of Ficino to Bruno's harsh Egyptian version, from Fludd's Mosaic-naturalistic theosophy to Böhme's Teutonic-cosmic variety, down to Swedenborg and Louis-Claude de Saint-Martin. The doctrines were disparate, sometimes opposed. But none of the pansophists ever cast any doubt on the principle of the universal analogy. Thought itself was offered as a variation on the "immense keyboard of *correspondences*." This implied a response, an attraction, and a repulsion among the dispersed elements of manifestation. No more was needed to inoculate the existent with the ambrosia, and the poison, of meaning.

Baudelaire therefore was only one of the last links in a long chain. His peculiarity lay in the addition of an element that until then had been absent or latent or in any case never claimed as such: literature. This ensures that ten lines of Baudelaire are more effective and memorable than one hundred pages of Swedenborg. That notwithstanding, the meanings of those ten lines and of those one hundred pages can coincide—even though Baudelaire, thanks to the passport of literature, permitted himself digressions and meanderings that the other esotericists had forbidden themselves, certainly to their detriment.

On analogy, we find the decisive word—calm, mordant, decisive—in Goethe: "Every existent is an analogon of the entire existent; and so that which exists always appears to us isolated and interwoven at one and the same time. If one follows analogy too closely, everything coincides in the identical: if one avoids it, all is dispersed in the infinite. In both cases contemplation stagnates, in the one case because it is too lively, in the other because it has been killed." As often happens in Goethe, the surprise comes from a single flash, at the end. In his carefully thought-out sentence, the shock is conveyed by the last word: *getötet*, "killed." How do you kill contemplation? And for Goethe this is tantamount to saying: How do you kill life itself? By *avoiding analogy*. Those who avoid analogy can mock the excessive liveliness—febrile, almost delirious—of those who instead abandon themselves totally to it. Everyone knows that analogy is not obligatory. You can simply ignore it. And this act of omission has a boundless power, like a blow delivered by a murderer.

Baudelaire was a lover of *depth*, understood in the strictly spatial sense. He waited, like some marvel always ready to flare into being, for certain moments in which space eluded its customary flatness and began to reveal itself in a potentially inexhaustible succession of stage wings. Then things—every single negligible object—suddenly took on an unexpected significance. In those moments, he wrote, "the exterior world offers itself with a powerful emphasis, a clearness of outline, a wealth of exquisite colors." As if to say that thought was possible only when the world presented itself in this way. These were also "the moments of existence in which time and extension are more profound, and the sentiment of existence has grown enormously." So, in Western terms, Baudelaire was getting close to describing what for Vedic seers, and later for Buddha, was *bodhi*, the "awakening." And in an equally literal Western spirit, he made this coincide with physiological awakening, with the moment in which "the eyelids have just been unburdened of the sleep that sealed them." This is what drugs are for: opium makes space deep ("Space is deepened by opium"), while hashish "spreads over the whole of life like a magic varnish" (perhaps similar to Vauvenargues's comment "clarity is the *vernis des maîtres*"?). Yet Baudelaire also pointed out that drugs are only a surrogate for physiology, since "every man carries within himself the right dose of natural opium, which he unceasingly secretes and renews."

But why should the opening up of the depths of space be such a precious phenomenon for thought? Baudelaire reveals this in passing: "the depth of space, an allegory of the depth of time." An illuminating example of the use of analogy. Only when space opens up in a succession of planes where single figures stand out with an inebriating and almost painful sharpness, only then does thought manage to seize, albeit fleetingly, something of that which is its first and last object: time, Father Time who eludes and watches over all things. Allegory is the artifice that serves to effect this delicate transition. And it is this that may reveal to us what Baudelaire was talking about when he spoke of "the deep of years." An expression at once evident and mysterious, it also appears in decisive passages in his work. It presupposed the existence—also perhaps allegorical—of a character who, faced with the "monstrous increase of time and space," was able to contemplate it "without sadness and without fear." Of this character one might have said, "He looks with a certain melancholy delight through the deep of years."

In days in which his major concern was to redeem from the pawn-shop some items of clothing that had been resold in the meantime—except for the garment he considered "the most indispensable, a pair of pants"—Baudelaire received from Fernand Desnoyers an invitation to send him "some verses on *Nature*" for a slim volume he was producing. Baudelaire did not try to get out of this; in fact, in the end he contributed to the book—which was a tribute to Claude-François Denecourt, known as *le Sylvain*, the discoverer and tutelary spirit of the forest of Fontainebleau—two poems and two small prose poems. But he accompanied the poems with a letter of uproarious *persiflage*, which seemed aimed not so much at poor Desnoyers, an exponent of the *bohème chantante*, as at a vast assembly of future worlds. What was he supposed to write about? asks Baudelaire. "About the woods, the great oaks, the greenery, the insects—and, I imagine, the sun?" Now the tone is insolent. Baudelaire moves on to a statement of principle: "You are well aware that I am incapable of waxing emotional over plants and that my spirit is impervious to this singular new religion, which will always have, I believe, a certain hint of the shocking about it for every *spiritual* being." Here his divinatory powers are manifest, behind the sardonic phrasing. Already we glimpse *naturism*, the form of intellectual handicap that emerged in the terrain of the sensibilities stretching from Rousseau to Senancour and later spread out in successive waves until it finally became a powerful economic enterprise. Baudelaire knew perfectly well that he was not talking about a harmless fashion of the Parisian *bohème*, but a "singular new religion." He anticipated the cult of the *vacances*, the deferential tone with which the word was to be uttered one hundred and fifty years later, and the blinkered reverence for "sanctified vegetables." Baudelaire was not one to encourage this cult. And obviously nature had nothing to do with it. If there was a poet who knew how to name nature, on those rare occasions when he was permitted to see it—and this right from the overpowering sight of that lake in the Pyrenees to which he dedicated one of the poems of his youth—that poet was Baudelaire. But the idea that Nature, once it had donned the capital *N* and was accompanied by a retinue of noble emotions, returned to spread itself over everything like the very image of Good was not for him, who so often found himself out of phase with even the commonest atmospheric manifestations—so much so that he wrote, "I have always thought, moreover, that in Nature, flourishing and rejuvenated, there was something impudent and distressing."

But Baudelaire's excesses with regard to Nature conceal something else—the golden thread of the poetry that was to be called modern, a thread interwoven with baser stuff into a luxuriant skein, but that sometimes disentangles itself from all the rest and resounds on its own. This happened in another letter, written eighty-two years after Baudelaire's, by another poet (Gottfried Benn to his friend Friedrich Oelze). With the same apparatus of harmonics and dissonances, with the same sovereign indifference and insolence: "Herr Oelze, once again the great fraud of nature is clear to me. *Snow*, even when it does not melt, offers little in the way of either linguistic or emotional ideas; all its undoubted monotony can easily be mentally liquidated from home. Nature is empty, deserted; only the petits bourgeois see something in it, poor dolts who must constantly go for a stroll in it . . . Flee from nature, it ruins the thoughts and is notoriously harmful to style! Nature—feminine in gender, obviously! Ever ready to squeeze out seed and use man for coitus, to exhaust him. But is *nature natural?*"

The "Nature" that Baudelaire talks about in "Correspondances," the one woven from analogies like an immense spider web, is that sacred, secret nature whose presence most people never even notice. Whereas the *"Nature"* (still capitalized but in italics) that Baudelaire rejects sarcastically in his letter to Desnoyers was the recent belief that embraced "the actions and desires of the pure natural man"—and it could not be other than "horrendous," even though the epoch tended to paint it in idyllic hues. That there may be a contradiction between venerating the first and execrating the second of these two Natures could become a torment only for Benjamin, still burdened by an Enlightenment inheritance that obliged him to see in sacred, secret nature—that of myth—only a *Verblendungszusammenhang*, a "context of delusion," as Adorno would have

defined it, employing to the utmost the potential of the German language. So the case was not that Benjamin discovered an invincible contradiction in Baudelaire. It was that Baudelaire invited Benjamin to
explore a territory that otherwise aroused in him an arcane terror. Like
a child singing in the dark, Benjamin then wrote that precisely in that
zone it was necessary to "penetrate, with the sharp ax of reason, and
without looking to left or right, in order to avoid falling victim to the
horror, which draws one from the depths of the forest." That exploration was never brought to a conclusion—and no "sharp ax" would have
served against what Benjamin described as "the brushwood of delirium
and myth."

That there is no contradiction between Nature strewn with "forests
of symbols" and Nature as man's fundamentally tainted constitution—
insofar as the latter is only one of the many parts of the former—
emerges with complete clarity in the ending of the letter to Toussenel,
where Baudelaire hints at how, in the animal kingdom, "baleful and
loathsome beasts" could be none other than "the vitalization, the mate-
rialization, the blooming of man's *wicked thoughts*" into material life. And
here the circle closed, bringing Swedenborg and Joseph de Maistre together: "In this way all of *nature* takes part in original sin." If nature is
born permeated by sin, man's privilege cannot be that of introducing
sin into the world, but only of elaborating upon it. To give it form—and
this was already a first definition of literature. And so Baudelaire's covert
metaphysics reconnected to the Vedic theory of sacrifice, which he could
not have known about (very few of these texts were available at the time).
For this reason, too, Baudelaire was the most archaic of the moderns.

For Baudelaire, verses flowed irregularly, welling up from a creaking
device, often jammed, and partly rusty. One of his virtues was a certain
lack of "fluency" in producing verse (to Poulet-Malassis: "Do you think
perhaps that I have the fluency of Banville?"). It's not hard to believe
him when he writes, "I am struggling with thirty-odd inadequate, disagreeable, poorly turned, poorly rhymed verses." Contrariwise, for his
friend Banville, words flowed to order. He was a vending machine of
poetry, which today slips over the reader leaving barely a trace, whereas
Baudelaire's memorable poems are so many *djinnis* who occasionally

escape from a workshop brimful of naked wires and phials of colorings. In a corner, an unmade bunk.

Baudelaire wrote a great many pedestrian, irredeemable verses, jumbled up in the mass of versification of his epoch. But it is this faded, generic, anonymous backdrop that makes his *other* verses stand out even more, like his elusive passerby in the midst of the crowd, she whose look has "the sweetness that fascinates and the pleasure that kills." They are verses—or sometimes fragments of verse—that establish an osmotic rapport with the reader; they emerge irresistibly, above all where they were born and still wander like tutelary geniuses among "those streets and those hotels that have taken on the gray patina of the insomnias they have hosted" (Paris according to Cioran). The young Barrès noted, "A bitter pleasure and one of the sweetest is to repeat a certain verse of Baudelaire on the morn of a Parisian night, in the shadows slashed by some rare carriage and by the ever feebler light of the lampposts, along the deserted boulevards, while the weariness of exhausted nerves, and a memory of the uninspiring hours, of shady complicities and of such a petty and vain struggle overwhelms you, always the same, and dragging along with it an unfulfilled ardor, an annoyance that defiles."

At the beginning of Renard's *Journal*: "Baudelaire's dense phrasing, as if laden with electrical fluids." A magnificent definition, placed by a master of lean, mordant, light prose on the entrance to his laboratory (which would have been his greatest work), as a tribute to one who had followed another path. Those "electrical fluids" were what Baudelaire's contemporaries lacked. At the heart of the generation of French Romantics, the fanatics and the disenchanted, we often come across a hint of something insipid, inconsistent, flabby. In the heart of Baudelaire there is always a magnetic storm at the very least.

The question of *weight* in Baudelaire's verse was brought up again almost one hundred years later by Julien Gracq: "No poetry is as *heavy* as Baudelaire's, heavy with that weight typical of a ripe fruit about to drop from a drooping branch . . . Verses that constantly bend under the weight of memories, vexations, suffering, and of joys recollected." Renard and Gracq are talking about two different weights. One is atmospheric, the other vegetative. Both are present in Baudelaire. His words are *laden*, whatever they say. There is an engorgement of sap, an accumulation of energy, a pressure from the unknown that sustains it—and in the end lays it low.

Moving on through Renard's *Journal*, we come across this entry, dated January 12, 1892:

"I detest," says Schwob, "people who call me 'cher confrère,' people who absolutely insist on putting me in the class they belong to."

Then he remarks:

"In a beerhouse Baudelaire said: 'There's a smell of destruction.' 'What?' they said. 'There's a smell of cabbage soup, of warm woman.' But Baudelaire repeated vehemently: 'There's a smell of destruction, I tell you.'"

What "destruction" meant for Baudelaire is expressed in the sonnet with the same title. It is a demon in the air, something *you breathe*. Similar to a virus: "He swims around me like impalpable air; / I swallow him and feel him burning my lungs." Something not unlike this happens with death—and Baudelaire had already hinted at this in the first verses of *Les Fleurs du mal*: "And, when we breathe, Death, that invisible river / Descends into our lungs with muffled moan." Evil is something physical, which we could even see and recognize if our eyes had a greater capacity to distinguish the minuscule. For this reason, too, Baudelaire's sufferings quiver with such an urgent, shocking thrill. They are reactions to powers that seize the body even before they seduce the mind. Most statements about Baudelaire are similar to the reactions of his companions in the beerhouse. Everybody is eager to put him "in the class they belong to."

Only in Proust can it be said that Baudelaire finds his antiphonic voice, which takes up and reconnects what was outlined in the "desert of men." Not so much in terms of form—even though on countless occasions we sense Proust extending Baudelaire's progression and sonority—but in terms of power. The "evocative witchcraft" that is writing invested his words with the power to impress themselves on the material of memory with a clarity and an imperativeness not achieved by any other, not even by Rimbaud, not even by Mallarmé. This is why Proust talks of Baudelaire as he who "momentarily had possessed the most powerful word ever to sound on human lips." A solemn expression, and an emphatic one for once, but couched within brackets, as if Proust despaired of conveying—and hence wished to reiterate in the firmest manner—what he saw as Baudelaire's particular character: "that subordination of the sensibility to truth" that is "basically the mark of genius, of power, of the art superior to individual compassion." This is the power that drives the "great verses" and hurls them into the race, like chariots devouring a "gigantic track." An image that gives a simultaneous impression of lightning speed and vastness. If Proust is so insistent about this aspect of Baudelaire, it is because one day he would be able to say the same about the *Recherche*, an immense arch of words held up by a single drive, like a stellar catastrophe that continues to resonate in constant waves of light.

The distinction between Baudelaire and Proust is in composition. Proust himself observed that Baudelaire proceeds "with confidence in the execution of detail and with the lack of it in the plan." Apart from some magnificent exceptions ("Le Cygne," "Le Voyage . . ."), none of Baudelaire's poems are borne up throughout by masterful composition. One often notices a dull rumble running through a verse or a cluster of memorable verses that then recedes—or falls back on feebler formulas comparable to the poetic jargon of the day. But an overall plan is lacking—or is irrelevant. This is not what we look for in Baudelaire. In Proust, instead, the demoniac sense of the great composition is at work, full of references, recurrences, reflections. The luxuriant denseness of detail is cultivated almost coquettishly, because the narrator knows that behind that forest we catch regular glimpses of the powerful framework of the construction. Everything has been prepared for observation under the microscope—or, alternatively, from a great distance. And both visions cause a sense of giddiness, which paralyzes. But the mercurial course of the narration immediately gets under way again, undulating and sinuous, like a protracted nighttime confession.

According to Baudelaire "almost all our originality comes from the stamp that *time* impresses on our sensibilities." For him, that "stamp" became a figure intricate as a Maori tattoo and brutal as the brand on a steer in Texas. He could not write a line without one noticing its presence. Perhaps for this reason, too, although he abhorred much of the *new* that the period incessantly produced, Baudelaire chose *nouveau* as the last word of *Les Fleurs du mal*.

"The writer of nerves": Poe defined by Baudelaire. A definition he could also have applied to himself. With the certainty of being recognized, Baudelaire stepped forward beneath the mask of the "nervous man and artist." But the insistence on physiology went even farther, all the way to a word that had not yet been admitted into the poetic lexicon: *brain*. No longer the *Idéal*, no longer the *Rêve*, no longer the *Esprit* (with or without capitals), now the brain seemed irresistibly to attract the sobriquet "mysterious." There was even talk of the cerebellum. "In the cramped and mysterious laboratory of the brain" . . . "The mysterious adventures of the brain" . . . "In the generation of all sublime ideas there is a nervous shock that makes itself felt in the cerebellum." The cerebral mass is inhabited. Not only by the traditional "people of Demons," but by creatures already inspired by Lautréamont: "Silent, foul spiders / Spin their webs in the base of our brains." Almost at the same time, Emily Dickinson wrote, "I felt a Funeral, in my Brain." But it was not metaphysics that became physiology. Rather, physiology had made a pact with metaphysics. And poetry would respect that.

"Genius is none other than childhood formulated with precision." It is possible to come across some of Baudelaire's stunning definitions (and the *art of definition* was the one in which he excelled above all) obliquely or hidden in a corner, sometimes amalgamated almost inseparably with the writings of another (who is De Quincey here) or camouflaged in an occasional piece, composed reluctantly. Generally they are not isolated phrases, with aphoristic pretensions, but fragments of phrases from which they must be detached so that their luminosity may expand. It is his way of protecting secrets: not concealing them behind esoteric barriers, but, on the contrary, throwing them into a promiscuous ambience, where they can easily get lost, like a face in the crowd in a big city, thus going back to breathe their unnoticed and radiating life. Thus the cell that emits vibrations is not the verse and not even the phrase, but the *suspended definition*, which we can find anywhere, set in a chronicle or in a sonnet, in a digression or in a note:

the act and the solemn and grotesque attitude of beings and their luminous explosion in space the feasts of Baïram, deep and undulating splendors beneath which there appears, like a pallid sun, the permanent ennui of the late Sultan

An immensity, sometimes azure and often green, extends as far as the boundaries of the heavens: it is the sea

The mysterious attitudes that the objects of creation adopt before the gaze of man

The green darkness on the damp evenings of the spring and summer.

In all these fragments of phrases we recognize a perceptual constellation that had never crystallized before. Not in Chateaubriand, or in Stendhal, or in Heine—just to name only three writers akin to Baudelaire, but incompatible among themselves. They were juxtapositions of sensations, syntagmas, phantasms, single words, sentiments, ideas, that moved away from current schemas, but without damaging form too much. Juxtapositions inaccessible even to Hugo, even though he possessed an impressive number of registers and blew out verses as a cetacean vents water. All this was not, if not only in a small way, the result of a will and a plan. Rather, it was the result of Baudelaire's ruinous exposure to everyday life. The most singular phenomenon, however, is not the crystallization of that sensibility, but its resistance to time. Today its substance remains, almost unscathed, as can be verified instantly in his critical prose, whereas in his poetry we must concede a part to those obligatory themes that the period slips into the cradle of every poet.

Baudelaire and Flaubert were born in the same year, 1821. And in the same months of their childhood they became writers. Flaubert was nine when he sent a letter to his friend Ernest Chevalier: "If you wish us to get together to write, I shall write plays and you shall write your dreams and, since there is a lady who visits Papa and always tells us foolish things [*bêtises*], I shall write them down." A few months later, Baudelaire told his stepbrother Alphonse about a trip to Lyon with his mother. He speaks like an adult who knows the world—perhaps he is already a bit weary of it—and protects his mother with affectionate irony: "Mama's first inadvertence: as she was having the luggage loaded onto the imperial, she noticed she no longer had her muff and she cried out, theatrically, 'Where's my muff?' And I reply calmly: 'I know where it is and I'll go to get it.' She had left it on a bench in the study." These are the first chords in the story of the son Charles and the mother Caroline. What follows is Baudelaire's entry into literature, through the high road of *chaotic enumeration*: "We board the coach, finally we're off. On my part, at first, I was in a foul mood because of the muffs, hot water bottles, foot rugs, men's and women's hats, cloaks, cushions, numerous blankets, caps of all kinds, shoes, padded slippers, bootees, hampers, jams, beans, bread, napkins, enormous poultry, spoons, forks, knives, scissors, thread, needles, pins, combs, clothes, numerous skirts, woolen stockings, cotton socks, corsets one on top of the other, biscuits, and I can't remember the rest."

Flaubert let little Chevalier write down his dreams and claimed as his own material the *bêtises* that his parents' friend came out with. Baudelaire gave precedence to the incongruous excess of the existent. But he got rid of that right away: "I soon became my usual cheerful self again." And he moved on to describe the evening, with the "fine spectacle" of the sunset: "that reddish color was in singular contrast with the mountains that were blue as the darkest pants." Only a writer—only the writer who was to be Baudelaire—could permit himself to associate the sunset with the color of pants. The next phrase already belongs to the Baudelaire of *Les Fleurs du mal*, which was to close with "Le Voyage": "After I put on my silk beret, I leaned back against the seat and it seemed to me that traveling would have always been a life I would have liked very much; I'd really like to write more about this to you, but a *damned essay* obliges me to end my letter here." Many other *damned essays* were to follow.

"Mama, I am not writing you to ask forgiveness, because I know you wouldn't believe me; I am writing to tell you that it's the last time that I'll lose my pass to go out, that from now on I want to work and avoid all punishments that might even delay my going out." These are the first words of the first letter written by the thirteen-year-old Baudelaire to his mother, Caroline. But they could also be the last words of the last letter, over thirty years later. Right from the start it is a matter of fault, captivity, work, and promises. It is also a matter of believing and going out. Going out (from the boarding school) was equivalent to freedom from debt, years after, or from his trustee. And the debts were the fault and the punishment at the same time.

When Baudelaire went to live alone in Paris—and the authority to punish was no longer in the hands of the boarding school but of his trustee, in the person of the notary Ancelle—this added one final characteristic to his relationship with Caroline: surreptitiousness. Like an unruly and unhappy lover, Baudelaire crossed the Seine and showed up in place Vendôme, in his stepfather General Aupick's apartment, taking care not to be noticed: it was a "big, cold, empty house, where I know no one except my mother," he wrote. And then: "I go in alone, cautiously; and I leave alone, furtively." For him, that surreptitiousness was to be the rule, not only with his mother but also with any event in life, as if every pleasure had to be saved from a powerful, omnipresent enemy.

The scorn for bourgeois manners within the bourgeoisie springs from Molière's *Les précieuses ridicules* ("*Madelon*: Oh, father, your words are those of the perfect bourgeois"), but it was only during the reign of Louis Philippe that the bourgeois rose to a pervasive, universal category, thereby arousing an equally vast rejection. This raged prominently in France—that is, in Paris, the capital of the century. Right from the start, the bourgeois was coupled with the *bêtise* (or *sottise*, as Baudelaire still said—and *sottise* is the first noun we come across in the first verse of *Les Fleurs du mal*), insofar as it can act as the moving force of history and progress. The bourgeois was not feared as a social class, but as a new being who put an end to all the previous categories and absorbed them without exclusions into a new humanity whose outlines were fuzzy because they were forever changing. This view was an accurate one and corresponds to the normal state of affairs a century and a half later, when the dominant societies happen to be based on various degrees of approximation to a ubiquitous middle class.

What happened to the *bêtise* in the meantime? Starting from Baudelaire in Belgium (a subtly distorted refraction of Paris), through Barbey d'Aurevilly, then the imposing material collected by Flaubert for *Bouvard et Pécuchet*, down to the exegesis of commonplaces in Bloy, there was an expansion of the *bêtise*'s epos, the only one in which modernity excels. But that, too, like many other things, was shattered on August 1, 1914. What followed, albeit steeped in *bêtise* right down to even its tiniest mechanisms, could no longer be attacked with the same stylistic acids. Karl Kraus could not treat Hitler the way Baudelaire treated the Belgian freethinkers. Nonetheless, the *bêtise* that beset Baudelaire and Flaubert was to remain a platform—invisible, implicit, and powerful—without which it would have been difficult to orient oneself in the new world. And in both authors the word always retained a certain mystic charge, almost that of a cosmic arcanum.

"Great poetry is essentially *bête*, it *believes*, and this is what makes its glory and strength": Baudelaire, 1846. "Masterpieces are *bêtes*. They have a tranquil air like the very productions of nature, such as big animals and mountains": Flaubert, 1852. At a distance of six years, one in a review, the other in a letter, and obviously unaware of each other, the two bards of the *bêtise* wrote similar phrases, which add a further dimension to the word. It is not a matter of pure "foolishness," as other languages are obliged to translate *bêtise*. But of something in which there lingers an obscure animal background, as if, on reaching its apex, art rediscovered something beautiful in nature, but veiled by an opaque film, impenetrable, and loath to take intelligence into account. In this, art is comparable to woman, thus celebrated by Baudelaire in 1846: "There are people who blush for having loved a woman, the day on which they realize that she is *bête*." Nothing more deplorable, because "the *bêtise* is often the ornament of beauty; it is the *bêtise* that gives the eyes the dark limpidity of blackish pools, and the oily calm of tropical seas." And this confirms the subtle distinction between *bêtise* and *sottise* that Mme de Staël suggested: "The *bêtise* and the *sottise* differ essentially in this, that *bêtes* submit willingly to nature and *sots* always delight in the idea that they dominate society."

But the meaning of *bêtise* was subject to constant oscillations. A letter written by Baudelaire to Soulary in 1860 has the impact of an electric shock: "*all great men are bêtes*; all representative men who represent, or men who represent multitudes. It is a punishment inflicted on them by God."

·

Baudelaire never wrote the ugly verses of adolescence. Nor did a vocation for poetry present itself to him as irresistible. After his *Baccalauréat*
he noted again, "I feel no vocation at all." When he left his family, he
said merely that he wanted to be "an author." Of the modern authors he
acknowledged he had read with enthusiasm he named only Chateaubri-
and (*René*), Sainte-Beuve (*Volupté*), and Hugo (plays and poetry). As for
the rest, to his mother: "I have learned to be disgusted by modern literature." The character of those "modern works" struck him as "false, ex-
aggerated, extravagant, and pompous." The practice of poetry came to
Baudelaire by an oblique route: from the composition of Latin verse. He
excelled in this (and he excelled in no other scholastic subject). All his
poetry is as if translated from a dead, nonexistent tongue, blended with
Virgil and Christian liturgy.

What was it about *Volupté*—a debut novel published without any
great stir, which simply "slipped away smoothly *like a letter for the mail*,"
according to the phrase used by Sainte-Beuve himself—what was it
about this book, written by someone who would never again chance
writing another novel, that made such a profound impression on Baudelaire the high school student? Because, for him, those pages had "gone
to the bottom of the most tenuous artery," a more radical and pervasive
effect than the one he attributed to Chateaubriand's *René*, whose sighs,
like countless contemporaries of his, he "fluently deciphered." The level
of assimilation is different. Those sighs were already "the beginning
of a wakening," according to Marc Fumaroli. But that "bottom of the
most tenuous artery" could be reached only by probing the most hidden
part of a sensibility. What route did *Volupté* follow to get there? One has
only to read the foreword, signed S.-B.: "The true subject of this book is
the analysis of an inclination, of a passion, even of a vice, and of all the
side of the soul that this vice governs, and to which it gives the tone, of
the side that is languid, idle, compelling, secret and private, mysterious
and furtive, dreamy to the point of fineness, tender to the point of softness, in short, voluptuous." Here we still do not know what he is talking
about. But we do know that this was to be Baudelaire's territory. At least
as long as the ambiguity of the title endures. Sainte-Beuve, who had a
tightrope walker's ability to protect his own respectability, immediately
safeguarded himself: "Hence the title *Volupté*, which has nevertheless the
problem of not offering itself in the right sense, and of creating the im-

pression of something that is more attractive than appropriate. But that title, published at first in a rather offhand manner, could not then be withdrawn." There is an Italian idiom that says, literally, "to throw the stone and then hide the hand," that is to say, to provoke a situation and then deny all responsibility. This was a technique that Sainte-Beuve was later to perfect. In this, Baudelaire was his opposite. He claimed the riskiest stones—and other stones he had never thrown were attributed to him. So there's no doubt that he would have understood *Volupté* in the sense that it was something "more attractive than appropriate." But this was to happen later.

Now, as long as he languished in the corridors of the lycée Louis-le-Grand, it was a matter in the first place of delving into a zone of words—especially nouns and adjectives—that came together following unusual trajectories. Words that in Baudelaire's prose and verse would soon find new vigor. Listing them is easy, if we extract them from the first sentence of *Volupté*: *languid, idle, compelling, secret, private, mysterious, furtive*—and also the sequence "dreamy to the point of fineness, tender to the point of softness, in short, voluptuous." From that pure succession of chords it would be simple to move on to judgment, even about the "times we live in," of which Baudelaire still knew only what little filtered through the smoke-darkened walls of the boarding school, but which would be presented to him from then on, still following in Sainte-Beuve's footsteps, as a "confusion of systems, desires, boundless sentiments, confessions, and nakedness of all sorts." These were the closing words of the foreword to *Volupté*. And they were already the premise for *Les Fleurs du mal*.

So it's no wonder that Baudelaire's inaugural poem is the one dedicated to Sainte-Beuve: perfectly mature, one of the most intense he would ever write. He sent it to the recipient as an unknown sender, accompanying it with a letter that opened with these words: "Sir, Stendhal said somewhere—more or less this: *I write for a dozen souls that I may perhaps never see, but I adore them without having seen them.*" Almost everything was said, including the indiscretion of naming Stendhal immediately upon introducing himself to Sainte-Beuve, who certainly did not *adore* him—and he did his utmost to keep his works at a distance, exactly as he would do with Baudelaire one day. At that time Baudelaire was living in the hôtel Pimodan. He had yet to publish under his own name.

His beginnings were anonymous or pseudonymous—and passably shady, too. The *Mystères galants des théâtres de Paris*, which he contributed to but did not sign, was a thinly veiled form of blackmail. Sometimes Baudelaire would read his poems to his friends, but plans for a book were still to emerge. Yet the capitals—those tonic, unpredictable, ominous capital letters that always stud his verses—had already appeared like a seal. And they fell on these words: *Solitudes, Enfant, Mélancolie, Doute, Démon*. It is almost a horoscope. And the distance from which the voice arrived was already fixed. A paradoxical phenomenon, for it wells up like a whisper inside the listener and at the same time comes from afar, exhausted after a long journey.

Raised "under the square sky of the Solitudes" (the sky is "square" because it was enclosed by the quadrangle of a courtyard in the boarding school), there was always something adolescent about Baudelaire, a certain bold and desolate rebelliousness. He never recounted those years, but he did hint at them by proxy, as was his custom, attributing his feelings of those days to Poe. He, too, had been subjected to those "torments of youth" that till the soil of all literature ("The hours in punishment, the sufferings of a frail, neglected childhood, the terror of the teacher, our enemy, the hatred of tyrannical schoolmates, the loneliness of the heart"). For Baudelaire—as it was for the young Talleyrand and for Balzac's Louis Lambert—boarding school was the laboratory where one consummated an irreversible dissociation from the surroundings. At the end of the corridor there appears the noonday hallucination of a young girl sitting with her chin resting on one hand and "her brow still damp with the languors of her nights": it was Melancholy.

The hôtel Pimodan—17, quai d'Anjou, in the Île Saint-Louis—was originally the property of the Duc de Lauzun, who had a hotly contested love affair with "La Grande Mademoiselle" (Anne, Duchess of Montpensier). Then, one owner after another, the building ended up in the hands of Baron Pichon, a diplomat, official, and bibliophile. Baudelaire was his tenant for some time. Baudelaire was just over twenty years old, and stood out for his good looks and elegance. On the first floor there lived

a junk dealer, Arondel. This last soon became one of Baudelaire's most pressing creditors. Baudelaire insulted him, and Pichon, too, in the anonymous *Mystères galants des théâtres de Paris*. Arondel discovered the ploy, and Baudelaire had to send Pichon a humiliating letter of apology. The landlord did not remember his tenant with fondness. Many years later he was to write to a friend, "If you knew what it meant to be landlord to Baudelaire and the life he led. His lover was a horrible black woman and he trafficked in paintings with Arondel."

In the hôtel Pimodan, Baudelaire lived in three rooms accessed by a service stairway. The study overlooked the Seine. Banville once declared that he "had never seen a house that more resembled its owner." On the walls, shiny wallpaper with a red-and-black floral pattern. Old damask curtains. Lithographs by Delacroix. Few but imposing items of furniture. A large oval table, in walnut. There was no library, nor were there any books to be seen lying around. They were all locked up in a cupboard, lying flat, together with a few bottles of wine. A large oak bed, without feet or columns, resembled a monumental sarcophagus. The study (and bedroom) was "lit by a single window whose panes, right up to the second-to-last row, were frosted, 'to see nothing other than the sky,' he said."

On going down to the main floor one found oneself in the "club des *Hashischins*." (The name was revealed by Gautier, who was a member.)

The hôtel Pimodan was a neglected marvel, a "gilded tomb in the heart of old Paris," when Roger de Beauvoir, the founder of the club, first rented it. A sickening miasma issued from a dyer in the first basement. Grass grew between the flagstones of the courtyard. But from the right-hand staircase, on passing through a door upholstered in faded green plush, one entered a den of delights. All was smoke-stained, owing to age and neglect, but all was enchanting. Stuccos, reliefs in stone, two Hubert Roberts, a stand for musicians in the salon, in a hanging niche. Decoration invaded every corner, like tropical vegetation. And it was interrupted only by a few mirrors in Bohemian glass, which multiplied it. On the ceiling: *Love Conquers Time.* Nymphs pursued by satyrs among the reeds. Ciphers, cherubs, greyhounds, spiraling foliage. The *hashischins* met in the *boudoir.* No background could have been better suited to letting the gaze lose itself and forget, aided by *dawamesk,* in the guise of a bit of "greenish jam, about the size of the thumb." Gautier observed how "time, which flies so fast, seemed to not have passed over that house and, like a pendulum-clock that has forgotten to wind itself up, its hands always showed the same date." In the enchanted period of the hôtel Pimodan the very young Aglaé-Joséphine Savatier attended swimming lessons held in the Deligny Baths, not far from the building. Radiant and dripping, she would sometimes show up in the "club des *Hashischins,*" where her lover Boissard lived for a while. Gautier recalls her being present when he met Baudelaire for the first time. Years after, the same Gautier called her "la Présidente"—and Baudelaire was to dedicate to her a brief, heartrending collection of love poems.

The *boudoir* in the hôtel Pimodan was in pure Louis XIV style, but it seemed to have been designed specifically for the visions conjured up by the *dawamesk*. Gautier, who had frequented it no less than Baudelaire, rediscovered its description in an episode of *Paradis artificiels* where the author presumes to compare the hashish experience to "a woman on the mature side, curious, with an excitable spirit." That woman "on the mature side" was Baudelaire himself, at twenty-three. The description reconstructs the contours of the walls with the loving persistence of a gaze that has used those same walls to lose itself in: "This *boudoir* is very small, very cramped. On the level of the cornice the ceiling curves to form a vault; the walls are covered with long, narrow mirrors, separated by panels painted with landscapes in the uninhibited style of the décor. On a level with the cornice, on the four walls, there are portrayals of various allegorical figures, some at rest, others running or pirouetting. Above them, resplendent birds and flowers. Behind the figures there rises up an illusionistic arbor, which naturally follows the curve of the ceiling. This ceiling is gilded. All the gaps between the moldings and the characters are covered with gold, and at the center the gold is interrupted only by the geometric network of the simulated arbors." And then, speaking to an unknown lady friend: "You see that all this looks a little like a highly refined *cage*, a most beautiful cage for a huge bird." Disguised as a lady "on the mature side, curious, with an excitable spirit," Baudelaire had unwittingly followed the teachings of Saint Ignatius on the *composition of place* and had slipped into this "place" like a "huge bird" happily imprisoned. Yet that place also existed outside his mind. It was hidden in old Paris, protected by the waters of the Seine. For this reason, too, for Baudelaire, Paris easily became allegory.

When Baudelaire, at twenty-four, tried to kill himself, he accompanied the deed with a letter of farewell addressed to the notary Ancelle, in which he writes that he is killing himself not because he feels "any of those troubles that men call *suffering*," but because "the effort of falling asleep and the effort of waking" were "unbearable" for him. Moreover, he is committing suicide because he is *"a danger to himself."* In closing, he states, "I am *killing* myself because I believe I am immortal, and because *I hope*." Many have deemed this to be rudimentary playacting. But whatever his reasons may have been, whether he was sincere or playing a part, a writer is he who inevitably reveals things—and himself, too—through the written word. In that farewell note, Baudelaire delivers the mark of that network of nerves and glorious *non sequitur* that would accompany him in every moment of his future life.

Regarding that attempted suicide, two pieces of evidence remain. One is the letter to Ancelle, indubitable as one of Pascal's fragments, modulated like a sequence of stabbing pains, excruciating in its complete lucidity. The other is that of Louis Ménard, steeped in ill will, like everything the "mystic pagan" was to write about his schoolmate. But there is a detail in his account, repeated almost in the same words by Philippe Berthelot and Rioux de Maillou, which seems like one of Baudelaire's most extreme, outrageously sarcastic inventions.

That evening, it seems, Baudelaire was with his mistress Jeanne Duval in a coffeehouse on rue Richelieu. At a certain point he tried to knife himself. Then he fainted. He apparently awoke before the eyes of a police chief, who said to him, "You have done a bad thing; you ought to give yourself to your country, to your neighborhood, to your street, to your police chief." The world was ready to welcome the young poet again, provided he agreed to *give himself* to the maternal arms of the police chief.

Gautier recounts that Baudelaire's first worry was not to look like an artist. He shunned anything picturesque. Even though he spent his life amid all kinds of *demi-monde*, from that of editorial offices to those of the cafés and theaters, one noticed clearly in him "the intention to separate himself from the artistic sort, with floppy felt hats and velvet jackets." He practiced a "sober dandyism that scrapes clothing with sandpaper to remove that brand new, Sunday best look."

On the other hand, Baudelaire never did anything to enter high society, as he could easily have done. It would have been enough for him to play up to his stepfather, General Aupick, who "wanted to see him attain a high social position," especially as the general was "a friend of the Duke of Orléans," as his mother, Caroline, was punctiliously to remind him one day. But for Baudelaire—as for the Russian *intelligentsia* that was forming in those same years—a certain déclassé air was essential.

While Baudelaire, a rare case indeed, showed no hint of attraction for high society, neither was he inclined toward the lower sort, amid whom he so often found himself as a result of the consequences of his life. Champfleury, an old friend of the *bohème*—whom Baudelaire once defined with icy neutrality as "one of the principal adepts of the so-called *Realist* school, which claimed to substitute the *Classical* folly and the *Romantic* folly with the study of nature and the study of themselves" (sarcasm in every word)—was not the kind to understand him. So they quarreled, because Baudelaire wrote to him saying that he didn't like low life. But the underlying reason was that Champfleury wanted to arrange a meeting between Baudelaire and a certain "philosophizing woman"—and his friend stubbornly resisted. Returning to the theme of "low life," Baudelaire pointed out, "My friend, I have always found it repulsive; riffraff and foolishness, and crime, possess an appeal that may please for a few minutes, but low life, but these, so to speak, eddies of scum that form at the edges of society! Impossible." In fact, everything was *impossible* for him. There was no occasion when Baudelaire felt at ease in any company.

A definitive sign of Baudelaire's sovereignty *d'en bas* was his total indifference to all forms of social life. Unlike Mérimée, who always had entrée to the right salons, all the way to the imperial ones; and unlike Flaubert, who couldn't manage to conceal his satisfaction at belonging to Princess Mathilde's circle, Baudelaire never tried to be *received*. The favors he solicited always had a sole aim: money. From the start, and with naturalness, his were the sensual pleasures of degradation. If he frequented journalists, he easily found himself with those capable of verging on blackmail. And the first publication in which Baudelaire's hand has been recognized was an allusive pamphlet whose aim was to spread insinuations about the private life of an actress, Rachel. Further, the only draft of an unpublished novel by Baudelaire tells the story of the young fop Samuel Cramer, who gossips about an actress, La Fanfarlo, to have her notice him and, in the end, to get into her good books as lover, protégé, and protector.

Baudelaire had trouble inspiring respect. It was as if everyone considered him to be in a state of perennial nonage. Even the less-than-sublime Maxime Du Camp permitted himself to define Baudelaire as "ignorant," perhaps because he had noted Baudelaire's refractory attitude toward the pursuit of any methodical study. "History, physiology, archaeology, and philosophy eluded him: to tell the truth, he had never paid any attention to them." And Du Camp wrote this in 1882, when Baudelaire had already attained glory. But in his account there immediately stands out the image of the poet as "he tried to shake off his creditors, who were numerous." (Du Camp had been one of them, for a few hundred francs, which he managed to get back from Ancelle.) So it's easy to understand certain wounding words on Baudelaire's part: "Those who have loved me were people held in contempt, or to put it a better way, contemptible, if I set any store by flattering *respectable people.*"

Many people thought Baudelaire was posing, whereas his attitude was only an attempt to keep them at arm's length. And to breathe. When Baudelaire was accused—by Champfleury and a few others—of being a mountebank or a play-actor, we can be sure that the allusion was to episodes where his words or actions had simply been misunderstood. It must have happened fairly often. Afterward, perhaps out of pure exhaustion, Baudelaire may well have come up with some mountebankery. It wouldn't have made any difference, after all. And in it there could even have lain some tiny pleasure in mockery.

But once the outcry of his contemporaries ceased, the profile of he who was Charles Baudelaire finally began to take shape. And great was the amazement. Because, while it is true, as Baudelaire himself wrote, that Balzac was the greatest of Balzac's characters, no one could compare to Baudelaire as a character, for the variety and peculiarity of his elements, for his tenacious centrifugal drive, which seemed to oppose any compromise. Yet that personality had an impressive unity, so sound and so deep that his every syllable appeared recognizable, as if it sufficed to observe it against the light in order to see in it an omnipresent watermark. Eugène Marsan once reviewed, with a sure eye, Baudelaire's wardrobe and showed how it differed from that of Barbey d'Aurevilly, who still remained incurably picturesque and never reached the peak of elegance, which is "'absolute' simplicity"—as Beau Brummell had taught. But what was it about Baudelaire that enabled him to distance himself so sharply even from his followers? An extremely strong chemical affinity among discordant elements. The *new* in Baudelaire was to be sought in that direction: "his women and his sky, his perfumes, his nostalgia, his Christianity and his demon, his oceans and his tropics, composed a material of sensational novelty."

Baudelaire was a supreme specialist in humiliation. No other writer, no matter how troubled his life, can compete with him in the practice of that condition. Baudelaire experienced it in every milieu: in the family (owing to the presence of his stepfather, General Aupick); in money (owing to his constant dependence on Ancelle and the struggle against debt); in his love life (owing to his cohabitation with Jeanne, who had no esteem for him); in literary life (owing to his relations with newspapers, magazines, publishers, the Académie Française and the Republic of Letters in general). There was no corner in which Baudelaire was allowed to breathe freely. It's pointless to wonder—as happened to Sartre, the unwitting pupil of an evening school "Will Is Power"—to what extent Baudelaire *wanted* all this. Certainly there were many times in which he could have recovered an existence within the established order. He could have imitated Mérimée, whom he admired and by whom he was not admired. While he was an artist in every fiber of his being, Mérimée had built himself an existence as a *grand commis*, which protected him like an impenetrable carapace. But Baudelaire could not have resisted. He would have suffocated before attaining any comfortable status. No less than *ennui*, humiliation inspired him. This last is linked to abjection, a mysterious sentiment—active and passive—that seems a natural part of "modern life" and has since the time of Baudelaire pervaded literature. It was a poisonous breath that began to circulate in the second half of the nineteenth century and was to permeate in different ways some indispensable authors: Dostoyevsky and Gogol first of all (for the Russians, abjection was the very air they breathed); Melville (in "Bartleby"); Lautréamont, in every syllable; Hamsun and Strindberg, in a hyperborean, wild-eyed version; and also Rilke (in *Malte Laurids Brigge*). And others again. But the originator, who gathered the magnetic storm over himself, was always Baudelaire.

•

Baudelaire was the solitary, fearless champion of the inalienable right to contradict oneself: "In the numerous lists of the *rights of man* that the wisdom of the nineteenth century returns to so often and with so much satisfaction, two rather important ones have been forgotten, namely the right to contradict oneself and the right to *go away*." This last, above all, could be Baudelaire's precious contribution to the ever-uncertain doctrine of the rights of man.

The *culture industry*—an expression coined by Adorno and Horkheimer that already sounded obsolete shortly after its introduction—had its official beginning in Paris in the first years of Louis Philippe's reign. That time marked the establishment of the conditions indispensable for the manifestation of the phenomenon: First of all the daily press, which in future was to branch out into the plurality of the *media* but at that time comprised them all, witnessed a marked increase in circulation and an equally marked reduction in price, having recourse for the first time to systematic advertising. To what brilliant mind do we owe this fateful innovation? Above all to Émile de Girardin, who halved the price of subscription to *La Presse* thanks to paid announcements. At the same time as this move, another novelty came along: the introduction of serialized fiction, the *feuilleton*, first in periodicals with *La Revue de Paris*, then in the daily papers with *Le Siècle* and *La Presse*. Three years later, in 1839, Sainte-Beuve was able to publish his essay "De la littérature industrielle" in the *Revue des Deux Mondes*. It was the first, masterful example of that sad discipline that was to become the sociology of literature. It was also the highly perceptive description of an epochal change in the literary landscape, which no one knew in detail better than Sainte-Beuve, who observed it every day. So, along with the steam engine and photography, advertising took its place among the decisive inventions of the first half of the nineteenth century. Advertising means above all that certain objects begin to speak and produce images. At first this was a laughable, clumsy process, but one whose developments were incalculable. Born as an adjunct to production, advertising was eventually to invert the relationship: objects are produced so that certain images, certain names, and certain words may find a medium. Fashion represents a way to make this constant overflow of images more erotic, assimilating it to the incessant mutability of desire. The model and foundation of advertising is the incurable restlessness of mental life, whose original homeland is the *delectatio morosa*. Desert Fathers did not have objects around them because they needed a uniform, austere surface on the outside, as they wished to isolate, on the inside, the mental mechanism that engendered simulacra. They would have considered advertising as a subtle theological response to their exercises. Nadar observed: "Another new word: *réclame*; will it be successful?"

Journalists were paid by the line, translators by the page. When someone accused Nodier of an excess of adverbs, which abounded in some of his cartilaginous sentences, he replied that those cumbersome polysyllables helped him fill the lines faster. And every line was worth one franc. Balzac, who in those years took frequent action—also because he was the injured party—on questions of authors' rights, cheerfully talked about certain writers who *"offer a certain commercial surface for exploitation,"* introducing an expression that managing editors of two centuries later must still envy him. This already allows us to perceive the oppressive alternative facing writers who for a few years, immediately after 1830, deluded themselves into thinking they could carry on living the irresponsible bohemian life forever. Now the situation had radically changed—and Albert Cassagne described it with epigrammatic pithiness: "The bohemian is either an artist without talent, that is, to use Balzac's expression, one without a commercial surface—or he is an artist of talent who has not learned how to exploit his commercial surface," hence a misfit, one who risks no longer finding a place for himself in the social machine. Just a few years, and everything had been turned on its head. It was at this point that the young Baudelaire arrived on the scene. He declared, "I who sell my thoughts, and wish to be an author"— and in the meantime he prepared to enter, without complaining about it at all, a cruel productive contrivance that seemed made specially to mistreat him.

It was the dawning of the "prostitutes of the intelligence," as the Creole Privat d'Anglemont defined himself and under whose name, protected by a dubious shield, Baudelaire was to publish some of his first poems. But Théophile Gautier was the clearest example of how a brilliant writer, with many talents, could deteriorate day by day as a result of the obligation to produce columns of words in papers and magazines, sprinkled with complaisant observations. Gautier had come to feel a physical repulsion for the act of going to the theater, even before he had to write about it. Thus the "perfect wizard *ès lettres françaises*" (which is the pompous definition in the dedication of *Les Fleurs du mal*) spent most of his life with the obsessions of the *pisseur de copie*. And it was precisely Baudelaire who gave Gautier the most cutting lash when he cited his enlightened and severe judgment of Delaroche, but adding a few mortally wounding words: "as was said, I believe, by Théophile Gautier, in a crisis of independence." One of those crises that, over time, became ever rarer.

Orate sine intermissione: this Pauline precept, which was to become the basis of hesychastic prayer, was transformed by Baudelaire into a different commandment: "You must get inebriated all the time." If the metaphysical element that wounds all appearances is the pure passing of the moment, it is necessary to wrap appearance, as if with a protective cloak, in the impenetrable veil of inebriation. But by now this notion no longer had any ritual or liturgical justification, as was instead the case for bacchantes and monks. Now "when you awake in the gloomy solitude of your room," getting inebriated again was "the only question," as if nothing else in the world mattered, but there were to be no more guaranteed, ceremonial, or traditional pretexts for the enterprise. It was necessary to give yourself over "to all that flees, to all that moans . . . to all that speaks," so that you are spurred on to return to the exceptional state that seems to be the only tolerable normality. *Les Fleurs du mal* is the chronicle of those ever-precarious, fragile, intermittent attempts. Every verse can fall within the category of what chemists call *unstable compounds*. But the aspiration they spring from is as near as you can get to St. Paul's precept. One day Baudelaire wrote to Flaubert: "You tell me I work a lot. Is this a cruel jest?" And he went on, with words that could have been those of Evagrius: "To work means to work unceasingly; it means no longer having senses or fancies; and it means being a pure will forever in movement."

To gainsay all those who have shown an inclination to consider Baudelaire's relationship with Jeanne Duval as a prolonged exercise in self-imposed subjugation to a crude idol and maybe not even a very attractive one, we need only consider a few lines from the letter of September 1856 in which Baudelaire tells his mother of the end of his relationship, almost as if he were talking to Jeanne herself, an absent, silent Jeanne. That irreparable break—"the idea of an irreparable separation had never clearly entered my head," he says—had produced in him something like "an obscure veil before the eyes and an eternal din in the ears." And he added a few direct and definitive words: "To this day—while I am entirely calm—I surprise myself on thinking, when I see a fine object, a fine landscape, or any other pleasant thing: Why is she not with me, to admire this with me, to buy this with me?"

Then there is a pentimento by Courbet. If we try to enter the *Atelier* following Diderot's suggestion, and start roaming around that vast, bare room crowded with characters, sharing different and isolated lives, but temporarily grouped around the painter, who, with incongruous assurance, is painting a luminous landscape before the eyes of a nude female model who is observing him (a model whom Courbet portrayed from a photograph, the technical novelty of the moment), once we reach the far right of the scene we come across a young man sitting at a table, completely engrossed in a book. It is Baudelaire, the only one among those present who flaunts his own absence. But beside his face, a photographic procedure has revealed another, which Courbet himself described as that of a "black woman looking very coquettishly at herself in a mirror": it is Jeanne, the indecorous mistress, whom Courbet had to erase, at Baudelaire's insistence—and so she is transformed into an occult, spectral angel. When she finally emerges from the canvas, her features are superimposed by two pen-and-ink sketches that Baudelaire was to make of her a few years later, on one of which we can read, *quaerens quem devoret*, "in search of someone to devour." Muse and vampire.

Narcisse Ancelle and General Aupick were the two archons looming closest to Baudelaire. Both shot through with a vein of the ridiculous, in their names alone. Both unsuited to the majesty of their task. They did evil with paternalism. This made them even more intolerable, revealing their complicity with the Parisian backdrop against which they stood out. They were *like many others*, dignitaries set in their social

niche—eminent, that of the general; average, that of the lawyer—satisfied with their function and equally incapable of imagining how they could feel otherwise. But this did not diminish the intensity of the torture they could inflict. When Baudelaire condensed the Revolution of 1848 (and all revolutions) with the exhortation "We have to go and shoot General Aupick!" he was under no illusion that existing powers hinged on the general. Yet his cry remains the most efficacious—and also the most precise—of all social rebellions since then. As for the memory of the humiliations he was subjected to, they were not dulled over time. This is what Baudelaire wrote to his mother, about Ancelle: "If you knew how much he made me suffer for some years. There was a period in which my person, my opinions and my affections were a perpetual cause for derision on the part of his horrible woman, his ghastly daughter, and those horrendous brats." A portrait of a mid-nineteenth-century family.

On the general's death, Baudelaire was obliged to recognize Evil in Ancelle, in that suburban lawyer, dominated by a "puerile and provincial curiosity," a man "at once mad and foolish," a busybody by vocation, hungry above all for gossip with anyone, for the pure pleasure of accumulating snippets of information. When Baudelaire found himself in the company of some acquaintance, Ancelle immediately interfered. He ensconced himself at Gautier's, at Jeanne's—and he talked and talked. He was the *voyeur* of Baudelaire's life. He was the bourgeois who wanted the artist to depend on him, even merely in order to survive, but he didn't want to miss a chance to sneak in, thanks to the artist, to places that would have otherwise been inaccessible to him. With respect to Baudelaire, Ancelle was nothing less than *the world*. Even though he certainly would have denied this, out of false modesty. But Baudelaire knew with whom he was dealing. Once he wrote it in all capital letters: "HE IS MY GREATEST ENEMY (and not out of wickedness, I know)." And one day, in subversive circles, someone will talk of the *greatest enemy*.

Above all, Ancelle wanted to buttonhole everyone and anyone. Preferably Baudelaire's friends in artistic circles, because then he could boast that he had met them. But at times he would content himself even with an innkeeper. As long as he could talk, as long as he was in the know. His technique had some perverse traits, which exasperated Baudelaire. With intellectuals, he would start talking without introducing himself, using a certain manner that seemed to suggest an old acquaintance. And above all he let it be understood that no one was as well informed as he, always, about every detail of Baudelaire's life. Ancelle's presence was not openly malevolent, but something worse: he cut off the air. Everything fed his curiosity and offered a pretext for satisfying it. With powerless dismay, Baudelaire told his mother of his conclusions:

"I have understood that he wanted to wrest from me the names of the people with whom I have certain very complicated affairs, solely to GOSSIP with them." Had his fateful role in Baudelaire's life not been evident, Ancelle could even have been overwhelmingly comic, a forerunner of certain characters in Feydeau or Courteline. But it was precisely this deceptive innocuousness that conferred an even more sinister air upon him, just as the brusque bonhomie of General Aupick made his shadow even more oppressive.

Ancelle's principal fault was that he had "no respect" for other people's time. His method was torture, hesitation. His weapon was a slight stammer that kept Baudelaire on tenterhooks for hours, dependent as the poet was on Ancelle in order to cash some small sum. There has even remained an—irresistible—sample of the way he spoke. Baudelaire wrote to Caroline: "I would have liked to do absolutely without those 500 francs. I would certainly have preferred that, rather than see him and hear him *stammer slowly, for hours*: 'You have a really good mother, don't you? *Do you love your mother?*—or even: *Do you believe in God*, there is a God, isn't there? Or even: *Louis Philippe was a great king.* They will do justice to him, one day . . .' Each of these phrases was diluted over half an hour. During all that time, people were expecting me in various quarters of Paris."

An evening on the Bosporus: The minister plenipotentiary of France, General Aupick, and his lady wife received two young men of letters who were making their *voyage en Orient*, as others before them used to make the Grand Tour in Italy. Their names were Maxime Du Camp and Gustave Flaubert. The general liked to appear an open-minded man, curious about the things of the world. He knew that the conversation would inevitably have to grant something to the profession of his two guests. After dinner, in coarse and protective tones, he asked a perfunctory question: "Has literature made any good recruits since you left Paris?" A question that did not necessarily require a precise answer. On the contrary, an answer would have made it necessary to go into detail; ever a sorry business on evenings like that one. But Maxime Du Camp felt honor bound to mumble something or other: "Recently, at Théophile Gautier's, I met a certain Baudelaire, who will make a name for himself." Sudden embarrassment. The ambassador's wife lowered her

gaze. The general had the air of someone about to react to a provocation. Shortly after, when the general and Flaubert had begun talking
about something else, Mme Aupick went up to Maxime Du Camp and
whispered, "He has talent, hasn't he?" Only at the end of the evening,
in front of Colonel Margadel's collection of lepidopteras, would Maxime Du Camp come to know that Charles Baudelaire was Mme Aupick's
son and that his stepfather, the general, had condemned and banned
him—and would not tolerate the mention of his name.

On returning to Paris in March 1853, by then no longer the wife of the
ambassador to Madrid, but of the newly nominated senator Aupick, Caroline found Charles in a "painful state" following a year that had been "a
real disaster." And she immediately showed an "admirable indulgence."

But there was an urgent question: according to Caroline, much of
Charles's pain had to do with the lack of shoes with rubber soles. On
this, too, his mother was to be gainsaid. This time, with the pride of the
true wretch, Baudelaire explained to her that he had become very skilled
at stuffing the holes in his shoes with straw, or even with paper. He made,
he explained stubbornly, real "straw soles or even paper ones." Not only
that: by then he knew how to "slip perfectly two shirts under a pair of
torn pants and a suit that the wind blows through." In this way, he
claimed, "I feel almost solely moral pains." He did not add, but perhaps
hinted, that this observation could be immediately grasped by a woman
of whom he had read in a paper that "the poor of Madrid would miss."

Immediately after, in the same letter, Baudelaire described himself
in a quick sketch (almost a Guys of dereliction) that remains fixed in the
memory of anyone who met him: "Yet, I must confess, I have come to
the point where I no longer dare to make sudden movements or even to
walk too much for fear of making the rips wider." Here was a young
man, good-looking and elegant, who walked too cautiously, as if hin-
dered by an invisible burden. It was Baudelaire at thirty-two. No one
knew that he thought only of the holes in his clothes, "which the wind
blows through." He is a first Buster Keaton in a frock coat, who moves
off, slowly, through the streets of Paris.

•

"In Racine's tragedy, the material element on which spiritual life must rest was that form of human society called life at court, that concentration of values, of beauty, of being in a whole country, in a small space, around a king, and this reaches its perfection in the first twenty years of the reign of Louis XIV. Now, Paris insofar as it is the capital, occupies in nineteenth-century Europe the same place as Louis XIV's seventeenth-century court." Paris as the modern equivalent of Versailles: this insight of Thibaudet's is the premise underlying Benjamin's title *Paris: Capital of the Nineteenth Century*. It also underlies the profound affinity between Baudelaire and Racine, which we see constantly in the air of their Alexandrines, but which is not easy to grasp. For Racine, humanity was to be observed within the court of Versailles, for that place, precisely because of its artificiality (which is that of all frames), enhanced the evidence of the passions, seen under a powerful magnifying glass. Baudelaire lived in Paris like a courtier-prisoner of Versailles. All that he wrote presupposed a prepared, intensely cultivated terrain, the only one that did not grant diversions, if not of the illusory sort.

Baudelaire's Paris is chaos within a frame. The essential thing is recognition of the chaos, of the pullulating forces and forms, of the benevolent hospitality accorded to all variations of the monstrous. But equally essential is the presence of the frame, of this artifice that delimits and separates. The metaphysical significance of this was more than clear to Baudelaire, insofar as it is the primary device that establishes a gap in reality, a gap that is produced in the mind as soon as a division occurs between the eye that looks and the eye that is looked at. The frame can be applied to a painting, to a woman (and then it is the entire ornamental apparatus that envelops her—and it becomes a powerful erotic artifice), or to any scene from life. In any event, it adds to the framed figure or scene a certain *"Je ne sais quoi d'étrange et d'enchanté / En l'isolant de l'immense nature."* This is the decisive operation: the act whereby something, anything, is carved out of the formlessness all around it and observed in itself, like a stone held in a hand. If all Baudelaire's poems tend to present themselves as a *tableau parisien*, it is because they are always pictures in which the frame unleashes in the picture itself an energy whose origin would not otherwise be evident.

All that happens within the frame intensifies the elements circumscribed by it, obliging them to crossbreed in combinations never before experimented with. And so the new is born. Thus it happens that the pure mutation of "the form of a city" opens up a chasm in the memory that makes it possible to join, in a moment, the prisoner Andromache as she desolately contemplates Troy reconstructed in miniature at Butrotus, the place of vain desire, which "has suddenly fecundated my fertile memory"—says Baudelaire—as he crosses "the new Carrousel." And Andromache has none of the period embellishments that used to accompany the evocation of names from history, but appears with the same immediacy as a "black woman, emaciated and consumptive, tramping through the mud and seeking, with bleak stare, the absent coconut palms of superb Africa behind the immense wall of mist." If these magnificent verses are set, as here, in prose, in a continuous discourse, not even marked by the capitals at the beginning of the verse, they reveal even more clearly what lies behind both figures: loss, an irreparable loss, harrowing for the figure who roams through the great city. No natural scenario could have aroused, or even alleviated, such keen suffering, which will not be healed.

If we were to ask people which of Baudelaire's poems is the first to come to mind, many would say "The Swan." And it would be hard to disagree. That intersection and collision of distant and disparate levels, in the memory and in perception, is something found only in Baudelaire— and after him it would no longer be presented with similar pathos within so ancient and formal a frame.

The beginning is blistering: "Andromache, I think of you!" Andromache is not the name of his beloved, even though she is invoked with such immediacy and intimacy. She is an epic character, thousands of years old. She is not Racine's Andromache, nor Homer's. She is the forgotten Andromache from a minor episode in the *Aeneid*: the woman who was passed like "base cattle" from one man to another after having "fallen from the arms of a great husband," Hector. Now she lives in a foreign land, a land of enemies, Epirus. Around her is a tiny simulacrum of Troy, which ought to mitigate but instead exacerbates her pain for the Troy destroyed by fire.

By then no one thought of Andromache. No one except Baudelaire, as he was crossing the new Carrousel. The modern reader cannot assess the dramatic implications of these words. Today the place mentioned by Baudelaire is the fast lane of a road. In passing, you have just enough time to see the snaking line of people in front of the Louvre, which plunges down into Pei's pyramid. There, once upon a time, there teemed another life. Adjacent to the metaphysical heart of Paris, which is the Palais-Royal, place du Carrousel had to be crossed by anyone wishing to go to the Tuileries. Around the square, there was a neighborhood that was razed to the ground so that the Louvre and the Tuileries could be linked. The square was a "a vast parallelogram" wherein were kept "the sovereign, the great powers of the state, the art treasures, like an Acropolis housing all that the empire contains that is most sacred, most august and most precious." The words are none other than those of Gautier, by now reduced by the Second Empire to an amenable pen. Yet those places meant something very different to him, as was also the case with Baudelaire. Alfred Delvau, a reporter of that time, remembered the places this way: "The place du Carrousel was enchanting, once: now it is populated by Saint-Leu's great stone men. Enchanting as disorder and picturesque as ruins! . . . It was a forest—with its inextricable tangle of shacks made of planks and shanties made of mortar, inhabited by a throng of minor businessmen and small businesses . . . I would often stroll amid this caravanserai of bric-a-brac, through this labyrinth of planks and these zigzags of shops, and I know its denizens almost intimately—men and beasts, beasts and things, rabbits and parrots, paintings and *rocailleries* . . ."

Between the two palaces, which represented the first-born and cadet lines of the royal family, the Tuileries and the Palais-Royal, there grew up an aggregate of the most formless and chaotic life, a fragment of "forest" proliferating alongside the heart of order. In the middle of that tangle, in rue du Doyenné, Gautier and Gérard de Nerval lived for a time. This was the precarious epicenter of the *bohème galante*. The rundown old salon had been restored and painted by some friends: two panels with Provençal landscapes by Corot, a Chassériau with bacchantes holding tigers on leashes like dogs, Châtillon's *Red Monk*, who is reading the Bible that rests on the curvaceous hip of a naked woman. There was also a portrait of Théophile (everyone understood it was Gautier) dressed up in the Spanish manner. The place swarmed with creatures called Cydalise I (like an empress) or Lorry or Sarah la Blonde. It so happened, Nerval noted, that "the *horrible* proprietor, who lived on the first floor, but over whose head we danced too often, after two years

of suffering, which had induced him to evict us, later had those paintings covered with a layer of tempera, because he maintained that those
nudes prevented him from renting to the bourgeoisie." But he did not
have many opportunities. Soon Nerval was to buy back from the de-
molishers some of those painted *boiseries*. Then everything would disappear. "We were young, always cheerful, often rich . . . But I have barely
touched the chord of bleakness: our building has been razed to the
ground. Last autumn I trampled over the rubble." Then Nerval decided: "The day they cut down the trees in the riding-school, I shall go
to the square to read Ronsard's *Adieu Vieille Forest*":

> Écoute, bûcheron, arreste un peu le bras:
> Ce ne sont pas des bois que tu jettes à bas;
> Ne vois-tu pas le sang, lequel dégoutte à force,
> Des nymphes qui vivaient dessous la dure écorce

An elegy that ends with cutting words, the toughest anti-Platonic
proclamation:

> La matière demeure et la forme se perd!

Nerval would have reread Ronsard. In the same places, Baudelaire
would write "The Swan." Two acts of farewell. Instead of the blood of
the nymphs, Andromache's tears, a meager brook. One of those days
Nerval was to meet Balzac: "Where did you lose so many beautiful
things? Balzac said to me. 'In misfortunes!' I replied, quoting one of his
favorite sallies." Balzac knew something of those places, because he had
set up his cousin Bette with a house there. And he had foreseen—in fact
almost wished for—its destruction: "The existence of the block of houses
along the old Louvre is one of those declarations of protest that the
French love to make against common sense, so that Europe will be reassured about the quantity of *esprit* it accords them and hence may no
longer fear them." Formidable sarcasm: the district of the Carrousel
would bear witness to the madness that still flourished in Paris, hence it
was a timely reassurance for foreigners intimidated by that *esprit*. And
Balzac already sensed that this strangeness was destined to be swept
away soon: "our grandchildren, who will certainly see the Louvre

finished, would refuse to believe that a barbarity of this kind could have existed for thirty-six years, in the heart of Paris, in front of the Palace where in the course of these last thirty-six years three dynasties have received the elites of France and Europe." But it did not elude his visionary eye that the ulterior significance of those places corresponded to the "need to symbolize in the heart of Paris the intimate alliance between wretchedness and splendor that characterizes the queen of capitals." Wretchedness and splendor. We are already very close to Baudelaire strolling along thinking about Andromache.

And not only her. From that improbable memory spring other images, other beings of extreme pathos. All emanating from something "ridiculous and sublime." Because by now, in the new age of Paris and the world, nothing could aspire to the *sublime* if not accompanied by the ridiculous, as it once was by terror. The first of these beings is a swan, escaped from some modest menagerie set up in the square, which stretches out its neck convulsively and vainly opens its beak close to a "rivulet with no water" and recalls with desperation "its fair native lake." And then an anonymous African woman, wasted and consumptive, in search of vanished places.

That which unites these figures, the thing that indissolubly binds the princess, the animal, and the slave, is not merely exile or their extraneousness to the world. Something more serious and irreparable can be glimpsed in them. It is pure grief for that which vanishes. As Baudelaire walked through the new Carrousel, defined by others in those years as "one of the glories of our epoch," he feels as if his feet are trampling something that has become forever invisible, like the feet of the swan scraping at the "dry cobbles" of the old place du Carrousel. Whatever the place, whatever the condition, there is always *another* place, there is always *another* condition that is lost forever. No unhappiness can compare with this, which is the pure realization of an absence. Even exile, even life as an inevitable foreigner (which pertains to those who write), is none other than a first revelation—still attributable to circumstances or misfortune—of something that instead belongs to all and to every moment. Something that belongs, distributed with impartial generosity, equally to whoever lives in time. This is the rock bottom that Baudelaire reached in his wanderings from the hôtel Voltaire, crossing the Seine by the Carrousel bridge, to the newly restored Louvre. And this explains why at the end, called up by the invisible, there appear around him not only the shades of Andromache, the swan, and the consumptive black woman, but also a horde of nameless characters, as in Hades. The shades of "whoever has lost something and will never find it again," all those who have lived, that is. The first to appear will be the shades of "castaway sailors on an island," "prisoners," and the "vanquished," but the crowd is much larger than that. All the dead belong to it. And so the last words can be the commonest and the most prosaic, but here they are sublime and no longer, because of their supreme sadness, ridiculous. The vision expands; one glimpses the shades of "many more still!"

It is natural to wonder why Andromache—the Andromache of the *Aeneid*—was so present, so familiar, so nearly akin to Baudelaire. Was Baudelaire that keen a reader of Virgil? It doesn't seem so—even though the poem pays homage to him, beginning with the epigraph "falsi Simoentis ad undam." But another shade stood between Baudelaire and Andromache. One with whom Baudelaire felt a steadily growing affinity as time went by: the creator of the "great school of melancholy," the "great lord great enough to be cynical," the "great gentleman of decadence" ("great" was obligatory for Baudelaire when speaking of him), the "father of Dandyism": Chateaubriand. More than in Virgil, it was in a few lines from *The Genius of Christianity* that Baudelaire had encountered Andromache: "Andromache gives the name *Simois* to a *stream*. And what a moving truth in *this little stream*, which mimics a *great river* of her native land! Far from the banks that saw our birth, nature is as if diminished, and it no longer seems to us as any more than the shade of what we have lost." For Baudelaire, this last phrase was decisive. The absent, the vanished—hence all the past—is placed in the hands of an incurable nonexistence. That which actually exists is doomed to be a *diminished* version of it. In this way all nature is attenuated nature, one that has already lost some of its color. The consequences of this paradox of absence are inexhaustible. Chateaubriand formulated it, but by applying it to the "instinct of the homeland," which is only one of the many applications of that paradox. With his metaphysical antennae, Baudelaire drew on all its desperate consequences. And so he wrote "The Swan."

For Baudelaire, the disappearance of the old place du Carrousel—
"camp of booths," a shapeless mass of men and animals, cluttered with
debris—is like the disappearance of Troy for Andromache; for the swan
transported into a menagerie, it is like the "fair native lake"; for the
"wasted and consumptive black woman" in Paris, it is like the "superb
Africa" of her memory; for anyone, it is like something that will never
be found again; for those who "drink of tears," for the "skinny orphans
who wither like flowers," for the "castaway sailors on an island," for the
"prisoners," for the "vanquished," and for "many more still"—it is like
what they have lost. This is the equation of "The Swan," a poem that
stands out for its dizzying acceleration, whereby the first to mourn an
apparently minor loss—Baudelaire himself, who cannot find a demolished fragment of Paris—ends by losing himself in an infinite mass of
the dead and the living. Absence has a cruel leveling effect, by virtue of
which the high walls of Troy and the painted planks of some shacks,
certain unnamable griefs and the loss of parents or freedom are all like
the "absent coconut palms," with an "immense wall of mist" between us
and them. This mist, in its majesty, is the obscure center where all converges: Troy, Paris, Africa, or freedom itself, seem almost not to matter;
what matters about all things is that they vanish.

Baudelaire had a knack for getting entangled in grotesque situations
that left him no way out. In the spring of 1853, together with his friend
Philoxène Boyer, a learned and boisterous bohemian, he decided to set
out for Versailles to compose a work whose success struck him as a sure
thing (as Boyer said to his friend Geidan before leaving, borrowing a
shirt from him in the meantime). Behind Boyer's words we feel we can
hear Baudelaire, a month earlier, assuring his mother that over the last
year "*he had had proof* . . . that he could really make money, even a lot of
money, by applying himself with constancy." Well, Versailles represented an opportunity. For Boyer, it was a matter of "going to Versailles
and preparing a story about Louis XIV there, basing the work on the
lives and deeds of the various personages whose portraits lend luster to
the galleries of the chateau." Boyer thought the project was "very original, very interesting." It remains unclear as to why the success of the
enterprise should be considered *certain*.

The first step was to install himself in a "grand hotel in Versailles." The first step and the last, because, Boyer acknowledged, "our resources were soon exhausted." So the proprietor threw them out, keeping their "modest baggage" in pawn. At this point, enter Baudelaire's talent. On their own in Versailles, "with empty pockets," what could the two friends come up with? Baudelaire's suggestion was that they have themselves put up in a brothel, where he decided to stay "in pawn." Let us pause to appreciate the perfection of the procedure: unable to pay, Baudelaire's idea was to take refuge in a place where everything is for sale and everything must be paid for. And there he transformed himself into a physical guarantee of payment. There is a perverse logic at work here, which only the pages of *My Heart Laid Bare* can illustrate. So poor Philoxène set off toward Paris to rake up some money. He returned three days later. Baudelaire treated him badly, because he found the sum "insufficient." Or perhaps it was because he wanted to stay on a little longer in that limbo of irresponsibility? After all, in those days he had written perhaps three of the finest poems in *Les Fleurs du mal*. In any case, Philoxène was ordered to stay, while Baudelaire assured him that he would find the rest of the money in Paris that very night. "But he never showed up again and my hosts showed me the door as if I were a criminal," Boyer was later to confide to Geidan, who was present at the beginning of the adventure.

"After a night of pleasure and desolation, all my soul belongs to you": words found in the epigraph of the poem plausibly sent from Versailles to Mme Sabatier and later published in *Les Fleurs du mal* with the title "L'Aube spirituelle" (but without the epigraph). Their flavor is even keener if we suppose they were written in the brothel in Versailles. And it is not diminished if we recognize in them an echo of a phrase of Griswold's in his account of Poe's death: "After a night of insanity and exposure . . ." The *spiritual dawn* to which the title refers is the result of the "work of an avenging mystery." But which? It is a mystery that Joseph de Maistre had called *"reversibility,"* daring to define it: "the great mystery of the universe." Reversibility refers to this: sins and virtues communicate, and so *"the virtues of the innocent can serve the guilty,"* even redeem them. It is this two-way subterranean circulation between misdeed and good that confers upon the world an "incomprehensible unity, the necessary basis of the *reversibility* that might explain everything, if it could be explained." De Maistre's tone already has us understand that here we have set foot in the most obscure and dangerous area of thought. And the fact that it remains obscure cannot have displeased de Maistre, convinced as he was that "the more the intelligence knows, the more it is capable of being guilty."

Baudelaire was not so scrupulous, but shared the doctrine with de Maistre, in fact he had discovered it in his books. And never in poetry did he reveal it as in the three poems for Mme Sabatier written in the brothel in Versailles. One reveals its secret in the title he eventually gave it in *Les Fleurs du mal:* "Réversibilité." Without that title—which makes sense only in light of de Maistre's theory—the poem might seem an invocation to a beloved, who appears as an "angel full of gaiety," written by a lover beset by "anguish, / Shame, remorse, sobs, ennui, / And the vague terrors of these atrocious nights." The mechanism of reversibility is triggered only at the end, where the lover says, "I beg nothing of you, angel, but your prayers." An exchange, therefore, could take place between the unwitting and happy beloved and her tormented lover: the sufferings of the lover could be counterbalanced by the prayers of his beloved. And so life could go on, instead of becoming paralyzed. It is an intimate and cryptic version (and all the more cryptic insofar as the beloved does not know *who* is addressing her) of another cosmic and metahistorical balance, about which de Maistre had written, "On the one side all the crimes, on the other all the satisfactions; from this spring the good works of all men, the blood of the martyrs, the sacrifices and the tears of innocence that accumulate unremittingly to balance out the evil that, from the origin of things, pours its poisoned waves into the other container." An exchange that can take place in both directions, when the prayers of the beloved redeem the sins of her lover, but also when the lover, to make an accomplice of his beloved, is prepared to open in her "a gaping, deep wound," in which "T'infuser mon vénin, ma soeur!"—to infuse you with my poison, my sister! (This verse horrified the court and persuaded it to include the poem in the *pièces condamnées*. The judges did not say as much explicitly, but Baudelaire himself made up for this in a note to the second edition of *Les Fleurs du mal*: nothing was easier, or falser, than to confer a "syphilitic interpretation" upon that *poison*, which "means *spleen* or melancholy.")

The daughter of a prefect and a seamstress, but officially the daughter of a soldier who had fought in the Napoleonic Wars—who had provided the prefect with a convenient cover, Aglaé-Joséphine Savatier became Apollonie Sabatier when her mother moved from the Ardennes. She changed her surname herself; her given name was conferred upon her by Théophile Gautier, who also dubbed her "la Présidente." This was how she was known in a circle of friends that included Flaubert, Bouilhet, and Du Camp, and the painters and musicians of the day. At eighteen she was a mistress—and she remained one for a lifetime, with no acrimony, no ostentation, no illusions. Mme Sabatier was a mistress just as one can be a surgeon or a botanist or an engineer. It was an available profession, one that could be practiced with greater or lesser grace. Probably out of a shrewd sense of strategy, above all she strove to appear carefree. Her opulent, silken beauty was a precious asset for her. Various sources concur in stating that she succeeded superbly well in her intentions. At ten years of age, Judith Gautier, daughter of Théophile (who was the *spiritus rector* of the place), was introduced in rue Frochot by la Présidente: "She was rather tall and well proportioned, with very fine joints and enchanting hands. Her hair was a very silky golden chestnut that hung down as if naturally in luxuriant waves dappled with highlights. She had a clear, compact complexion, regular features, with a hint of something gamine and witty, and a small laughing mouth. Her triumphant air created an aura of light and happiness around her." This last sentence connects directly with Baudelaire, for whom Mme Sabatier— this woman *qui n'était pas son genre*—emanated that rare kind of happiness that did not disgust him, an aura that could strike him as a blessing in its very existence.

After he had been sending unsigned letters for over a year, Baudelaire wrote Mme Sabatier something that revealed his primitive idolatry: "what's more there's no doubt that you have been so inundated, so saturated with compliments that by now only one thing can flatter you, that is to know that you do good—even without knowing it, even when sleeping—simply by living." In the cosmic economy as perceived by Baudelaire, the pure existence, the happy breath of Mme Sabatier, must have acted as a power strong enough to resist the regular scourges that fell on him every day.

This would explain why, when Baudelaire saw the date of the trial for *Les Fleurs du mal* looming nearer, and he realized his most serious weakness (*"I lack a woman,"* he wrote to his mother in those days), his thoughts could only have turned to Mme Sabatier. At the trial for *Madame Bovary*, Flaubert had been saved by the intervention of Princess Mathilde. Now Baudelaire decided to rely on a lady of the *demi-monde* (whom the Goncourts, with their unsleeping malevolence, defined as "a peddler of fauns"). And the connection was not that unfounded, because, after all, this was the age of Offenbach, and Mme Sabatier's lover *en titre* was the brother of the woman who had been for many years the mistress of the duc de Morny, the man whom popular opinion, rightly for once, held to be the most powerful personage of the Second Empire. But like all of Baudelaire's enterprises in his own favor, the ploy didn't work. Instead, it obliged him to present himself before Mme Sabatier in person, even though he knew he had already been recognized. (Bébé, Apollonie's little sister, had said to him one day: *"are you still in love with my sister, and do you still write her marvelous letters?"*) Even though the reason for writing a letter was, this time, an urgent request for help, Baudelaire could not resist referring to certain dogmas of his amorous theology, declaring *"fidelity is one of the marks of genius,"* or describing himself as someone who "is a little vexed with you on account of your artful *gaiety*." But it is in the envoi that the letter illuminates, with superb simplicity, the obscure and lofty function that Mme Sabatier performed for Baudelaire: "You are my constant Company, and my Secret. It is this intimacy, where for a long time I have been replying to my own questions, which has given me the audacity to use such a familiar tone." Since Petrarch, no one had been capable of speaking in such a disarming way to his Muse, *"née* language," which as such is the precedent of every beloved.

Baudelaire never used the poems for Mme Sabatier as an "applied art" in Brodsky's sense, in other words as a pretext and an artifice for winning his beloved. For six months, with long pauses, but doggedly and with perfect coherence in tone and imagery, he elaborated a brief cycle of variations around a mental phantasm. Such and so many were the possible occasions that might have brought him close to Mme Sabatier, so numerous were their mutual friends, from Gautier to Flaubert, that we must believe Baudelaire when he writes that for a long time his efforts were aimed at coming up with expedients for *not* seeing her. So, still in 1857, Mme Sabatier could encounter Baudelaire on the street and greet him with an elusive *"Bonjour, Monsieur,"* like a casual acquaintance, even if "with that beloved voice whose timbre enchants and torments." If the *Les Fleurs du mal* trial had not come up, if Baudelaire—in any case too late—had not thought of her as a last resort in the hope of getting a hand from the powerful, perhaps the poems for Mme Sabatier would have gone on distilling themselves as the work of one of those "poets who have spent their entire life with their eyes fixed on the beloved image." Otherwise they would have dried up forever like a wellspring lost among the brambles.

A little over three years after Baudelaire sent his last unsigned letter to Mme Sabatier, he wrote her again, signing the letter this time and attributing all the previous ones to himself. But now the reason, as almost always in Baudelaire's letters, was eminently practical. The trial for *Les Fleurs du mal* was scheduled for two days later, and Baudelaire found it hard to imagine he would be acquitted. He had never been acquitted in any circumstance of his life, so why should he be acquitted in this case, which was symbolic? So he took up his pen and wrote to Mme Sabatier, asking her to intervene in his favor with some powerful person. The result was a love letter even more poignant than the earlier ones, as were some letters to Caroline, complete with frantic requests for money. That Mme Sabatier might in the end also serve some purpose, that her benefits were not limited to her pure existence and her beatific breath: this was enough to bring her closer to Baudelaire's customary tone, which was that of a hounded man. In this way it would have been possible to put Mme Sabatier's ultimate power to the test, a power that consisted not only in her being "an image, dreamed of and beloved" (how many women had been thus, between Musset and Lamartine . . .), but something far more archaic and binding, which only Baudelaire could adore: a superstition. "You are more than an image, dreamed of and beloved; you are my *superstition.*" And here Baudelaire added a brief passage in which we notice a vibrant trace of infancy: "When I do something really stupid, I say to myself: My God! If she knew about this!"

In the space of a year and a half, at intervals of every few months, Baudelaire sent Mme Sabatier six poems, each accompanied by a few lines in prose, without ever revealing his name. In doing this, he complied with an archaic schema, not unlike the one used by Dante with Beatrice in the *Vita nuova*, albeit adapted to the times. In other words, he used the mail. The first poem, "To She Who Is Too Gay," sounds the chord that engenders all the others: the beloved is asked to do nothing other than let herself be punished for being "too gay." Behind this amorous fencing, which Sainte-Beuve understood immediately and correctly as an Alexandrine variation, we glimpse the tormented relationship between the poet and, no less, nature. More precisely: "The insolence of Nature." Unlike the adherents of the Enlightenment, Baudelaire knew that nature was first and foremost the bearer of guilt, followed by the procession of all ills. But this was not enough to deprive nature of a patina of splendor, which many misinterpreted, considering it a sign of innocence. Hence it happened that spring and luxuriant greenery *humiliated* the poet's heart. And he, as always, wanted to be understood literally: the mocking aspect of nature lies in its capacity to ignore the melancholy that is instead propagated by it. For this reason, woman, the figurehead of nature, is accused mainly of lacking an essential element: melancholy. It's easy, almost obligatory, to translate this in rather naïve psychological terms. Nor does Baudelaire prevent this; in fact, he almost encourages it, by coming up with the scheme of anonymous letters addressed to a lady who was very well known in the incorrigible *demimonde* of the artists. By virtue of a spell whose secret he guarded, in his work the closest he gets to the angelicized woman (one verse dedicated to her even reads, "Her spiritual flesh has the perfume of the Angels") is a representative of *haute bicherie*, who had allowed Parisians to peek at the unseemly image par excellence (the female orgasm) in a notorious sculpture by Clésinger.

Then there is another detail. In "Confession," one of the most ill-treated and beautiful poems addressed to Mme Sabatier, for the first and the only time Baudelaire gives voice to a woman. It is as if the enchanting and unknown passerby of this poem were leaning on Baudelaire's arm to whisper some secret to him, something Jean Prévost found "extremely banal." But he was too hasty, because rather than considering the concept, one should listen to the rhythm, which cannot be deleted. Here are the words of Mme Sabatier during the nighttime stroll called up—and perhaps invented by Baudelaire:

> Que c'est un dur métier que d'être belle femme,
> Et que c'est le travail banal
> De la danseuse folle et froide qui se pâme
> Dans un sourire machinal;

Is this extremely arduous task, this military mission "to be a beautiful woman" really so banal? And in accounts of Mme Sabatier, when we unfailingly read of her eternal gaiety, helpfulness, benevolence, when we read the kind of coarseness her devotees permitted themselves in her regard, certain that they would not be blamed, do Baudelaire's words not return to mind as the authentic "horrible secret" that Mme Sabatier might have whispered "to the confessional of the heart"—Mme Sabatier, this woman of whom we know nothing except that she was liked by many men (on a par with many other women) and whose voice is heard only in a few lines uprooted from three letters to Baudelaire that are now lost?

Mme Sabatier's devotees ritually convened for dinner at her house on Sunday evenings and declared in unison that they adored her. But in all of them Mme Sabatier irresistibly aroused some vulgar allusions, as is borne out in Gautier's *Lettres à la Présidente*, where more than the insistence on the obscene, the distressing aspect is the author's puerile self-satisfaction at his own wit. We do not know what the recipient made of Gautier's letters, because la Présidente never had a bad word to say about her friends.

Only through Baudelaire, when the anonymous poet declared himself and, in a night of love followed by a few turbulent August days, their passion flared up and burned to ashes, can we hear, albeit for only a moment, the voice of Mme Sabatier, in three fragments of letters that have fortunately survived. A voice that reveals itself to be in tune with that of her lover; even in irony, when she reproves him for showing "too much subtlety for a blockhead of [her] stamp." She goes on, and from her words one gathers that she knew all about the psychic agony that obliged Baudelaire to back away with the maximum celerity from an affair that threatened to offend him with the insolence of happiness: "What mortal chill has blown on this beautiful flame. Is it perhaps simply the effect of wise reflections?" For Baudelaire, "wise reflections" implied the decision not to touch on "certain knots that are difficult to loosen" that had been impeding his movements for years. Jeanne, his creditors, Ancelle: through a perverse and tortuous silent logic, that daily weariness frightened him less than the "tempest" of which Mme Sabatier was the bearer. And at this point Baudelaire added the phrase that served as his definitive leave-taking: "But what I know well is that I have a horror of passion—for I know it, with all its ignominies."

"Is there not perhaps something essentially comical about love?" wrote Baudelaire to Mme Sabatier, still under the protection of anonymity: an example of one of those irresistible sentences that well up everywhere—in letters or in sonnets. And often they are sentences that no one before him had managed to say, due to some mental or physiological obstacle, some fear of damaging the proprieties and the genres. Yet they are expressions that we cannot do without, corresponding to something inevitable, to an experience lying in wait for all, which otherwise would remain mute.

Only with Baudelaire would the "manly dough" of poetry recognize its inadequacy—until womanly hands came to knead it. At the start of everything there is the physical contact with the "undulating, scintillating and scented apparatus" that underpins all erotic perceptions. Without the "precocious taste for the female *world, mundi muliebris*," Baudelaire insinuates, without an attraction, even before that for the mother, "for the pleasant titillation of silk and fur, for the scent of the bosom and the hair, for the tinkle of jewelry, for the play of ribbons, etc.," even the "ruggedest and most virile genius remains, in proportion to the perfection of art, an incomplete being." Here, for the first time, a certain clumsy male *pruderie* is unearthed, something we come across everywhere around Baudelaire—and certainly it was not dented either by Heine or Hugo. This is the premise of Mallarmé's *dernière mode*, and this is what was to triumph in Odette and in the shots of Max Ophuls. This is what confers an unmistakable air upon some of his female visions, which in Baudelaire may also present themselves as allegories. In the worst cases, they resemble the figures portrayed in the monuments of great cities, suitable for separating deafening and indifferent traffic; or they have a hint of the cemeterial; or of the ornamental. And in any case, of the solemn and imprecise. For example, Beauty, evoked in the sonnet of the same name in *Les Fleurs du mal*, after having declared that it unites "a heart of snow with the whiteness of swans," goes as far as to confess its weakness by acknowledging that its "grand poses" look as if they were borrowed "from the proudest monuments." Here the allegorical figure seems to anticipate, lucidly, the parody of itself.

But there are also opposite cases—the most surprising, most peculiarly Baudelairean ones. In such cases the allegory allows itself to be absorbed into a single, unrepeatable figure, singled out down to the tiniest details of gesture. This is what happens in "Amour du mensonge," six allegorical quatrains almost devoid of capital letters. (There is only a forlorn "Heavens" in the twentieth line.) The allegory is declared in the title: the entire poem is a gesture of amorous homage to the *lie*. Let's take a look at the memorable opening lines:

> Quand je te vois passer, ô ma chère indolente,
> Au chant des instruments qui se brise au plafond
> Suspendant ton allure harmonieuse et lente,
> Et promenant l'ennui de ton regard profond;

Here no one thinks of an allegory. We simply glimpse a *woman*, captured in her secret rhythm, as she crosses a scene to the sound of music "that breaks against the ceiling." And in fact commentators doggedly persisted in trying to identify her: maybe Marie Daubrun? Or a certain Madame B——, to whom another of Baudelaire's poems was dedicated? Or an unknown actress? A dancer? Wisely, Claude Pichois concludes, "So, for now we must resolve not to know the identity of the heroine." The only sure thing is that the poem deals with a woman of mature beauty, if for no other reason than the fact that she appears as a turreted Cybele. The "regal and heavy tower" resting on her head is "massive memory." And, already, here—almost without noticing—we have stepped over into allegory. The female figure is no longer passing before us, with slow and indolent gait. Now she is still and seen head-on. We see her heart, which is certainly not the incongruous "heart of snow" of Beauty, but a heart "bruised like a peach" (a perfect Baudelairean touch). And her eyes reveal the strange phenomenon of an *empty melancholy*. Now, the most precious quality that Baudelaire denied women was melancholy. But here we feel that we have gone beyond the female being: we are in a land of "jewel caskets without jewels, medallions without relics." It is the land of pure appearance, happily oblivious to all substance. The land yearned for by "a heart that flees from the truth." The fact is that in this profound emptiness he *cheers up*. A singular sensation, and one attributable to another solitary visitor to that land: Nietzsche. For it was he who was to write, "*We have art* in order that we may not perish from truth."

"Moved by contact with those raptures that resembled memories, touched by the thought of an ill-spent past, of many mistakes, of many quarrels, of many things to conceal one from the other, he began to weep: and his warm tears ran down in the shadow of the naked shoulder of his dear and still attractive lover. She started; she too felt touched and shaken. The shadows reassured the vanity and the Dandyism of a cold woman. Those two decayed creatures, who still suffered owing to a remnant of nobility in themselves, embraced each other spontaneously, blending in the rain of tears and kisses the sadness of the past with highly dubious hopes for the future. It may be presumed that for them rapture had never been so sweet as on that night of melancholy and charity; a rapture full of pain and remorse.

"Through the black of the night he had looked behind himself into the depths of the years; then he had thrown himself into the arms of his guilty friend to find there the forgiveness that she granted him."

These lines arrive like a meteorite, on the pages of *Fusées*. What are they? The beginning of a novel? The end? Baudelaire claimed he had "twenty or so novels" in his head, with which he would have liked "to overwhelm souls, leave them amazed, like Byron, Balzac or Chateau-briand." But not much remains of them other than a few lists of titles. And this is no great loss. Baudelaire was rather clumsy and impatient when it came to weaving stories. He was not cut out for the novel. He could talk only of "eternal situations" that knew of no "resolution." His only Muse was the "irremediable." There is something static and hypnotic in the pictures that fill his pages. There is an "atmosphere of truth that hovers over the whole," the same atmosphere that Baudelaire recognized in De Quincey's visions. But there is no way out; nor do we wish for one, for it would spoil his evocations, break their spell. Baudelaire had no talent for any form of linear development, even a polyphonic one. He was the man of submersion, in time and in space; of the instantaneous vision that reveals many stage wings and loses itself in them. Hence those few lines marooned in *Fusées* can stand as an example of a hypothetical novel of his. No novelist of those years so ably fuses the sexual and the sentimental. This is eros steeped in the "singular benevolence" brought on by hashish, a feeling hinted at in *Artificial Paradises*: "a kind of philanthropy made more of compassion than love (here is where the first germ of the satanic spirit manifests itself)." In this parenthesis we recognize the cold theological eye of Baudelaire, who identifies the first germ of Satan in the prevalence of compassion over love. But benevolence is commingled with remorse as a "singular ingredient of pleasure" of which hashish encourages "rapturous analysis." What is at work here is a subtle chemistry of the mind, akin to abjection in Dostoyevsky. If Baudelaire had ever written a novel, this would have been it.

On three pages of the notebook in which Baudelaire jotted down the lists of his creditors, in ever-changing and ever-similar sequences, with the sums owed, and notes about things to do, we come across lists of women's names, sometimes with addresses. Jean Ziegler plausibly maintains that these are "bonnes addresses," taking refuge behind quote marks. If this is how it was, Baudelaire was not only a client, but sometimes a creditor and friend of these *filles* (Louise, for example, to whom he dedicated the *Fleurs* of 1861 with the words "To my dear and good Louise, old friendship. C.B."). The dedicatee was probably Louise Villedieu, "a five-franc whore" who once accompanied Baudelaire to the Louvre, where she had never been. Faced with the nude sculptures and paintings, she blushed, tugged her friend by his sleeve, and kept asking "how they could show obscenities of this kind in public."

Baudelaire took two weeks before sending *Les Fleurs du mal* to his mother. The copy on *grand papier* he had promised her ended up in the hands of the minister Achille Fould, who was to act as Baudelaire's high protector given the imminence of the legal case against him. There was always an impediment, something erotic in nature, as Baudelaire acknowledged when, finally, he decided to send the book to Caroline: "Modesty on my part would be just as mad as *pruderie* on yours." But, in addressing his mother, he did not want to spare her the precise, incisive cruelty he used in defining his book. He offered her a single precautionary sentence: "You know that I have never considered literature and the arts as other than things whose ends are extraneous to morality, and that beauty of concept and style are enough for me." Those are words that could be found strategically placed in any of his essays. Whereas the sentence that follows is decisive in its dryness, and seals the fatefulness of the moment: "But this book, whose title: *Fleurs du mal*—says it all, possesses, you will see, a sinister and cold beauty; it has been written with fury and patience."

Until the death of General Aupick, Baudelaire addressed his mother as he would a volatile and occasional lover, but one who always turned up, generally with a request for money. On the death of his stepfather, which he felt was "a solemn thing," his attitude changed. He saw in that event a "call to order." With impassive gravity he offered to fulfill the role of a third husband to his mother, after his father, Joseph-François, and General Aupick. He felt "from now on naturally responsible" for Caroline's happiness. So he wrote to her in the tone of a mature, protective, solicitous man who wanted to look after a lost young woman: "All that is humanly possible, with the aim of creating for you a new and particular happiness for the last part of your life, *shall be done*." Lest his intentions be mistaken for "filial duty," he hastened to set the matter straight: "The sale, your debts (of the moment), your health, your isolation, all interests me; that which is great or important, that which is trivial or minor, I shall attend to, believe me; not out of filial duty, but passion."

In the endless letter to Caroline of May 6, 1861, amid lists of debts and promissory notes, as if among underbrush and tangles of thorn bushes, we find a paragraph that is a vibrant and shameless declaration of love. Addressed from a forty-year-old son to his mother, it reads like a letter from one lover to another: "There was in my childhood a period of passionate love for you; listen and read without fear. I never spoke of this very much to you. I recall a trip in a carriage; you came out of a nursing home where you had been confined and you showed me, to prove to me that you had been thinking about your son, some ink drawings you had done for me. I have an amazing memory, don't you think? Later, place saint-André-des-Arcs in Neuilly. Long walks, constant tenderness! I recall the riverside embankment, so sad of an evening. Ah! For me it was the good time of maternal tenderness. I ask your forgiveness because I call a *good time* what was certainly a sad one for you. But I was always alive in you; you belonged solely to me. You were at once an idol and a companion. Perhaps it will surprise you that I can talk with passion about such a remote time. It surprises me too. It is perhaps because, yet again, I have conceived the desire for death that old things paint so graphically in my mind." Pure intensity, yet not dissociated in sentiment and thought. It is the word *passion*—otherwise denigrated by Baudelaire—that unleashes everything; to develop, to exercise, to exacerbate an "amazing memory" is the sole contribution that the writer's art can grant on its appearance. His words have the wayward vehemence of a wave: from celestial oceans, they came to break on a crumbling cliff in Calvados.

Left a widow, Caroline took up residence in Honfleur, in a villa that Baudelaire dubbed the "toy-house." For him it would be the only safe refuge, sheltered from the "horror of the human face." It stood "perched over the sea," and the garden looked like a small stage. Baudelaire concluded straightaway, "It's what I need." From then on his days would be punctuated by plans and promises to go to Honfleur. Then there were consignments of furnishings, drawings, papers, declarations that he had to wait. But the symbol is lurking everywhere. The house threatened to collapse, overwhelmed by the constant subsidence of the cliff. The garden was eroded little by little. Baudelaire was obsessed by the place: "The only serious thing that struck me in your letter *is the cliff.*" In Paris one moved as if in quicksand. But what if the distant refuge were to fall apart? The symbol's ironic power continued to act even posthumously. After Mme Aupick's death, the "toy-house" was purchased by the hospice of Honfleur, which built a contagious diseases ward in its place.

The air of Honfleur was good for Baudelaire, but it did not make a profound change in his moods, as he soon became himself again: "I'm really down, my dear fellow, and I have brought no opium with me, and I have no money to pay my pharmacist in Paris" (to Poulet-Malassis). But the time spent there gave him a little more breathing space, let him take his mind off things, if only by talking with the men at work in the garden. And straight off he set down the outline of a story, one of those abbreviated and swift narratives of which Baudelaire would have been a master if he had had the opportunity to practice them. A letter to Asselineau: "Local news: I have come to know from some men who were working on the garden that, some time ago, the mayor's wife was caught while having a fuck in a confessional. This was revealed to me because I asked why the church of Sainte-Catherine was closed during the hours in which there were no services. It seems that the curate had later taken precautions against sacrilege. She is an unbearable woman, who recently told me she had known the painter of the pediment of the Panthéon, but who ought to have a superb ass (she). Doesn't this story of provincial fucks, in a holy place, have all the classic flavor of good old French smuttiness?" Moreover, the parish priest of Sainte-Catherine was Caroline's spiritual director. At the time, Baudelaire spoke of him as a "good man . . . almost a remarkable man and even erudite." But soon he would dismiss him as "that damned curate." It seems that the priest wanted to burn a "precious copy" of *Les Fleurs du mal* that the poet had given to his mother. Possibly the priest really did this. ("As for burning books, no one does that anymore, except for maniacs who want to see paper in flames.") Always the same story, even in that corner of Calvados where Baudelaire hoped only to obey the "Muse of the Sea." The "toy-house" in Honfleur was also a modest parallel of Hugo's residence on Guernsey. Both of them overlooked the sea—or rather, the ocean. As always, Hugo's was far more imposing. His rocks were solid and defied the breakers, whereas Caroline's garden was eroding day by day.

There was another disquieting parallel. Precisely when Baudelaire was living in Brussels, Hugo decided to set up house there. Two poets abandoned the ocean: a good subject for a dissertation. Baudelaire, who was a vitriolic chronicler if need be, took note of the event: "By the way, this last [Victor Hugo] is coming to live in Brussels. He has bought a house in the Léopold district. It seems that he and the Ocean have quarreled. Either that or he wasn't strong enough to bear the Ocean, or the Ocean *itself* was tired of him. It was really worth the effort of carefully building a house on a cliff! As for me, alone, forgotten by all, I won't sell my mother's little house if not at my last gasp. But I still have more pride than Victor Hugo and I feel, I know, that I will never be stupid [*bête*] like him. One is fine anywhere (as long as one enjoys good health and has books and engravings), *even overlooking the Ocean*."

There is absolutely no sign that Baudelaire aspired to some sort of family life (not even a sigh like that of Flaubert: "Ils sont dans le vrai"). At most, he yearned for a quiet domestic life, orderly, repetitive: the opposite of that which was offered him every day. The all-too-brief spells with his mother in Honfleur were the only hint of that inclination, as if they cohabited like an old couple, disturbed only when the bailiffs came to knock on the door of the "toy-house," urging Baudelaire to pay his debts. Having reached forty, Baudelaire missed no chance to call himself *"an old man."* His first gray hairs had begun to appear. "To make them white," Baudelaire thought of powdering them, another way to become like Caroline. Maybe they would have been taken for a couple who had seen the world and had now retired to the provinces. He apologized to her for the "inanities of an old man."

In some of the poems added to *Les Fleurs du mal* for the second edition of 1861—whatever the theme, from "Voyage" and "The Swan" to "The Seven Old Men" and "The Little Old Ladies"—we note a change of pressure. The gauge has risen to the last notch before the intolerable. Baudelaire sought to take a few steps beyond, toward the "atrocious." He hinted at this with impassive irony: "I try to be like Nicolet, ever more atrocious." Nicolet was an actor who came up with bolder and bolder quips and excesses to attract the public. Hence the saying "Stronger and stronger like Nicolet." A constant surge, but to what end? Baudelaire did not fail to point this out, in a letter to his publisher Poulet-Malassis: "New *Fleurs du mal* done. They smash everything, like a gas explosion in a glassmaker's."

Baudelaire was a dandy, especially in ruin. Nothing resembles his voluntary exile in Brussels so much as Brummell's last years in Caen. Hounded by creditors, they both obeyed the same perverse impulse: they chose a place of unmitigated squalor, which they were sure they would abhor. *Ennui*, the tutelary power of *Les Fleurs du mal*, is traceable not only to René de Chateaubriand. It is found, penetrating and bitter, in one of Brummell's letters from Caen, where he speaks of wandering "in the desolate regions of *ennui*." There is a harrowing sign of Baudelaire's physical deterioration in Brussels, in the months preceding the crisis: a *lapsus calami*. In one of the many letters full of talk about the contracts due to arrive for his books, he stated that his critical essays were *easy to sell* (*d'un débit facile*); he wrote that they were "*d'une défaite facile*" (an easy defeat). A harbinger of imminent disaster.

"Dizzy spells and falls": this is how Baudelaire described to Sainte-Beuve the premonitory symptoms of the disease that would fell him a few weeks later in Namur. In the same letter (referring to pompous authors such as Thiers and Villemain), he posed the first question that should be asked about anyone who reads a book or looks at a picture: "Do these gentlemen really feel the *dazzlement and the enchantment of an art object?*"

On March 15, 1866, Baudelaire returned to Namur, especially to see the church of Saint-Loup, a very rare gem amid the horror of Belgium. As he was showing his friends Rops and Poulet-Malassis the confessionals of the church ("all in a varied, refined, subtle, baroque style, a *new antiquity*"), he tripped and fell. He did not laugh at himself, as he should have, according to his own precepts, had he been a philosopher. Instead he reassured his friends, saying that he had just slipped. That moment was the sign of the end. After that day, he was not to recover again. In falling, Baudelaire attempted to lie down in his last bed, because for him Saint-Loup was "a terrifying and delightful bier." More precisely: "The inside of a bier embroidered in *black*, *pink*, and *silver*." He wanted to end up in the place that was most similar to the essence of his work, which could be defined, no less than Saint-Loup, as a "sinister and elegant marvel."

On two occasions, when he attempted suicide at twenty-four and when he wrote a long, unwittingly testamentary letter a few days before he collapsed in Namur, Baudelaire chose Ancelle as the recipient of his words. This exasperating good man, the *"horrible affliction"* of Baudelaire's life, for some obscure reason could also serve, on occasion, as confessor and final companion. In that last letter, Baudelaire defined him as the "only friend" he could "insult." The remark he made next, ending the letter, was none other than Baudelaire's last judgment of his epoch. A judgment before which, in all its details, we can only bow: "With the exception of Chateaubriand, Balzac, Stendhal, Mérimée, de Vigny, Flaubert, Banville, Gautier, Leconte de Lisle, all the modern riffraff horrifies me. Virtue, horror. Vice, horror. A fluent style, horror. Progress, horror. Never talk to me anymore about those who say nothing." Many people have condemned their epoch since then. But no one was capable of listing "fluent style" among the horrors.

Countless attempts have been made to subject Baudelaire to some kind of psychological dissection, all of them clumsy and inopportune. Psychology stops at literature. And Baudelaire went beyond literature. But it remains indubitable that from every line of his there emerges the profile of a person, of a psychic climate, of a certain way of feeling alive. On leaving an exhibition on Baudelaire, Cioran recalled that once he had written, in one of his Romanian books, "From Adam—down to Baudelaire." Balkan pomposity? No, something that sounds right.

II

INGRES
THE MONOMANIAC

Ingres was one of those extremely rare people who are *nothing but* genius. Apart from that, it would be far too easy to be merciless about his stiffness, pettiness, overweening self-confidence, and pomposity. Attitudes to which genius was juxtaposed with the very characteristic of "fatality" that, according to Baudelaire, was exactly what Ingres lacked. Which is a notable oddity. Had it not been for Ingres, the nineteenth century would seem even more desperately nineteenth century, docked of that metallic and abstract light of his, which is neither natural nor supernatural or contrived, but has something in common with the tautological display found in Elinga or Torrentius.

"A Chinese painter, in the nineteenth century, lost among the ruins of Athens": this definition of Ingres, formulated by Théophile Silvestre when Ingres was still alive, has echoed down to this day. Yet Ingres showed no interest in China or in chinoiserie. His devotion, as everyone knew, was directed first and foremost at Raphael and the Greeks. So why did he seem like a Chinese to a contemporary, and a perceptive one at that? Perhaps it was Silvestre's contorted way of hinting at a most disconcerting fact: the more humbly Ingres submitted to diverse canons—he was a Greek with the Greeks or otherwise Nazarene, or Gothic, or Renaissance, according to the epoch he was portraying—the more his talent seemed extraneous to influence. His gaze fell on the successive cartoons of history like that of a Chinese "with a limpid and fine heart" (as Mallarmé was to observe one day) who took note of everything and proposed to copy everything, but kept an incommensurable distance from the subject. That distance is intrinsic to Ingres's painting—and the work is so deeply rooted in it that Ingres himself never showed any sign of noticing it. On the contrary, he vigorously stated rules and principles that would have excluded and condemned such distance as a recent perversion.

In Ingres's most felicitous works the paint deposited on the canvas does not seem to have passed through any verbal or conceptual filter, but rather, it looks like ectoplasm. Right from the start, critics saw some congenital shortcomings in Ingres. They found nature lacking, even though the artist continued to refer to the holiness of nature. Or at least they found in Ingres a "radical incapacity to perceive almost all that is a joy to the eye in nature," as Robert de la Sizeranne wrote in 1911, giving voice to an opinion widely held for decades. Yet that judgment had something that did not quite convince even the man who made it. Because, as Sizeranne himself observed, "this devil of a man was able, more powerfully than anyone else, to express what little he perceived." But what could that "what little" have been, that thin slice of reality that, in Ingres, stood out so plainly? And what other aspect—of reality—could expect as much? These questions have always been stifled. Perhaps because they are no longer even artistic questions, but metaphysical ones prompted by an artist (and we can state this without any fear of denial) who imperturbably ignored metaphysics altogether.

According to Valéry, who had heard it from Degas, "Ingres used to say that the pencil on the paper should have the same delicacy as a fly wandering across a window."

Théophile Thoré is remembered above all because it was he who, long before Swann, *recognized* Vermeer and rescued him from an obscurity in which all was uncertain, starting with the spelling of his name. But Thoré was also much more than this. When Baudelaire made his debut with the *Salons* of 1845 and 1846, the only rival from whom one could expect something comparable was Thoré. Baudelaire often used to meet Thoré in that period, before political reasons drove the latter into exile in Belgium, where many years later Baudelaire found him again, with "immense pleasure." In a letter to Ancelle, he described Thoré with an admirable *pointe*: "Thoré, although a republican, has always had elegant manners."

At the Salon of 1846, both Baudelaire and Thoré, as a matter of principle, could show only hostility to Ingres. In Baudelaire's view, it was necessary to side noisily with Delacroix; in Thoré's view, Ingres was the new tyrant who, when "the ashes of Louis David and his dynasty" were "still warm," had already claimed his crown. But nothing written then in praise of Ingres was as precise or as stimulating as Baudelaire's and Thoré's malevolent observations. No one was able to describe Ingres's paintings as well as Baudelaire did, albeit in hasty, almost reluctant glances. And no one explained better than Thoré the theory Ingres secretly complied with—and it was a theory wholly opposed to the one he professed. With assurance—and also with nonchalance, almost as if it were obvious—Thoré saw in Ingres the exemplary physiognomy of the *fanatic of form*. And this is the only aspect of the man to survive, the one that confers upon Ingres an Egyptian timelessness: "Basically, M. Ingres is the most Romantic artist of the nineteenth century, if Romanticism is an exclusive love of form, absolute indifference to all the mysteries of human life, skepticism in philosophy and politics, and egotistic detachment from all commonly held sentiments. The doctrine of art for art's sake is, in effect, a kind of materialist Brahmanism, which absorbs its adepts not in the contemplation of eternal things, but in the monomania of external and perishable form." There is no word that is not right there—and the last are almost alarming in their precision. Yet nothing is so far from the widely held opinion that Ingres and his adversaries squabbled over. The doctrine of *art pour l'art* had been thought up by Gautier—starting with the foreword to *Mademoiselle de Maupin*, which is from 1835—as a defensive stratagem for use against the steadily growing throngs of the obtuse who demanded that art *be useful*. But there was also an esoteric aspect to the doctrine, and it hinted at something else: the emergence of the fanaticism of form, to the exclusion of all other concerns.

But when Thoré was writing, it had never even crossed anyone's mind to think of applying the doctrine of *art for art's sake* to Ingres, to whom critics rather applied the magniloquent and disdainful image of a strenuous defender of classical antiquity—*any* classical antiquity—

against the corruption of the modern age, which found its banner in Delacroix.

Ingres lived through the most turbulent epochs without leaving a trace of evidence—not even a remark in a letter—that he grasped what was happening around him. For him a change of regime meant a decrease or an increase in commissions. This was the only reason why the fall of Murat was one of the ill-starred events of his life (largely because it involved the disappearance of the splendid *Sleeper of Naples*, which Ingres had painted for Caroline Murat and which was never found again). Thoré was a diehard republican—"always a republican, before, during and after," and after 1848 he would pay the consequences of his political actions. So he had absolutely no sympathy for Ingres's way of being. But it is to him that we owe a first mention of the physiognomy of the monomaniac artist: "M. Ingres therefore goes entirely against the mainstream with respect to the national tradition, and especially with respect to Louis David's recent doctrine. Yet in the French school what should have survived of David is this: love for generous things, enthusiasm for all acts of heroic abnegation. Brutus, Socrates, and Leonidas have been succeeded by Odalisques. The artist no longer has opinions; he follows only his imagination and, thus isolated from other men, disdains, from the heights of his pride, all the cases of everyday life." A perfect diagnosis, an involuntarily comic turn of phrase. Finally the Brutuses and the Leonidases go to ground and the curtain opens on the odalisques. This was the dawning of a new art, which was introduced by a painter who inveighed *against the new* every day. An enchanting comedy of errors, hanging among the rooms of a Salon and noticed by no one. But Thoré had done more than grasp that singular changing of the guard between two opposite forms of art. Even in the individual paintings of Ingres he saw something that others did not see: "M. Ingres's painting is more closely related than people think to the primitive painting of the Oriental peoples, which is a kind of colored sculpture. Among the Indians, the Chinese, the Egyptians, the Etruscans, whence do the arts begin? From bas-reliefs to which color is applied; then the relief is eliminated and there remains only the external outline, the brushstroke, the line; apply color to the interior of this elementary drawing and you will have painting; but air and space are not present at all." Now, that exclusion of air and space, that transposition of the painting into a second nature, without atmosphere and without depth, was exactly what Ingres had been covertly pursuing for years, even though he continued to declare himself a *"peintre de haute histoire"* and craved official commissions for solemn celebratory themes. But in the meantime he had ensured that the odalisques discreetly occupied the place reserved for the deeds of heroes.

Ingres corresponded fully to the description of the fanatic of form in Thoré. But he neither knew nor cared; no more than he cared about knowing what happened inside him as he breathed. He breathed, and that's all. As for the rest, he had his repertoire of sound principles—not of evident theoretical interest—that he trotted out as soon as possible, with the air of someone who, for one reason or another, is always offended. His contemporaries believed him. Above all they believed that his painting was true to his words. And so he sailed through his epoch like an astonishingly new ship that observers took for an old galley.

Written sources agree in presenting Ingres as a comical figure. But Théophile Silvestre certainly showed an excess of zeal (perhaps to please Delacroix) in making a portrait of the master that sounded outrageously malevolent, caustic, and hyperrealistic: "M. Ingres is a robust old man, of seventy-five years, stocky and ill-treated by time; of a vulgarity of aspect that clashes amazingly with the affected elegance of his works and his Olympian tendencies; one would say, on seeing him pass by, that he is someone who lives on a private income after having retired from business, if not a Spanish curate in civilian clothing; dark complexion, liverish; black, sparkling, suspicious, fiery eyes; sparse, contractile eyebrows; a narrow brow, sloping back to the top of the skull pointed like a cone; short, bristly hair, once very black, now graying, parted in the middle in the manner of women; big ears; pulsing veins in his temples; a prominent nose, a little short and hooked in appearance, owing to the distance separating it from the mouth; muscular, jowly cheeks; very marked chin and cheekbones, craggy jaw, thick surly lips.

"This elephantine bourgeois, composed of shapeless stumps, moves stiffly, with brusque jerky movements of his short legs, dashing down the stairs without holding on to the banister, hurling himself into the coach with one bound, his head lowered. If he had less violence in his blood, he would live for a century. The perfect care he devotes to his person and his disconcerting manners take at least twenty years off him. It's difficult to remain serious in the presence of this coarse majesty whose brow is girt with a triple crown: the nightcap, the laurel wreath and the halo. He never laughs, for fear of compromising his dignity; but he shows an amiable familiarity with models, housewives or the bookseller around the corner." And here Silvestre stops, as if to get his breath back, after having buried Ingres in the grotesque.

But, shortly after, he goes back on the attack, shifting it onto the theoretical level: "David had put form at the service of thought, now M. Ingres comes to establish the cult of form through the abolition of thought itself; to reduce the mission of Art to the sensual and sterile contemplation of brute matter, to an icy indifference to the mysteries of the soul, the turmoil of life, the destinies of man, the intimacy of creation, and to pursue, by means of straight and curved lines, absolute plasticity, seen as the beginning and end of all things. But, after creating his new Adam and Eve, he apparently didn't even notice that he had forgotten to give them a soul. To what aberrations has he thus dragged the French school, and what a responsibility will fall upon him!"

As shown by other noble examples (including Nietzsche's Wagner and Adorno's Stravinsky), the most significant praise may come from the most ferocious adversaries—and at exactly the moment when they feel they have landed the hardest blow. Of course Théophile Silvestre is not Nietzsche or even Adorno, as we can already infer from his prose. But if we isolate some snippets, perhaps we can get rather close to the mystery of Ingres. "The cult of form through the abolition of thought itself": is this not already a statement that hints at what set Ingres apart from his contemporaries? The sovereign, inflexible "abolition of thought"—understood as the ultimate tribute, in the liturgical sense, that can be made to form—is the decisive point where Ingres stands out alone. It is the Zen "no mind" applied to the "cult of form," something like a secret doctrine of Western painting, already noticeable in Vermeer or in Chardin. But here it is ventured in portraits with a name and a story, in which the human figure is given the greatest significance. And in the end this doctrine is not erased, but finds its place alongside a vase, a shawl, or some fold in silk—where all the elements are oriented, by virtue of an obscure and unexplained complicity, toward "absolute plasticity, seen as the beginning and end of all things," just as Théophile

Thoré said. And that "sensual and sterile contemplation of brute matter"? This shows a new way to approach the inanimate. As for the "icy
indifference to the mysteries of the soul": here Ingres is presented as an
unwitting dandy, one all the more admirable given the incessant and
indecorous overflowing of "beautiful souls" around him.

Ingres: a "compact and stocky" man, devoid of a sense of the ridiculous,
ran through his studio in Villa Medici thinking he was Seleuchus, and
hurled himself onto a mattress to create an interesting effect in the folds
of a drape.

Ingres said—and was pleased when others said the same—that he was
extraneous to his own time. But that sly and malevolent soul Sainte-
Beuve did not fall into the trap: "M. Royer-Collard, exactly like M. Ingres, belongs to our time, if for no other reason than for his constant
concern with distancing himself from it . . . One still has much to do
with one's own time, and highly intensely, even when one rejects it."
This point is cleared up as soon as we move on to other times: Ingres's
extremism is a quality that implies the modern—or at least the brief
moment when in the word "modern," if uttered by Baudelaire, we notice
an all-embracing vibration, bewitching and daring. Ingres could speak
of Raphael and the "probity" of drawing as much as he wished, but he
kept on giving off that insistent and powerful vibration.

Ingres was more akin to Bronzino than to his revered Raphael. In
truth there was very little of Raphael about him. He did not have Raphael's lifelike delicacy, his fluidity. Ingres's world was made of metal,
gem stones, fabrics, enamels. Psyche appeared as if irresistibly drawn
toward the visible, not because it existed in itself. While not forgetting to
pay homage to ideal beauty, like many of his contemporaries, on the
canvas, Ingres showed a provocative indifference and extraneousness to
the idea, as if it were an intrusive element, rather inappropriate to the
pure, sovereign exercise of painting. Of course, his dicta and his anath-
emas suggested something very different, but a painter such as Cabanel,
who was a member of all possible academies, was not, a few years later,
any less drastic or furious in condemning the degeneration of the painting

around him (Manet, in this case). Each artist chose the most congenial measures to exorcize what surrounded him. In general, these were as stentorian as they were vacuous.

Deep down, Ingres was uncultivated—in fact, impervious to culture, just as Baudelaire was naturally steeped in culture, without any need to cultivate himself. Certainly, Ingres's boast was that he worshipped the classics and always kept some with him (not many—a score of books, and only the most obvious ones, in run-of-the-mill editions). But when he took up his pen, all he could use was a "violent, tormented ferociously energetic language, without spelling or grammar." It is as if in his head a most ancient stratum were still powerfully active—something like the reptilian brain, with a massive exclusion of the left hemisphere. Ingres was only apparently a contemporary of his epoch, whereas he could have found a place and a role in any civilization devoted not so much to art as to the production and use of talismans.

Owing purely to an accident of birth, Ingres happened to live under all the regimes that were also those of Talleyrand and Chateaubriand. In fact, one more than they did. From the Ancien Régime to the Second Empire, he passed through all the canonical phases of the modern, and one of the first parodistic repetitions of them as well. But in his case there were no questions of loyalty, no betrayals or metamorphoses. A man of integrity if ever there was one, "with absolute impartiality he had put his pencil and his talent at the service of all the powers, the First Empire, the Restoration, the July dynasty, without making any distinctions regarding the principles that those governments represented, except that he felt a greater inclination for despotism." These are the words of Charles Blanc, devoted to the point of perfidy. And none of Ingres's adversaries made him look ridiculous the way this supposed champion of his did: "As far as regards questions of public rights, Ingres had the blinkered ideas of the most reactionary bourgeois; verging on Prudhomme. The slightest movement that came to disturb the apparent equilibrium of things struck him as an unpardonable crime and hurled him into a kind of epilepsy. He, who wouldn't have hurt a fly, in his childish fury, talked of nothing but arresting, executing and exterminating the entire universe."

.

Ingres corrected the drawings of his pupils with his thumbnail, "leaving a deep furrow" on the paper. This *deep furrow*, inscribed without using any instrument, was an ultimate mark of form as a still-mute and self-sufficient power, which pervades the psyche and *precedes* all art. "The precision of those corrections amazed us all," noted Amaury-Duval.

This was Ingres's silent work. If he spoke, instead, his speech was merely "disconnected words, exclamations, disjointed gestures"—for example, when he argued in vain with the eloquent Thiers about Raphael. It did not matter if he was right; even if he was, he wouldn't have managed to make his arguments count. Inarticulate in speech, Ingres was dominated by a thought of perfection that eluded words. It was a kind of perfection that should have contained a "throng of strokes that were priceless for what they had cost or because they cost nothing." Strokes ignored by most, except by a few connoisseurs who "enjoy them alone and in secret." What was Ingres alluding to? Those words seem to be the premise of an esoteric doctrine, which has nothing to do with his proclamations about drawing as the "probity of art" and about the artist's duty to imitate nature.

It is as if Ingres were telling us that his secret was a secret to himself first of all. In a letter, he remarked on the "incomprehensible sensations" that set him against all that surrounded him. In the unexpected manner of their utterance, these words recall the moment in Stendhal's Italian travel journal when, writing about an ordinary day, he pauses to say brusquely, "These secrets are part of the interior doctrine that must never be communicated." In the case of Ingres we may suppose that what was at work was both an exterior doctrine, expressed several times in apodictic form and all in all of minor interest; and an "interior doctrine" so secret as to impinge upon his verbal awareness only rarely, but capable of inflexibly guiding his hand in the drawn and painted work.

"He who can copy, can do" is a phrase Lorenzo Bartolini is said to have repeated constantly, when he attended David's school together with Ingres. But for Bartolini that maxim was of no great consequence. With Ingres it assumed a metaphysical sense, which escaped him first of all and escaped almost all of his contemporaries. Today time has transformed it into the "manifest mystery" of Ingres, which offers itself as something like a challenge to anyone who looks at his portraits and many of his other paintings (when they avoid the *style troubadour*).

"He had raised the rule of copying to an absolute principle, slavishly copying what was before his eyes": mingling with the students in
Ingres's studio, Amaury-Duval heard these words several times—and
he reproduced them in the pithiest form. The overwhelming power of
Ingres did not lie in faithfulness to nature, which he himself had proclaimed many times, trusting in the fact that the word *nature* would confer a nobler aura upon the precept. It lay in copying, in "slavishly copying,"
in copying *everything*. The maxim Ingres picked up from his friend
Bartolini was perhaps the only principle held by this man who claimed
to be made solely of principles. It is as if Ingres wanted to take advantage, with devouring passion, of the last moments granted the world
before it entered the era of the indefinite multiplication of images, so as
to show the world that everything could also be reproduced *in another
way*: not by dispersing and disseminating its power through reproduc-
tion, but by concentrating that power in a copy that was, paradoxically,
unique. Ingres's slavish submission to the visible, whatever it may be,
made it possible for the artist to superimpose a glossy layer upon it that
snapped shut upon itself without referring to anything else. Hostile critics found fault with Ingres's painting for an irremediable lack of depth.
But after a lapse of time, Ingres looks "Chinese" for a completely different reason: as a master of the copy and the emissary of a culture that
tends to annul the difference between the copy and the original. None
of this so much as crossed Ingres's mind—and nothing would have
sounded more aberrant to him. But that other being within him, the
one who moved his hand—and the nail that traced a furrow on the
page—acted in that sense. And the two beings did not interfere with or
recognize each other, owing to a secret pact upon which Ingres's art was
based.

The *dicta* of Ingres, or at least those that traditionally pass for such, reveal the same strident discordance with his work that was observed in
his physical aspect. Even Charles Blanc, Ingres's celebrator, saw him
like this: "Small of stature, stocky, brusque of manner, devoid of distinction, Ingres's person had everything that might clash with the elegance
of his thoughts and the beauty of his female figures. His head, with a

wide jaw and a narrow skull, bristly hair over a low brow, short nose, enormous cheekbones, big mouth, sensual and sulky and set at an enormous distance from his nostrils, his head, I say, which was the opposite of beauty, had great character and surprising power; but his expression usually seemed harsh, and while his deep and penetrating black eyes spoke of a man far above the common herd, nonetheless they revealed no tendency toward affability, indicating rather the extreme susceptibility of a touchy spirit." That is a zoological portrait of rare vivacity, which brings to mind a delightful painting by Jean-Baptiste Deshays showing an ape busily painting a nude woman seen from behind. That said, however, the women painted by Ingres were far more attractive.

Talking about Ingres means talking about Ingres's women. Baudelaire insinuated this when he wrote of Ingres's "intolerant and almost libertine taste in beauty." He was a fanatical libertine, the maximum approximation, in painting, to the fetishist. But not in the sense of the eighteenth-century voluptuary. In Ingres, something implacably primitive was at work, which the apparatus of glory has tried to wipe out, like a disgrace. But only that background, wordless and dissociated from culture, makes it possible to understand the intensity the fetish had for him. Ingres was fundamentally extraneous to the word, in the sense of articulate speech. His friends and devotees have concealed as much as possible the fact that the revered painter never acquired an acceptable knowledge of French spelling. But there is always a chink that these evasions trickle through. Charles Blanc could not restrain himself and pointed out in a note that Ingres had "almost always mangled proper names. For example he never knew how to spell the name of his best friend, M. Gatteaux."

Without an erotic and maniacal background, Ingres's painting stiffens into an "immense abuse of the will." But everything changes if, behind the thunderous declarations on Beauty, we discover a fundamental devotion to the female being. This was a topic his contemporaries disregarded, save for Baudelaire, who made it explicit on at least one occasion: "In our view, one of the things that, in particular, distinguish the talent of M. Ingres is love for women. His libertinage is serious and full of conviction. M. Ingres is never so happy nor so powerful as when his genius finds itself at grips with the charms of a beautiful young woman. The muscles, the folds of the flesh, the shadows of the dimples, the hilly undulations of the skin, nothing is missing. If the island of Cythera were to commission a painting from M. Ingres, it would certainly not be frivolous and charming like that of Watteau, but robust and nutritive like the love of olden times." That might already suffice, as a bold start—the words are those of Baudelaire at twenty-five, who still signed himself Baudelaire Dufaÿs in the "Corsaire-Satan"—but he immediately adds a note that delves into intimacy: "In M. Ingres's drawing there is a search for a particular taste, a certain extreme refinement, perhaps due to singular means. For example, it wouldn't surprise us if he had used a black woman to lend a more vigorous emphasis in the *Odalisque* to certain forms and a certain slenderness." It is as if Baudelaire wished to propose Jeanne Duval to Ingres as a model.

"A terrible and incommunicable being like God," swinging between a uniform vacuity and a "shining of all of nature's charms condensed into a single being," woman was a theological scandal. Not only for her contribution to the mise en scène of original sin, which only the speculative ineptitude of the Enlightenment had dared to deny, but also because her body has the singular capacity to prolong itself in metals and minerals as in the "clouds of fabrics in which she wraps herself." Woman's complicity with nature is such that all the materials she uses to adorn herself become part of her physiology. This is the unceasing marvel of fashion, insofar as it is the progressive and systematic appropriation of inanimate material by an agent of the human species, which would otherwise risk losing contact with the outside world.

This vision of woman, applied by Baudelaire to the figures of Constantin Guys, could be confirmed above all by Ingres's portraits. In no other place did the mysterious relationship between the female complexion and the precious stones, shawls, feathers, fabrics, stuccos, woods, and metals that envelop her or frame her or serve as a background for her appear in such full evidence. Yet again, while Baudelaire's prose and Ingres's painting seemed born to eulogize each other, their intentions were diametrically opposed: on the one hand Ingres, who made

suffocating proclamations of loyalty to Raphael; and on the other
Baudelaire, who took his provocative gesture—and precisely in the
course of his digressions on women and fashion—so far as to claim with
regard to Raphael (and Winckelmann) that "here we do not know what
to make of them," whereas he was prepared to make important sacrifices as long as he could maintain the privilege of "savoring a portrait by
Reynolds or Lawrence." But intentions are the most ephemeral and in-
ert part of the history of intelligence and sensibility. Combinations,
tests, and convergences occur far more often between figures who are
inimical to or unaware of each other than in the circle of presumptive
affinities.

•

The author's signature is inevitably a weak point of the painting, unless the painter manages to come up with a suitable artifice. The most elegant of all was the one Ingres thought up for his portrait of Mme de Senonnes. This lady with the asymmetrical gaze and turbulent life, who was born in Lyon but lived long enough in Rome to pass for a native of Trastevere, "does not pose like a woman who is looked at; on the contrary she seems to be looking vaguely at the viewer and telling him about whatever trifle that crosses her mind and barely disturbs her expression"—without distracting the viewer from the show of her rings (eleven of them, spread over five rather plump fingers, since Ingres never edulcorated what he saw) or from her décolleté, which merely pretends to be veiled by a gauze ruff that the peasants of southern France called a *modestie*. In working on the portrait, Ingres did not miss the chance to dedicate to Mme de Senonnes an enchanting drawing in which her breasts appear wholly revealed and are held up only by her red velvet dress abundantly adorned with silk ribbons.

Behind the lady, who seems to be borne up upon a billowy plateau of amber-colored silk cushions, there opens out a large mirror, in which

we see the reflection of a hint of her profile and can recognize the outline of a pilaster. But the remainder is plunged into a vast obscurity, as if
the cushions Mme de Senonnes is sitting on were on the brink of an
abyss. The female body could not be more in evidence, but the raven
hair does not stand out from the background mirror, painted in a compact black in which gleam only the gems of the diadem. As in an allegory, the reflection adds the shadowy part to the full light of the figure.
But the relatives of the Vicomte de Senonnes did not care for this, and
for a long time the painting of that intruder of dubious reputation was
hidden in an attic.

Slipped into the lower part of the frame of the mirror, like a message from a lover, or at least a habitual visitor, we see a slightly curved
card on which is written, "Ing., Roma."

On Christmas Day 1806, Ingres's head was full of pagan thoughts.
From Rome he wrote to his friends the Forestiers: "I have therefore
thought that when Thetis goes up to Jupiter, she clasps his knees and his
chin for her son Achilles . . . it would be a fine subject for a painting and
wholly worthy of my projects. I shall not yet go into the details of this
divine painting with you, which should smell of ambrosia one league
away, and of all the beauties of the characters, and their divine expressions and forms. I leave it to your imagination. Apart from this, there
would be such a physiognomy of beauty that all, even the rabid dogs
who wish to maul me, should be moved by it. I have almost composed
it in my head and I can see it."

A young boarder in Villa Medici, Ingres wanted to paint a picture
that might "smell of ambrosia one league away." But how to do this? In
those days, antiquity meant David: eloquent poses, frozen gestures. Ingres knew something about this: he had practiced it. But ambrosia?
Absent on principle, David's antiquity was incompatible with ambrosia.
At that time, Ingres jotted down possible mythological subjects in a
notebook: Hercules and Achelous, Hercules and Hebe, Pandora and
Vulcan, and also various episodes from the life of Achilles. None of
them satisfied him. His attention became fixed on *that gesture* described
by Homer: Thetis implores Zeus in favor of her son Achilles, "clasping
his knees with one hand and brushing his chin with the other." In the

meantime—still according to Homer—Hera is spying on the scene. Ingres had made a pencil mark alongside the passage in his Bitaubé translation of Homer. No painter, over the centuries, had dared to portray that gesture while sticking to the letter of Homer's text. And maybe, as Caylus insinuated, painters had ignored it because they thought the pose "too simple, too familiar, perhaps too coarse to avoid the criticism of sophisticates"? Shortly before Ingres, Flaxman had tackled the subject, but bashfully. Thetis's hand is suspended in midair—and Zeus brings his *own* hand to his chin, like a puzzled patriarch. On the contrary, Ingres has one of Thetis's fingers reach nearly to Zeus's lips. Her white breast rests on the thigh of the sovereign of the gods with the familiarity of an

old lover. And her right big toe brushes that of Zeus. Neoclassical eros had never gone so far. What Ingres had composed in every detail in his head had to be an epiphany spread over imposing dimensions (over 3 by 2.5 meters). It is as if, perfectly defined in its details, the entire painting had been detached from Ingres's mind to be deposited upon the canvas, without any mediation on the part of the hand that painted it.

But the work was not well received in Paris in 1811. It aroused feelings swinging between apprehension and embarrassment. Moreover, on reading the comments in the report of the Académie des Beaux-Arts, the doubt arises—and it was to arise on many other occasions in the years that followed—that contemporaries were stricken by scotoma before Ingres's paintings. And above all they did not perceive the *color*, as if it were too outrageous to be noted. Baudelaire once got furious about this blindness, and wrote, "It is an acquired and recognized fact that M. Ingres's painting is drab. Open your eyes, O foolish nation, and say if ever you saw more dazzling and more sumptuous painting, as well as a greater exploration of tones?" Yet on *Jupiter and Thetis* the Académie des Beaux-Arts decreed, "It lacks contrast and depth; it has no mass: the tone of the color is feeble or unvarying. The blue sky has a uniform and hard hue." "Feeble or unvarying," that color? If anything, it was irritating because of its ostentatious excess. The French state, which already possessed the painting, didn't know what to do with it, and returned it to Ingres. But twenty-three years later the state bought the painting back, and after a laborious exchange, it ended up in the museum of Aix-en-Provence, thanks to some scheming on the part of Ingres's old friend Granet, to whom the artist had dedicated one of his great male portraits. Several decades were to pass before Louis Gillet dared express what it was about that painting that disconcerted people: "That more than human scene, those gigantic and vaguely terrifying dimensions, that wild eagle, that Empyrean in a savage and almost black ultramarine above the regions of the tempests and vapors." The painter who preached an unwavering devotion to classicality and balance offered a vision where "all is unusual, all is made deliberately to grate on the nerves: that provocative color, that ozone, that cruel ether, that harmony of indigo and gold." Even more than, one day, in Manet's *Déjeuner sur l'herbe*, in Ingres's painting one could have found cause for scandal. If there was no scandal, it was because the state locked the picture up in its secret recesses and because no one dared to associate the name of Ingres with *that* kind of scandal—erotic, chromatic, theological. The scandal of the "cruel ether." But the painting is anomalous in another way: its complete disconnection from history before and after it. If *Jupiter and Thetis* anticipates someone or something, it is only an American illustrator with whom art historians are not accustomed to dealing: Maxfield Parrish. Otherwise the painting might as well be a meteorite fragment.

Today, those who stand in front of *Jupiter and Thetis* get the impression that they are not looking at a painting but a huge decal. Something detaches that three-meter-high rectangle from everything around it, from both space and time. The expanse of sky behind the sovereign of the gods has nothing to do with the one you can see through the museum window. That sky is an impervious, unchangeable enamel, perhaps descended, as Homer says, from "the highest of the numerous peaks of Olympus." As for Zeus and Thetis, they are no longer characters in the style of David that Ingres also used to paint, in his early days, ready to issue solemn judgments. On the contrary, their silence is profound, as if they belong to a geological era in which the word was yet to be born and would seem superficial. They have a mineral fleshiness. Zeus is resting his left arm on plump clouds, which support it like rocks. While the little toe of one foot seems monstrous, because it is too small in relation to the other toes, it's because that's how toes were then. The gaze of Zeus's eagle and that of Hera, who peeps out from an edge of the sky like a howitzer hanging in midair, engrossed and calm in her thoughts of revenge, converge on Thetis's arm, boneless, unfolded in its whiteness to the point that it penetrates Zeus's beard. The gazes are slightly oblique, like the ecliptic with respect to the axis of the world, which is Zeus's flowered thunderbolt, clutched in his right hand. What is immediately noticeable is in fact what the academics held to be absent: contrast, depth, mass, vibration. We can agree with them only on this: that the sky has a "uniform and hard hue." A hardness that smacks of ambrosia.

Ingres chose the subject of Zeus and Thetis because his eye had identified a gesture in Homer. And to that he stuck, inflexibly. He was not disposed to further mythological or theological inquiry, but with the unwitting boldness of the greats he had stumbled across a great gamble.

Zeus and Thetis were the only erotic couple in the classical world that he would ever paint. Otherwise, his female figures are solitary or surrounded by other women—with the exception of Aphrodite *wounded* by Diomede and Angelica waiting to be *delivered* by Roger. In both cases, the premise is some act of violence. Whereas Zeus and Thetis are caught in a situation of amorous intimacy (Antiope instead is merely an odalisque spied on by Zeus).

But Zeus and Thetis are also the first and foremost of impossible couples. Zeus desired Thetis, but he had to give her up because, according to the prophecy of Themis (and of Prometheus), Thetis would bear "a son stronger than his father" and hence one destined to supplant him. Zeus was obliged to see in Thetis the end of his reign. In that case *alone* he had to curb his desire.

If we observe Ingres's painting, we realize that although Zeus emanates a prodigious energy, he appears defenseless. His vast torso is exposed, passive, motionless. The only, minimal, movement comes from Thetis. The fingers of one hand that penetrate Zeus's beard like a soft octopus, the other wrist leaning on his thigh, her big toe brushing that of the god. In this case alone, Zeus cannot act. If he yielded completely to Thetis's seduction, it would spell his end. At the same time, Zeus clearly desires Thetis. His gaze is fixed straight ahead, and he sees nothing of her body. He emanates not merely power, but also utter melancholy. Charles Blanc saw this, even though he did not know the mythic reason for it, when he spoke of that "face at once formidable and infinitely sad." But the god approves the subtle pleasure of that minimal contact: the finger toying with his beard, the arm resting on his thigh, the big toe that brushes his. Now we begin to see why the painting gives off an extreme, almost painful erotic tension. What is shown is the intensity and gravity of desire. For the vision is highly paradoxical. The scene represents something forbidden or, in any case, secret: the unfulfilled desire of the supreme god. The one who had spied on, seduced, and possessed nymphs and princesses; the only invincible seducer, who had only to worry about eluding the eye of Hera—even that god could evidently encounter an obstacle. And here we touch on the limit of polytheism, its dependence on cosmic cycles, which subjects all sovereignty to a greater power: time. That Ingres was aware of the hidden bond between Zeus and Thetis is not at all certain. In reality he probably did not know about it. But mythic images live through a power of their own, and can guide a painter's brush just as the delirium of a schizophrenic.

In his huge canvas, which invades the spectator's visual field and attracts it like a magnet, Ingres showed the *nefas* of desire, thereby crossing the boundary of that which is allowed. The painting was never shown to the public during Ingres's lifetime and it never found a buyer. Many critics ignored it. Delaborde, author of the first monograph on Ingres, hardly mentions it. Even today, the voluminous *Oxford Guide to Classical Mythology in the Arts* makes note of all Ingres's mythological paintings, except this one, which is the most grandiose. The prophecy of Themis and Prometheus did not strike the god alone, but also his simulacrum.

Ingres's *La Baigneuse Valpinçon* could be any model seen from behind. She is slightly plump—and without a doubt less attractive than Kiki de Montparnasse, whom Man Ray had adopt a similar pose for his *Violon d'Ingres*. But the painting has an unassailable absoluteness. Among all Ingres's female nudes, it is the closest to a Vermeer. In the first place, the resemblance is due to the fabrics that gird her and, marginally, enfold her. Her head is partly covered by a white kerchief with red stripes, wound around like a turban. It is "the only high note of this refined, circumspect and soundless painting." It is the proof that no one knew better than Ingres how to adorn a woman's head. But up to this point we are in the traditional order. The head is seldom shown without ornament in painting. Artists can have recourse to ribbons, bands, circlets, tiaras, hairnets, fabrics, architectonic headgear. And in Ingres the hair flows free only twice: in the *Odalisque with Slave Girl* and in *Jupiter and Antiope.*

But if we let our gaze move down from the head to the bust of the *baigneuse,* we come across another fabric: light, delicate, it envelops the woman's left elbow and then hangs down to the ground. Its function is unfathomable. And the reason why it has ended up around that elbow is obscure. Unless it is this: in order to highlight the uniform smoothness that runs from the nape of the *baigneuse*'s neck down her back, buttocks, and thighs, all the way to her feet, Ingres needed folds. He put them in from the top, in the turbaned kerchief; and in the middle of her body, in that fabric around her elbow, which is perhaps more erotic than the *baigneuse*'s body. But that's not all. That fabric ends up lying on the floor covering one of the *baigneuse*'s feet. And after all, she appears to us in her full and calm nudity except for three points: the rear part of her head (that most delicate area, which is the base of the neck), the left elbow, and the right foot. There is something marvelously incongruous in that arrangement. Yet we realize this slowly, because every detail is in exactly the right place. Here the fabric—this remote device humanity conceived in order to move through the world—celebrates its freedom from any function. Here it exists only to serve as a counterpoint to skin, so that the continuity of the flesh is modulated by folds, wrinkles, ruffles. And so some shadows allow themselves to be evoked—and through these shadows, the element that forms the sovereign substance of the painting and the point of whose origin we can never identify: the light.

The secret of the *Baigneuse Valpinçon* is the space in which she finds herself: not a room, but a shelter protected by drapes and bathed in a uniform clear light. It is inevitable to suppose that no one is permitted to set eyes on her other than the painter and, after him, the spectator, both of whom are ignored by the *baigneuse*. There is another striking thing in that space: the background of the painting, which appears at first like a gray drape with rippling folds. Charles Blanc thought that it looked like a "wall that is unfortunately in a rather cold gray." Now, a wall that ripples to hint at the folds in a fabric is not found in nature. Yet the illusion into which Blanc falls has a basis. The point where the drape meets the floor is not distinguishable from a gray wall. Nearby, we see a water spout that pours into a tub. We are in a *hammam*. It is the first sign of *The Turkish Bath* that was to continue to grow for over fifty years in Ingres's mind. But the origin was to remain. In *The Turkish Bath* of 1862, the largest figure and the one closest to the spectator is a variant of the *Baigneuse* of 1808. This time she is holding a mandolin with which to play for her companions, but she has not given up the white kerchief with red stripes, wrapped around the nape of her neck exactly as it was fifty years before. Now someone has pulled the drape aside, and from utter silence and solitude we have moved on to a scene containing twenty-four nude women. Yet those bodies *do not form a group*. Each figure has retained something of the pensive and self-sufficient isolation of the *Baigneuse Valpinçon*. It is as if, in the course of fifty-four years, one by one, those twenty-four women slowly and silently assembled in the same place while, outside, Napoleon triumphed and fell, regimes followed one another, photography was born—and they knew or wanted to know nothing about all this, absorbed as they are solely in the noble task of fixing their pose on a canvas, which in the end would be round like the eye that had always been observing them.

The *Baigneuse Valpinçon* would not have arrived at *The Turkish Bath* if not through intermediate stages, as if to get some air, emerging from the waters of the mind. In 1828, Ingres painted the *baigneuse* again, still with the same white kerchief with red stripes worn down to the nape of her neck, the same red slippers of twenty years before, and the same day bed (even the folds have been left intact). But the pillow has disappeared. And above all, the drapes are pulled apart like a stage curtain, allowing the appearance of a scene that perhaps was always there. In the background we see six figures, including a woman immersed in a swimming pool.

The *baigneuse* was to spend another twenty-three years in concealment. In 1851, however, she reappeared in a further variant, now lost but testified to by an etching by Réveil and a watercolor by Ingres, now in Bayonne. Here the scene changes again. Undaunted, the *baigneuse* has kept the same pose and her white kerchief with red stripes, but the bed has disappeared. Now it has been replaced by a Turkish stool, partly covered by items of clothing left lying around. One garment is still faithfully wrapped around the left elbow of the *baigneuse*. In the background now are eight women, one of whom is dancing, and the swimming pool. This was the last epiphany before the female bodies multiplied to occupy the entire space, right to the edges of the painting, which at first was rectangular. "It's too much," decreed Princess Clothilde. So Napoleon III, who was supposed to receive the painting, had to have it removed from the Palais-Royal. After its return to Ingres's studio, where the painter worked on it again, transforming it into a tondo, it was acquired by Khalil-Bey, the repository of all that was deemed excessively erotic at the time (including Courbet's *The Origin of the World*), and finally put to auction by him in 1868 in a catalog with a preface by Théophile Gautier. The buyer, for twenty thousand francs, was Constant Say. To a friend, Khalil-Bey said, "How funny life is! Women have deceived me, gambling has betrayed me, and my pictures have made me money!"

The Turkish Bath seems to possess the gift of stirring up material that seldom reaches the surface of the psyche. Even the impeccable sophisticate Jacques-Émile Blanche felt obliged to apologize for the images his pen sought in his description of the painting: "These ladies with troubled eyes are animals of pleasure, amorous cats whose limbs are mingled in a tangle of worms, if I may express myself thus regarding these damned souls . . ." What perturbs Blanche is not the erotic vibration, but that "tangle of worms," as if the lower part of *The Turkish Bath* still belonged to a remote phase in zoological evolution, prior to any individuation of species. Women, *Ciliophora*: the gap might not be that wide. Perhaps those torsos and those faces of "animals of pleasure" spring from some teeming and undifferentiated matter. This is the impression given by *The Turkish Bath*. It is, Blanche adds with sudden vexation, a matter of the "morbid and perverse vision of an old man who was a priest excited by female beauty." This unseemly outburst ought to close the case.

The path from the *Baigneuse Valpinçon* to *The Turkish Bath* bears witness to Ingres's monomania. The images were engraved in him, definitively occupying a space that could then have expanded or varied, but always following a trail already marked and almost tattooed on his mind. Two months before his death, Ingres retouched a study of Jupiter (made fifty-six years before for *Jupiter and Thetis*) that no one had wanted for decades, and regarding which the painter Martin Drolling, when he saw it for the first time in Villa Medici, had written to his son, "Perhaps Hingres wished to make fun of everyone?" Certainly Ingres never wanted to make fun of anyone, if only because he had no sense of humor. What he wanted to do was always and only what his monomania obliged him to do.

Thus *The Turkish Bath* was born: twenty-four female nudes without a center. They had alighted on the canvas over five decades, like flies on fly paper. While they had no center, there *was* a center: but it was over toward the left. It is the large Chinese vase with blue figures, in the niche. Its position is comparable to that of the hanging egg in the Brera altarpiece by Piero della Francesca. Only on the surface of the vase do we see a reflection: the last piece of evidence that an outside world still exists.

Ingres was eighty-two when he finished *The Turkish Bath*, by then a tondo and no longer a rectangle. After that, no member of the public

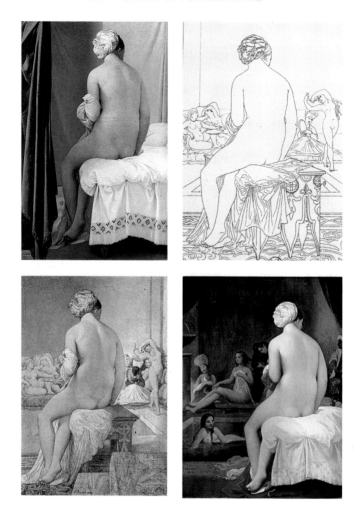

saw the painting for nearly a half century, until, at the Salon d'Automne of 1905, "a room was reserved for two painters from whom much was expected." They were Ingres and Manet. Visitors seemed irresistibly drawn to *The Turkish Bath*; Paul-Jean Toulet, a delightful chronicler on occasion, observed that the public "thronged around it so closely that it looked as if they wanted to lick it."

A few years ago, four daguerreotypes were found in a drawer of Ingres's desk. One, the work of Désiré-François Millet, depicts a lost painting

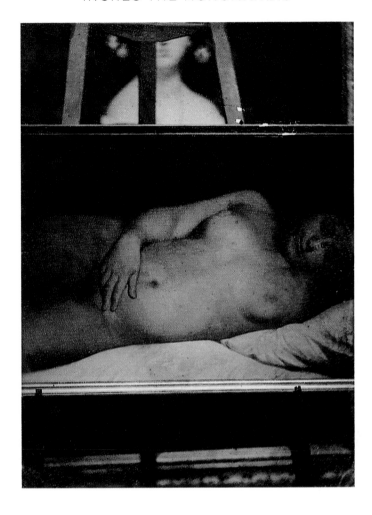

resting on an easel. In the background we can see the portrait of Mme Moitessier, now in the National Gallery of Washington. The setting is indubitably Ingres's studio in Paris. The lost painting portrays a nude woman stretched out on a bed. Her left arm is behind her head; her right hand is between the navel and the pubis. From her face, with eyes shut, we recognize Ingres's first wife, Madeleine Chapelle. The painter had done away with the picture—and apparently had kept only the daguerreotype, tucked away in a drawer, out of discretion, at the time of his second marriage. This is suggested by the man who found the image, Georges Vigne, considering the closeness of the date of the daguerreotype and that of Ingres's second marriage. If we look at the daguerreotype without knowing the circumstances, it immediately emerges as one of the most erotic images of the early days of photography. Its remarkable strangeness is due to the woman's pose: she is not stretched out on the bed, or even resting on one side, but has attained an improbable equilibrium whereby she appears to be resting almost vertically to one side and to be stretched out before the observer at the same time. The effect is created by a certain angle formed by the body, which gives the illusion of a double pose. We would search in vain through the history of painting for such a successful optical mix between an outstretched nude and one lying on her side. Was there a reason why Ingres chose that angle? All we can say is that this pose shows the largest possible surface of the body—and all with the same delicate luminous value, where the focus of the light is concentrated transversely between the right breast and the left part of the belly. The center of the composition is the woman's navel, and her eyelids are lowered, as if to prove one of Ingres's dicta: "the navel is the eye of the torso." The effect is that of a total view, like the one we would have on contemplating the body from above, whereas here the body is inclined toward the observer. All that remains is to wonder why no painter before Ingres sought for or found that angle. And why Ingres decided to get rid of the painting, while keeping proof of its existence in the form of a photograph—a medium that (like many of his contemporaries) he so abhorred that in 1862 he joined twenty-six other artists in signing a petition in which they solemnly protested "against any likening of photography to art." Then there is a chance detail: the dark, almost mulatto complexion of the woman portrayed is in correspondence with the whiteness of the sheet and the cushion below, and above, enclosed between two uprights of the easel, the whiteness, even more accentuated, of the opulent and arched shoulders of Mme Moitessier. This, too, stresses the phantasmal character of the image.

The artifice used by Ingres in the pose of the vanished nude of Madeleine is a significant deviation in the history of painting. The nude woman outstretched and resting on cushions is a recurrent theme that appears, among its supreme variations, in three paintings: Giorgione's *Sleeping Venus*, Titian's *Venus of Urbino*, and Manet's *Olympia*. In all three cases, even given the disparity of the stylistic preferences, we observe

some constants: the hand covering the pubis is the left one, and the right hand can gird the head (Giorgione) or rest against the cushions (Titian and Manet). And in any case, the woman's left breast appears in profile, thus giving the entire figure the nature of an oblique view. Ingres apparently respected his two illustrious predecessors (Giorgione and Titian; Manet painted *Olympia* ten years after the daguerreotype of Ingres's lost nude), especially Giorgione, from whom he takes three elements: the closed eyes, the arm behind the head, the hand on the pubis. But he does this in order to divert them, transforming the oblique view into a frontal one. He brings the right hand to the pubis instead of the left, and puts the left arm behind the head. This way, the two breasts appear frontally and the profile outlined against the dark background is formed by a relief that runs from Madeleine's right arm to her thigh. Giorgione's and Titian's Venuses, and even more so Manet's Olympia, do not repudiate the world, and far less deny it. The Venus of Urbino and Olympia are ready to turn to someone who might enter their room, Giorgione's Venus might shake off her sleep and instantly take note if a passerby were to venture into her landscape. Instead, Ingres's Madeleine, in her compact frontality, is like a playing card figure, closed in on herself and her sealed eyelids. All she wants is to bare the expanse of her skin to a tenuous light, as if beyond the folds of her bed there were not a room but emptiness. One might say that Ingres was aiming to eliminate nothing less than space itself. There is no longer Giorgione's airy landscape; there is no longer Titian's spacious room where two women in the background are rummaging around in a chest; there is no longer even the cramped and dark room where Olympia waits for her clients. There is the pure encounter between a female body (which stops halfway down the thighs, even though the painting, presumably, measured over a meter at the base) and a gaze, which is engrossed in it.

If we took Ingres's lost nude, as it is revealed to us in Désiré-François Millet's photograph, and eliminated the frame, the easel, and the fragment of the portrait of Mme Moitessier glimpsed in the middle ground, Madeleine Chapelle's naked body on the bed might be taken for something born as a daguerreotype, comparable to those of certain models that appear in the photographs of Durieu, such as the celebrated Mlle Hamely, included in the album prepared by Durieu for Delacroix and copied by Delacroix in the *Odalisque* of 1857. Thus a painting by Ingres could have become photographic material for Delacroix, and the two mortal enemies would have found themselves communicating in the mysterious substance of a female body, that of Ingres's first wife; just as a pose of Mlle Hamely, Delacroix's odalisque, her arm raised around her head, would be renewed in drawing number 2,001 by Ingres.

Baudelaire came to speak on Ingres at the Exposition Universelle of 1855—forty-three paintings hanging one beside the other like stamps, according to the custom of the time: *The Great Odalisque* crushed beneath the rosy *Joan of Arc* in full armor, which obliged the former to touch the skirting board; the highly respectable Mme Gonse beneath the nude *Venus Anadyomene*, Cherubini and Monsieur Bertin oppressed by the *Apotheosis of Napoleon I*, while, to one side, the back of the *Baigneuse Valpinçon* was turned to the convex belly of the adolescent Venus. Faced with this, the poet coined the term *heteroclitic* to define the painter, adding that by then Ingres enjoyed "an immense, indisputable renown," as if to let it be understood that this renown was based on radical incomprehension. And he observed, stressing the point even more, that Ingres obliged the viewer to tackle "a *heteroclitism* far more mysterious and complex than

that of the masters of the republican and imperial schools, where he had taken his first steps." In short, that painter who was by then celebrated by all—nobles, bourgeois, and academics—was *stranger* than anything painting had produced since the time of David, the "cold star," whose disconcerting ways led other painters to bathe their improbable characters "in a greenish light, a bizarre translation of the true sun." This painting was so *strange* that, setting foot in the "sanctuary assigned to the works of M. Ingres," the visitor was seized by a rare "malaise," a kind of swoon like those caused by "rarefied air, by the atmosphere of a chemistry laboratory or by the awareness of a phantasmal ambience." These words take us very far from any idea of *nature.* Yet we are talking about a painter who referred to *nature* obsessively. What's more, no one had ever objected. Now Baudelaire was talking about a "phantasmal ambience," using an adjective that was making its first appearance in an essay on painting (and it's delightfully ironic that it was applied to Ingres). The word did not bode well; in fact, the text added that that ambience was inhabited by "a mechanical population and one that would perturb our senses owing to its overly visible and palpable extraneousness." One might say that the description refers to a crowd of mutants. Instead, it refers to Ingres's characters (bourgeois ladies and noblewomen, illustrious men, goddesses or heroes from history). Everything that Baudelaire was to write about Poe's short stories is less disturbing than those few words, which correspond to a "powerful feeling," a kind of primordial terror. But not a noble feeling, which one would expect from a work of art. Instead, it was something "of a lower order, of an almost unhealthy order." From "ideal beauty," which was still discussed by Winckelmann's modest epigones, important at the time (Baudelaire had noted shortly before, "we are full of them, the nation is overflowing with them, and lazy people are crazy about them"), we are plunging into psychopathology. How to account for this? Baudelaire came up with a daring explanation: Ingres's undeniable power was due to an amputation. His painting posits an event that would seem inauspicious: "The imagination, this queen of faculties, is dead." With this, Baudelaire had already said enough to disorient his readers, certainly of those days but also of today. But he wished to take his provocation even further, to bring Ingres closer to the painter most incompatible with him: the unsophisticated, fascinating Courbet. What, supposedly, did they have in common? Their works allegedly had "this singularity, that they manifest the spirit of a sectarian, a slaughterer of faculties." Following the psychopathological allusion, Baudelaire moves on to the political one. Ingres and Courbet prefigure those who one day would become the Russian nihilists and the agents of the Okhrana: devoted to opposite ends, but prepared to use the same means: "In their war on the imagination, they comply with different motives; and two opposing fanaticisms lead them to the same immolation."

It's no surprise that the article on Ingres was rejected by the editorial board of *Le Pays*. They could not have understood much, but they certainly noticed that in those pages there was something—indeed, a great deal—that was irregular and irreverent. The art criticism that Baudelaire employed here was metaphysics in disguise. Nobody noticed this, but it disrupted the order of the prose. And Baudelaire worked out metaphysics in that form alone, slipping it in in phrases about painting, the psyche, politics—or any other topic. He could not have done otherwise. In the report on the Exposition Universelle of 1855 he had confessed, "I have tried more than once, like all my friends, to close myself up in a system so as to expound it conveniently. But a system is a kind of damnation that drives us to unceasing abjuration; it is always necessary to invent another one, and this effort is a cruel punishment." So systems were not suited to Baudelaire. For him, metaphysics was rather a potent drug distilled in solitude, a doctrine dense with paralogisms no less than dreams. But it was also the only possibility that ensured that he was always willing to grasp every "spontaneous, unexpected product of universal vitality." And this was the only power before which he would bow: "multiform and variegated beauty, which moves in the infinite spirals of life." At the Exposition Universelle, together with Ingres, this could be represented by a collection of Chinese objets d'art (it was the collection owned by Montigny, the former consul in Shanghai) that the critics of the day unanimously ignored, with the exception of Gautier. Or otherwise it could be revealed by one of those "mysterious flowers whose deep color despotically enters the eye, while their form stimulates the gaze." Yet again, nature and art followed each other as alternating forms of "universal vitality."

It was not only his aversion to every system that kept Baudelaire far from "philosophism." With painful understatement he wrote, "I do not have the time, nor perhaps the necessary knowledge, to seek out the laws that shift artistic vitality from one place to another." In this way he alluded to the fact that he never had the tranquility, the ease, to work out a theory in an articulate, balanced, exhaustive way. He always had to take advantage of an occasion—a Salon, a book to review, an exhibition—to invade the scene obliquely, by surprise, with thoughts that were sudden, persuasive, and often distant from the subject he had committed himself to dealing with. As a result, thought was always a stowaway, which had to make its way ahead for a few paragraphs, digress feverishly, and then vanish or conceal itself. Having abandoned the halls of philosophy, thought entered a phase of concealment, of successive disguises, of camouflage, as if it wished to regenerate itself in many lives under a false name.

Ingres proclaimed that "drawing comprises three quarters and a half of that which constitutes painting" and spent his life deprecating colorists, behind whom his number one enemy was thinly veiled: Delacroix. But he who looks at Ingres's paintings today immediately thinks of the brilliant use of color. In fact, the initial impact, at least in the portraits, can come from the color more than the drawing. This is one of the most sensational examples of how Ingres stubbornly refused to understand himself. But the matter is even more complex. Because on this point, exceptionally, Ingres was in line with the trend of the century. For most of his contemporaries and for the first of those who came after him, Ingres's color was often a source of mockery, as if the artist were incapable of using it, owing to his blind devotion to drawing. Robert de la Sizeranne found that, in the sublime portrait of the Princesse de Broglie, Ingres makes "the blues and the yellows . . . scream," referring to the contrast between the yellow damask of the little armchair in which the princess is sitting and her superb light blue dress. A hypnotic contrast, which one cannot tire of admiring. The change that time imposes upon the perceptual apparatus is seldom so evident.

Ingres's color was disquieting, and so people did not want to perceive it. In *The Salon of 1846*, Baudelaire began to explain this (albeit with a few malevolent touches, because that *Salon* was centered on the exaltation of Delacroix): "M. Ingres adores color, like a haberdasher. It is a torment and a pleasure at the same time to contemplate the efforts he makes to select and match the tones. The result, not always dissonant, but bitter and violent, pleases above all the corrupt poets; yet, after their weary spirit has taken lengthy pleasure in these perilous struggles, it desires absolutely to rest on a Velázquez or a Lawrence." The allusion is as far as you can get from Ingres's current view at the time. No one had dared say that Ingres's color is "bitter and violent." Worse still, that that color might please the "corrupt poets." But who was closer to the image of the "corrupt poet" if not the young Baudelaire himself, in the Paris of 1846, still not sufficiently intoxicated by *décadence*? And where there was already talk of a book of his poems titled *Les Lesbiennes*? The thrust of Baudelaire's allusions is clear: Ingres's color is something highly unnatural, a distortion that has something disturbing, perhaps sinister about it—and it serves to introduce us into a space where "all these things do not appear to us save in a light that is almost frightening; because it is neither the gilded atmosphere that permeates the fields of the ideal, nor the tranquil and measured light of the sublunary regions." Bold words, which Baudelaire had to camouflage in his account, instantly moving on.

Line versus color, color versus line: this dispute, which runs like a scar across the history of painting, reached new heights with Delacroix and Ingres. Two factions formed, which exchanged insults and deprecation. No one wondered, at that time, what line or color might be without launching into appeals to nature, appeals that always smacked of black-mail. On drawing, at least, one day Valéry would venture to say, "Draw-ing is an act of the intelligence." But color, then? Insofar as it is the enemy, must it be abstracted from the intelligence? And why does one always notice an underlying *moral* dimension in this dispute? Certainly never as in Ingres's pompous apothegms: "Drawing is the probity of art"—one celebrated example.

But even if we avoid all moralizing, the contrast remains. In fact, Poussin and Rubens point to two diverging and opposite paths. As do Delacroix and Ingres. Having arrived at that irredeemable point of con-trast, painting introduces itself into strata of the sensibilities where im-age clashes with image and perception with perception, almost without further recourse to the word. It is easy to substantiate all this in Ingres. His realm precludes the word—his and that of his contemporaries. What happens with him is an act of submission and devotion to the vis-ible that has the violence and the anguish of an archaic superstition. In-gres marks the triumph of the mystique of tautology. This was already noticeable, two centuries earlier, in certain Dutch interiors. But now it becomes a ubiquitous tautology. It invades social and family life. It is ready to go out for a *diner en ville* or a ball. With equanimity, it spreads over gloves, folds in silk, shawls, lorgnettes, fans, ribbons, cameos, fringes, bows, handkerchiefs, rings, feathers, and ruffs, and also the women who wear them. Objects, stones, fabrics, and people possess a sole nature. The nature of the fetish.

Some portraits by Ingres convey a certain sense of indubitability, as happens with Velázquez. Yet they are two very different painters. Of Velázquez it was said that he could *paint the air*. And Thoré also tried to explain how: "It is a matter of 'creating a void' around figures and ma-terial things so that they may appear in the air. Velázquez never risks a positive color in his backgrounds, always neutralized by mixed and elusive colorings, sometimes greenish or off-pink or covered by a patina

of pearl or silver." An impeccable description, which one could not trans-
fer to Ingres. Because in Ingres *there is no air.* But this is not why there is a
sense of oppression. And so the doubt arises that in him the void is not
only near the figures, but behind them. As if all of them, despite the
precision of their every wrinkle and fold, were of a hallucinatory nature.
This does not imply that they do not have psychological substance, a
substance that is sometimes imperious, as in *Monsieur Bertin.* Other
times, it is as if some secret signal is there to warn us that the individual
characters are so many emissaries of the play of forms, with respect to
which the social function of the sitter—and this also holds for the Duke
of Orléans—becomes a pretext, as if they were professional models taking turns among the drapery of the studio. The figures whose portrait
Ingres painted constitute a population apart, genetically distinct, of the
animal kingdom, as is hinted at in a few far-sighted words penned by
Baudelaire: "His figures have the air of outlines marked by extreme cor-
rectness of form, full of a soft matter that is not alive, extraneous to the
human organism." If the "painter's painter," as Manet called him, is
Velázquez—the painter without adjectives, without definitions, without
qualities—his counterpart in a planet without oxygen is Ingres. Opposite in everything, they reach, by different paths, of which they have
transmitted nothing to us, the ultimate goal of painting: evidence.

Ingres did not *react* to photography, as did his peers—and generally did
with repulsion, save for exceptions such as Delacroix. Ingres *incorporated*
photography into his painting long before it was invented.

Charles Blanc pointed this out to the artist one day (in Ingres's
apartment at number 11, quai Voltaire). He was looking at the lead pencil portrait of the Forestier family "assembled in a bourgeois drawing
room: the father without his hat, with his tobacco jar in his hand, the
mother dressed for the occasion, a young girl at the harpsichord and a
visitor" (but there is also the housekeeper at the door, caught in the act
of turning around). Blanc said, "You had foreseen photography thirty
years before photographers came along." Naturally, Ingres denied this
and spoke of nature: "The drawing you admire I found ready made in
nature: I changed nothing." But Blanc was right. Otherwise it is difficult
to say why Ingres's lead pencil portraits are so cleanly detached from

the centuries-long tradition that preceded them. To measure that sudden and profound gap, we need only compare the portrait of the Forestier family, which is from 1806, with the portrait of Alexandre Lenoir and his wife, drawn by David in 1809.

Ingres had trained at David's school. The candelabrum in the portrait of Mme Récamier is said to have been painted by him. But he barely had the time or the need to shrug this off, given that the portrait of Barbara Bansi—signed "Ingres. Élève de David"—can be dated to 1797, since in the background we glimpse the first parachute, tried out by André-Jacques Garnerin in October of that year. And this shows that a radical divergence was already under way. David's portraits refer back to Fragonard, if for nothing else than the technique of parallel and splintered shading, just as Fragonard referred back to Watteau. Whereas with Ingres, we enter another space. The Forestiers' drawing room is hinted at solely by the harpsichord and the doorjamb, yet its presence is palpable. The family, including the little dog at Mme Forestier's feet, is caught in a snapshot, even though after a prolonged pose. And it is an image of the new bourgeois universality in its manifold variations. In contrast, the Lenoir couple drawn by David offers itself to the paper like the last descendants of a family whose every generation has been por-

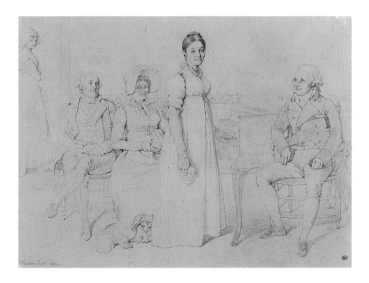

trayed, each one in a slightly different style and dress adapted to the times.

Just as the burdensome *style troubadour* of Ingres's historical paintings presupposes the proximity of melodrama and Walter Scott, his lead pencil drawings usher in the heyday of the novel. As soon as they left his studio, the English ladies vacationing in Florence (who paid him forty-two francs for a half-length portrait and sixty-three for a full-length portrait) went to enroll in the Republic of Storytellers, waiting to be summoned to the pages of Jane Austen and the Brontës or of Stendhal and Balzac, all the way down to the as-yet-unborn Henry James and Proust.

Ingres was in the habit of defining himself as a *"peintre de haute histoire,"* and nothing made him angrier than to hear someone knocking at his door to inquire: "Is this where the portrait painter lives?" Yet, while all his pictures of historical subjects sank without a trace, painting and the eye could also pretend they did not notice this. But what if the roughly 450 lead pencil portraits—the ones Ingres generally produced for money—were to vanish? It would be a catastrophe, like the disappearance of some zoological species, devoid of close kin, that stood out for its perfection and self-sufficiency, like the extinction of a liturgical language. About this part of Ingres's œuvre, Amaury-Duval said that "there is nothing comparable in any epoch." The population of Ingres's drawings does not belong to *"haute histoire"* but to *haute vie*—if something of that sort can exist—like a silent and indelible *comédie humaine*.

In the year in which Ingres showed his *Henri IV Playing with His Children* (1824), another twenty-one paintings showing episodes from the life of Henri IV were presented at the Salon (a chilling thought). In choosing his subjects, Ingres only rode the wave of the times. He obeyed—and executed, and suffered if he was not sufficiently appreciated. But at the same time another being was at work within him, a being who knew very well the hypnotic power emanated by his lead pencil portraits—and it was for precisely this reason that he did not want to include them in his retrospective of 1855. ("They wouldn't look at anything else," he said.)

We can also suggest another, less evident reason for the way he avoided and shelved the topic. One day Amaury-Duval asked Ingres if he had finished the lead pencil portrait of a lady friend of his. Ingres replied, "Ah, my friend, don't talk to me about that . . . it's awful. I no longer know how to draw . . . I can't do anything anymore . . . A portrait of a woman! Nothing in the world is more difficult, it's not possible . . . I shall try again tomorrow, because I'll start from scratch . . . One feels like weeping." Amaury-Duval added that in that moment tears really did come to Ingres's eyes.

If a *secret doctrine* of Ingres existed—and we are persuaded to think this by the immense gap between his works and his declarations of principle— this ought to have included, as its first article, that a portrait of a woman is the hardest task in the world, for theological and cosmic reasons that perhaps the last articles of the doctrine, unknown to us, might have explained. Hence the dogged tenacity and the supreme mastery of Ingres in portraying women, throughout his lifetime. And perhaps one reason why *The Turkish Bath* accompanied him right to the end was that that place was the very emblem of the challenge—and hence also the most sought-after place. According to certain sources that Ingres had in mind, in a Turkish bath one could see up to "two hundred women bathers" all at once. So the most terrible moment, the one in which the ordeal began, was repeated every time an unknown lady of polite society came to pose for Ingres in order to have her portrait done in lead pencil.

We can consider Ingres's last words to be his remark at the door of his house in quai Voltaire, whence he had accompanied some lady guests after a musical soiree to help them put on their fur coats, as a bitter January wind swept over the group and everyone insisted that their host go back inside as soon as possible: "Ingres will live and die a servant of ladies," he said. A few days later, he was dead.

III

VISITING MADAME AZUR

For some time Delacroix and Ingres battled it out before a public that surrounded them and egged them on like "two wrestlers." And, without hesitation, Baudelaire immediately sided with Delacroix. But why was his prose so sharp and precise when he wrote about Ingres, while it became nebulous and emphatic when dealing with Delacroix? Delacroix had the disadvantage of being not just a painter but a cause. It was incumbent upon him to represent "the melancholy and ardent part of the century." A part that otherwise would have risked being smothered, given that it was "a century for which nothing is difficult to explain, by virtue of its dual character of incredulity and ignorance." With Delacroix, instead, one was overwhelmed by a tremor and a surge. But toward what? It was not clear. Baudelaire knew this—and on one occasion he showed his hand. He wrote that Delacroix was the only artist able to "faire de la religion." Indeed. Religion had become a *genre*. And Delacroix wasn't even the first. Before him, Chateaubriand had been a master when it came to "making religion," starting with *The Genius of Christianity*.

As long as Delacroix was alive, Baudelaire marched behind his name as if it were a sumptuous and bloodied banner. And in the meantime he formulated his metaphysics of art. Delacroix then became, over and above his role as a painter, the devotee of the "queen of faculties," the imagination, understood as the capacity to assimilate and elaborate, using the devices of *composition*, that boundless warehouse of images and signs that, for the sake of brevity, was called nature. In Baudelaire's hands, the imaginative process became a modern variant of the alchemical *opus*, a theurgical practice proposed by a new Giordano Bruno.

But the way Delacroix is described in the essay on the artist's death is very different. Here the man enamored of passion and ardent things is also assigned traits previously associated with Talleyrand, his presumed father. These are the first touches: "Eugène Delacroix was a curious blend of skepticism, courtesy, dandyism, burning will, shrewdness, and despotism." In him, for Baudelaire, the stamp of the eighteenth century was clear—and, paradoxically, more in the manner of Voltaire than of Rousseau. References to his descent from Talleyrand sometimes verged on insolence: Delacroix "had at least twenty ways of pronouncing '*Mon cher Monsieur*,' which represented, to a practiced ear, a curious range of sentiments," Baudelaire wrote, when legend already had it that Talleyrand had as many formulas for offering a plate of roast as there were guests. It is possible that Delacroix and Baudelaire were secretly congenial to each other also because of the vague air of the previous century that clung to them; Delacroix as the reputedly illegitimate son of Talleyrand, Baudelaire as "the son of an old man who . . . had seen the *salons*" (his father was sixty-two at his birth). Hence even the most banal misunderstandings: "His courtesy seemed affected because it was a legacy of the eighteenth century."

A man with a "complexion like that of a Peruvian or a Malay," Delacroix roamed around a vast studio where all bric-a-brac was forbidden and where one still breathed "the austerity typical of the old school." He was "too much of a *man of the world* not to disdain the world." So he was afraid to yield to the pleasure of conversation as if it were a libertinage that was enchanting, but harmful because it was a distraction. The Talleyrand blood and the *sprezzatura* of the dandy culminated in a trait that only Baudelaire has shown us: "I believe that one of the great preoccupations of his life was to conceal the fits of anger of his heart and not to seem a man of genius."

One Sunday, at the Louvre, Baudelaire caught a glimpse of Delacroix absorbed in explaining "the mysteries of Assyrian sculpture" to a woman who followed him with candid tenacity. Baudelaire recognized her as Jenny, "the maid with the big heart" who had been looking after Delacroix for thirty years.

Delacroix was suspicious of Baudelaire. He kept him at a distance, as if in fear of being exposed. The latter's praise always had something insinuating about it, which he found disturbing. When, for example, Baudelaire celebrated the women in Delacroix's paintings, saying that "almost all of them are unhealthy, and they shine with a certain inner beauty," Delacroix remarked, "He ends up by irritating me," as Buisson tells us. He was irked by the fact that his painting was praised for a "je ne sais quoi of the unhealthy, the lack of health, stubborn melancholy, the wan hues of fever, the anomalous and bizarre luminescence of disease." Baudelaire probed Delacroix's forbidden zones, and Delacroix, even in his diary, defended himself by calling him Monsieur Baudelaire (and in the salutations, "Mon cher Monsieur").

Delacroix's relations with women were neither easy nor happy. In his epicedium, Baudelaire wrote, "In all probability [Delacroix] had loved women a lot in the turbulent days of his youth. Who has not sacrificed too much to that fearful idol? And who does not know that it is precisely those who served it best who suffered even more on its account? But long before the end he had already excluded women from his life." That divinatory sureness *in psychologicis* would certainly not have pleased Delacroix, forever barricaded behind the mask of a wary feline.

In his middle twenties, Delacroix was tormented by his body, "a silent, demanding and eternal companion." In his private lexicon, *body* meant sex. "It's probably a joke in poor taste that the heavens have permitted us to observe the spectacle of the world from this ridiculous window," he wrote. Sex was associated with two terrors: syphilis and impotence. The parade of female models in his diary—Laure, Adeline, Millie, Hélène, Sidonie—was often accompanied by a note in dubious Italian: *"Dolce chiavatura"* (sweet screw), followed by the tariff for the double service. The artist was meticulous. Every so often he became gloomy: "I have spent two hours in the studio. Great desire for sex. I am totally abandoned."

Apart from the case of the superb *Lit aux amours* by Fragonard, painting had never felt any need to portray an unmade bed. Then, suddenly, in the mid-nineteenth century, two painters poles apart in training and taste, Delacroix and Menzel, drew the image of an unmade bed. It is as if they portray, with radical differences in style and variations in point of view, the same bed. It is the rumpled and abandoned world of the human presence that finally shows itself in its self-sufficient wholeness, without requiring any additional significance. On the contrary, it is all but relieved and freed of any function as support and background. Only an unmade bed grants us this prodigy: the absence of the human figure, and at the same time the impression of the body. This was the Delacroix hidden behind the coruscating historical or literary fancies that occupied his most famous canvases. And perhaps this aspect of his was the one most secretly akin to Baudelaire.

The young Odilon Redon was told that Delacroix would attend a ball held in the Préfecture (in 1859). He recognized him instantly. He was "beautiful as a tiger; the same pride, the same elegance, the same power." More soberly: "average height, thin, sinewy," long, dark hair. They kept their distance. Redon and his brother Ernest did not lose sight of him for a moment: "We spied on him throughout the evening amid the throng, and we went so far as to leave at the same time, right after him. We followed him. He crossed Paris by night alone, with head bowed, walking like a cat on the narrowest sidewalks. A poster bearing the word 'Paintings' caught his eye; he went up to it, read, and moved on again with his dream, I mean to say with his idée fixe. He crossed the city as far as the street door of an apartment in rue La Rochefoucauld, where he didn't

live anymore. Distracted to the point of forgetting habit! Then he tranquilly returned with his thoughts as far as rue Furstenberg, the silent little street where he now lived."

"There is nothing more cosmopolitan than Eternity," Baudelaire once wrote, solving with a meteoric flourish some serious questions that were vainly to occupy the minds of many anthropologists of the century to come. Some problems have no answers because they don't need any. Among these, one is that of the clear affinity among the myths of the human species. Baudelaire's view was that these myths should be seen as the branches of "a tree that grows everywhere, in all climes, under all suns, spontaneously and without any grafts." If myths are, as Lévi-Strauss once suggested, *that which is not lost in translation*, one can say that, among alleyways, forests, tents, and caravanserais, those stories have also been the most reliable lingua franca, and maybe the only one used since earliest times, efficiently and without interruption. For sure, when one arrived in Belgium, for Baudelaire the geometrical locus of the modern *bêtise*, all this became rather hard to see, a subject for the professors. Then his verdict on the Belgians rang out, two phrases that ought to be separated by a slight pause:

"Everything they don't understand is mythology."

"There's a lot of that."

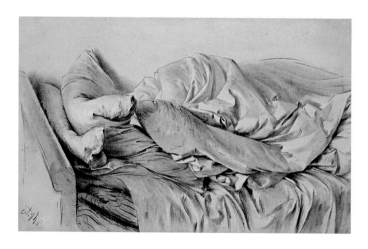

When Delacroix died, Wagner took his place in Baudelaire's mental theater. The peculiarity of his music was hinted at in certain words—*"will, desire, concentration, nervous intensity, explosion"*—the same words he had used to define Delacroix years before. But at the same time, Baudelaire grasped the relentless novelty of Wagner. To him only did he devote a digression on myth (*"myth* as the ideal material for the poet"), which would have been out of place regarding Delacroix. And straight off he illuminated the sense in which Wagner's leitmotifs act as coats of arms, emblems that clash with one another, something closer to the hexagrams of the *I Ching* (of which there was still no translation) than the arias of melodrama. Wagner's characters were first of all the vehicles of those powers: "Every character is, so to speak, blazoned by the melody that represents his character."

On New Year's Day, 1861, Delacroix was already working on his last great enterprise, the Chapelle des Saints-Anges in Saint-Sulpice; he made an entry in his diary: "Painting obsesses and torments me in thousands of ways, to tell the truth, like the most demanding lover; for four months I have been running off at daybreak to rush to this seductive task, as if to the feet of the most adored mistress." And a few days later, in a letter to George Sand, he again spoke of painting in erotic terms: "This constant distraction and the ardor I put into my work and my cart-horse exertions make me believe that I have gone back to that enchanting age in which one flees always and above all from traitorous women who murder and bewitch us." He rose at five and, in the mud and cold, headed for the scaffolding of his fresco, his bristly shell turned against the world.

Delacroix moved to rue Furstenberg to be closer to Saint-Sulpice. He built a studio that gave onto a little garden. The full light of midday was filtered by a curtain. The studio gave onto the garden. Redon took note: "No sound comes in from outside; one has the impression of being far from Paris. Certain letters from the solitary one, written to a distant friend, show that he felt really well in the silence of those calm places, where his last works were conceived and completed."

Delacroix used to say, "Rest often."

.

With alarming confidence, Baudelaire managed to associate—indeed, to superimpose—two figures as different as Delacroix and Stendhal. Both worshipped passion, albeit each in his own way. Both were tormented by the same nagging fear: "One can say of him [Delacroix], like Stendhal, that he was really scared of being deceived." But deceived by what? By passion itself, by the soul, by the supernatural—all of which raged through his painting. Flaming splashes of color, bloody vapors, blazes—on the canvas. But restraint and diffidence in the mind of the painter. And at this point the decisive phrase appears: "Skeptical and aristocratic, he knew passion and the supernatural only through his obligatory frequentation of dream." Without wishing to emphasize it, here Baudelaire provides a formula that makes it possible to follow Delacroix's stubborn, secret, demanding quest: it was "an obligatory frequentation of dream," as if dreams were not something that by definition come to visit us, but something that we try to unearth. No one ever said anything as precise about Delacroix—nor anything that went so far.

Stendhal called her Madame Azur, because her address was number 11, rue Bleue. "Neither coy nor sugary" (according to Mérimée), Alberthe de Rubempré at twenty-four was the mistress, in rapid succession, of Delacroix, Stendhal, and Mérimée. Each of them spoke too well of her to his best friend—and was then promptly ousted by him. Two revolutions later (1830 and 1848), Delacroix went to call on her one evening: "I went to call on good Alberthe, and I found her without a fire, in her large alchemist's room, wearing one of those bizarre getups that always make her look like a witch. I have always had a passion for this necromantic apparatus, even in the days when her beauty was the truest magic. I still remember that room with its black hangings and funerary symbols, her black velvet dress and that red cashmere scarf wrapped around her head, all accessories that, together with the circle of admirers whom she seemed to keep at a distance, had fleetingly exalted me. Where's poor Tony [Johannot]? Where's poor Beyle? . . . These days she's crazy about turning tables: she told me all kinds of things about them. The spirits lurk inside there; at your pleasure you can oblige the spirit of Napoleon or of Haydn and of many others to answer you! I quote the two she mentioned to me. How everything is being improved! Even tables are

making progress! . . . She spoke to me of long manuscripts whose authors are the tables, and which will certainly make the fortunes of those
sufficiently endowed with fluid to infuse all this spirit with matter. So it
will be possible to become a great man for next to nothing." Even Hugo
would take advantage of them.

Then there was the blood. "Lac de sang hanté des mauvais anges" is the
stunning scroll that, in *Les Phares*, offers the essence of Delacroix in
words. Startling because it penetrates the psyche of the painter, even
more than his works. Baudelaire decided to explain it: "*Lake of blood*:
the red; *haunted by wicked angels*: supernaturalism" (a decisive term that
Baudelaire borrowed from a French translation of Heine). But the tricky
point was still the lake. That red was the red that so often permeates
Delacroix's canvases. It was blood. No one had enlarged upon the fact
that *The Death of Sardanapalus*, more than portraying the despot's end,
showed the slaughter that came before it; a scene in which Sardanapalus still played the role of he who observes, almost as if he were the outpost of the person viewing the painting. In Delacroix's source (a drama
by Byron, in its turn based on a few words from Ctesias), none of this is
mentioned. It is said only that Sardanapalus died in a blaze with his
concubines rather than surrender. But Delacroix's painting fixes the
moment in which one concubine is about to have her throat cut, another
is about to hang herself, and a slave is plunging his sword into the breast
of a white horse. It is as if the entire picture had been conceived to show
not a collective pyre, but only the moment in which an individual wit-
nesses the killing of the creatures he loves. Above all, the touch of having the blood spurt from the woman and the horse at the same time has
something archaic and terrifying about it, a far cry from the innocuous
historical paintings that afflicted the Salons.

A concealed sacrificial fury is implicit in all of Delacroix's painting,
but only in rare cases was it authorized to show itself. *The Death of Sardanapalus* provided an exemplary opportunity. Never again would Delacroix attempt something so daring; never again would he portray
Liberty with her bosom bared on the barricades of Paris (even though
Thoré was to ask him to do so in 1848). In any event, no one dwelt on
the details of his ferocity. The gaze was distracted by the cascades of

gems and plate trampled upon by the concubines and by the enchanting
pose of the favorite prostrating herself on the bed to beg mercy for the
despot.

"To look at the *Sardanapalus* again is to find youth again," Baudelaire wrote many years later, at the height of the Second Empire. But the
painting did not resuscitate only the "happy time" of the great Romantic
school. The bond was even closer: "Many times," wrote Baudelaire, "my
dreams have been populated by the magnificent forms that struggle in
this vast painting, itself as marvelous as a dream." In that coruscating
oneiric scene, Delacroix and Baudelaire understood each other—perhaps
too well—and it was precisely this that made Delacroix uneasy. It is as
if he already knew some of the revealing words that Baudelaire was to
write in commemoration of him: "More than once, on looking at it, I
have dreamed of the ancient sovereigns of Mexico, that Moctezuma
whose skill in the sacrifice could immolate in a single day three thousand human creatures on the pyramidal altar of the Sun."

In a note to the *Salon of 1846*, Baudelaire recalled, "They have told
me that for his *Sardanapalus*, years ago, Delacroix made a quantity of
marvelous studies of women, in the most sensual poses." So it was: Delacroix had drawn various nudes for his *Sardanapalus*, exactly as, about
thirty years later, Degas would draw some magnificent sketches of women

tormented by arrows for his *Medieval War Scene*. It was as if, twice, the most intense and most perfect image of the female body could appear for only an instant before it was slaughtered. In Degas, those bodies assume, in the painting, poses very similar to those of the drawings, except for one figure, which in the end vanishes from the picture. In *Sardanapalus* the composition is far more uncertain, and some shortcomings appear evident: the horse is out of proportion, the figure of a man with a raised arm on the right seems incongruous. Delacroix was riddled with doubts about the painting. And one can understand why. Whereas, in Degas, the arrangement of the figures corresponds to a moment of terror that immobilizes the scene, Delacroix had conceived the *Sardanapalus* as a kind of vortex, a cyclonic spiral at whose center is the eye of Sardanapalus. This can also be seen in an ink drawing of formidable boldness, which makes one think of Picasso at his best. But it was still too soon for something like this to be at the Salon. So, in the end, the painting was the result of a compromise with the canons of historical painting. But its most scandalous element did not elude Baudelaire: that "Asiatic despot . . . with his black plaited beard" was also "as beautiful as a woman." In fact, he appeared "draped in his muslins, in an effeminate pose," as if that circle of sensuality and slaughter were self-sufficient and peculiarly

feminine. The male role was reduced to the pure imperative of self-destruction.

Delacroix and Chopin were bound by an intense friendship. But there was a fine difference between the two: Delacroix "never tires of listening to Chopin, he relishes him, he knows him by heart," observed George Sand. Whereas Chopin looked at Delacroix's paintings without managing to utter a word. Not because he disapproved of them, but out of a total insensitivity to art in general. Everything struck him as eccentric, and "all that he found eccentric scandalized him"; another remark by George Sand, who added, "He closes himself up in all that is most blinkered in conventionality." Chopin did not even like it when people told him that his "genius is the most original and individual that exists." This struck him as suspect. And he would open his eyes wide, dumbfounded, when Delacroix spoke of the "mystery of reflections," and applied this to music, too. As if he thought, "Oh well, he's a painter . . ."

Delacroix always enjoyed spending a few days as a guest of George Sand and Chopin, in Nohant, deep in the province of Berry. He would set to painting flowers, whose "fine *architecture*" he said he admired. They all played billiards and cards, took walks, or withdrew to their rooms. There were suspended, perfect moments. Delacroix wrote to Pierret, "every so often, from the window open onto the garden there would come gusts of the music of Chopin, who was working on his own account; and this blended with the song of the nightingale and the scents of the rose garden."

Ennui, the Tedium that Baudelaire set as the tutelary divinity on the threshold of *Les Fleurs du mal*, was the allusion, the lingua franca of all sensibilities. It was the water table that made it possible to reach the common stratum, the equivalent of the class struggle for Marx.

Delacroix went to visit Chopin when the latter was on his sick bed, a few months before his death: "An evening with Chopin; I found him much dispirited, he can't breathe. After a little my presence cheered him up. He told me that for him boredom was the cruelest of torments. I asked him if he had ever experienced the unbearable emptiness that

I sometimes feel. He told me he always found something to do. And something to do, no matter how unimportant, kills the time and keeps the vapors away. Pains are another thing altogether."

In their friendship, Delacroix and Chopin found themselves sharing many confidences, even the most disagreeable kind. And never so much as on the evening when George Sand had the idea of obliging her lover and Delacroix to listen to her read passages from her novel *Lucrezia Floriani*, in which she mocked Chopin in the guise of Prince Karol. One day Delacroix confided to Madame Jaubert: "That reading was a torment for me." But how did the other two react? she asked him. Delacroix replied, "Believe me, I wouldn't know. The torturer and her victim amazed me to the same extent. Mme Sand appeared perfectly at her ease and Chopin never ceased to admire the story. At midnight, we left together. Chopin wanted to accompany me and I took the opportunity to sound out his impressions. Was he acting a part with me? No, he really hadn't understood, and he continued in his enthusiastic eulogy of the novel." It was up to other friends to make the point clear to him. Sometime later, short of breath and sobbing, he left place d'Orléans, where he had lived with the prolific novelist, never to return.

But when they were alone and relieved of the burden of society, Delacroix and Chopin also spoke of very different things. We find precious signs of this in a note in Delacroix's diary. It was April 7, 1849, and Chopin was already seriously ill. The two friends took a long ride in a carriage, beyond the Champs-Élysées and the Étoile. Thinking about Chopin, Delacroix felt happy "to be useful to him in some way." That day, Chopin had talked at length, and Delacroix, usually disinclined to fill his diary with lengthy discourses—his or those of others—decided to transcribe the words in detail, with rare involvement. If you listen to them as if they were one of the *Études*, you can sense this pair, whom an insensate tradition assigned to the exclusive cult of the sentiments and the passions, as they waxed enthusiastic at the thought of an almost scientific self-consistency in art (in any art), of a knowledge that makes it possible to treat even inspiration with impatience.

À quoi rêvent les romantiques? They are rigorous *jeunes filles* who talk about logic and "higher laws," exactly as Proust was to do one day. And in this case we can easily hear the narrative voice as if it were a *dual voice*, that of Chopin but also of Delacroix: "During the day he talked to me about music, and this restored his spirits. I asked him what logic established in music. He explained to me the nature of harmony and counterpoint; and that the fugue is like pure logic in music, and that being expert in the fugue signifies knowing the element of every reason and every concatenation in music. I thought how happy I should be to learn about all this, which mediocre musicians abhor. This awareness gave me an idea of the pleasure that the learned, if worthy of that name, find in science. The fact is that true science is not what is commonly understood by this word, that is to say a part of knowledge that differs from art. No, science considered in this way, of which a man like Chopin is the proof, is art itself, and so art is no longer what the common man believes; I mean a kind of inspiration that comes from who knows where, which proceeds at random, and presents no more than the picturesque outward appearance of things. It is reason itself adorned with genius, but it follows a necessary path borne up by higher laws."

When Baudelaire, three years later, introduced Poe to France, he did not fail to contrast him with the formal slackness of George Sand, the forerunner of those authors whose "style drags itself along and sways like their dresses." Whereas "in the books of Edgar Poe the style is concise, *concatenated*; the reader's lack of goodwill or his laziness will be unable to pass through the mesh of this net woven with logic." So Chopin and Baudelaire were united by a *golden chain* through Delacroix. Chopin, whom Baudelaire mentioned only once, in a few words. But what words they were, talking as they did of his "light and impassioned music that resembles a varicolored bird wheeling above the horrors of an abyss."

IV

THE DREAM OF
THE BROTHEL-MUSEUM

On March 13, 1856, a Thursday, Baudelaire was woken at five by Jeanne, who was making a noise shifting a piece of furniture in her room. His awakening interrupted a complex dream. He immediately wrote it down in a letter to Asselineau, the trusted friend who would one day collect his papers. Baudelaire set great store by good manners. He knew very well that people who recount their own dreams are generally a nuisance. Monsignor della Casa was also of this opinion. So why did Baudelaire choose Asselineau to tell him immediately and in complete detail—he was never to do this again, nor had he ever done it before—about that dream of his? "Since dreams amuse you" are the first words of the letter, and they hint at an allusion: Asselineau was Baudelaire's accomplice in dreams. Two years before, Asselineau had published in a magazine a short story, "La Jambe," which describes the preparations for the execution by firing squad of a general in the Tuileries. One might define this as the dream of the shooting manqué of General Aupick: a dream *lent* by Baudelaire's psyche to that of his friend. Perhaps also because the lender would not have been able to tell it directly. But one day he would isolate it from the story and comment upon it in a review that is also the text in which Baudelaire delivered his most penetrating words on dream in general.

ASSELINEAU'S DREAM

One day I dream I am watching, on the wide avenue of the Tuileries, in the middle of a dense crowd, the execution of a general. Among the onlookers there reigns a respectful and solemn silence.

The general is brought in inside a trunk. Very soon he gets out of it, in full dress uniform, head bared, chanting a funeral dirge in a low voice.

Suddenly there appears a charger, saddled and harnessed, which prances on the right hand terrace, on the side of place Louis XV.

A gendarme goes up to the condemned man and respectfully hands him a loaded rifle: the general takes aim, fires and the horse slumps to the ground.

The crowd disperses, and I too move off, inwardly convinced that *it was customary, when a general was condemned to death, that if his horse were to appear in the place of execution and if he killed it, then the general would be saved.*

During the insurrection of February 1848, when Jules Buisson came across the dandy Baudelaire in rue de Buci as he was shouldering a "fine rifle" and inciting the insurgents to go and shoot General Aupick, those who were listening to him probably did not object, in principle, to the idea of shooting a general. But they probably did not even know General Aupick, who, for his usual good fortune, was not based in Paris at that time and besides, for other reasons, was not sufficiently known to the masses. Above all, those who chanced to meet Baudelaire were unaware that General Aupick's original fault was that of having taken Caroline Baudelaire as his second wife.

Eleven years passed between that day of revolution and the review of Asselineau's work. In the meantime, Baudelaire had come to the conclusion that 1848 had been "attractive solely for the very excess of the Ridiculous." But a fixed point remained: General Aupick. Every revolution is a renewed attempt to stage the sacrifice of a king. And just as a king can be substituted for by one of his generals (therefore also by General Aupick), so can the general be substituted for by his horse, which is the animal closest to man according to the doctrine of the Brāhmana, and so the one most suited to replace him in the sacrifice. This was the basis of the *ashvamedha*, the horse sacrifice, which was the founding rite of sovereignty in Vedic India. If, at the end of a highly complex and detailed sequence, which lasted one year, the horse was sacrificed, the king obtained sovereignty over all. But in Baudelaire's time, Vedic India was as remote as could be, and the texts that tell of the *ashvamedha* were still to be translated. Yet the dream seems to know about all this—and adapts it to the new times. Now the king was not sacrificed, but guillotined in place Louis XV (place de la Concorde), toward which the horse moved. And to avoid the killing of the king, it was necessary to sentence one of his generals to death, just as to avoid the killing of the general, it was necessary to kill his horse, with a rifle shot. In fact, it was necessary for the general himself (the king's substitute) to kill it with his own rifle, just as, in ancient India, they sacrificed the horse to avoid sacrificing the king—and it was the king himself who organized the rite. This passage from sacrifice to the death sentence represents a lightning transition from ancient times to the new day—eras which diverge in every way, except for a single but essential point: the need for the substitution of the victim. Baudelaire came to recognize this dizzying condensation of all history through a friend's dream. Or rather, through the dream that his friend Asselineau recounted in his short story, but which Baudelaire seemed to have understood as his own dream, *substituting himself* for his friend through one of those "monstrous paralogisms" that dreams themselves have us accept as "wholly natural things"—and that then wind up, through a network of subterranean channels, nourishing all literature.

Now, instead, Baudelaire took on the task of telling Asselineau about one of his dreams while it was "still warm." He defined it as a fragment of "an almost hieroglyphic language, the key to which I don't possess," as a succession of "confused words," like those that issue from the temple of nature in "Correspondances." The dreamer is surrounded by them; he observes their "familiar gaze." He recognizes that they are hieroglyphs, images laden with significance. He knows he does not have the key to them. He can only contemplate them, at length; he can only present them in succession, and so *narrate* them, as Baudelaire tried to do just then with Asselineau. Such was the chronic condition of his life, immersion in the "natural obscurity of things." So it is for everyone, even those who do not know that they live amid hieroglyphs. The crucial difference has to do with one's awareness of this condition, as with the difference between pure evil and the "consciousness of Evil." The act of telling a story is the first, perhaps even the last, form of consciousness.

This is why Baudelaire sat down at his table, at five in the morning, and wrote to Asselineau. He was not a storyteller. He spent years promising novels (to himself, to his mother, to magazine editors) in vain. But his œuvre as a novelist flows wholly into this dream, as if into its estuary.

BAUDELAIRE'S DREAM

It is (in my dream) 2 or 3 in the morning, and I am walking alone along the street. I meet *Castille*, who, I believe, had various things to attend to, and I tell him I shall accompany him and take advantage of the cab to see to a personal matter. So we take a cab. I felt it my *duty* to offer to the madam of a great house of prostitution a book of mine that had just come out. On looking at the book I was holding in my hand, it *turned out* to be an obscene book, which explained to me *the necessity* to offer the work to that woman. Moreover, in my head, this necessity was basically an excuse, a chance to screw, on finding myself there, one of the girls of the house, and this implies that, without the need to offer the book, I wouldn't have dared to go into a house of that kind. I say nothing of all this to *Castille*, I have the cab stop in front of the door of that house and I leave *Castille* in the cab, promising myself not to make him wait long. Immediately after ringing and going inside, I realize that my prick is hanging out of the open fly of my pants, and I decide that it is indecent to present myself that way, even in a place of that kind. In addition, since my feet feel very wet, I realize that I am *barefoot* and that I have stepped in a wet patch at the foot of the stairs. Bah!—I say to myself—I'll wash them before I get laid, and before leaving the house. I go upstairs. From this moment on the book no longer appears.

I find myself in immense galleries, adjoining, poorly lit, with a sad and run-down look, like old cafés, the reading rooms of once upon a time, or squalid gambling dens. The girls, scattered around those immense galleries, chat with various men, among whom I spot some high school kids. I feel very sad and very intimidated; I'm afraid they will see my feet. I look at them, I realize that *one* is shod. After a bit I realize that I have shoes on both feet.

What makes an impression on me is that the walls of these immense galleries are adorned with all kinds of drawings, framed. Not all are obscene. There are also architectural drawings and Egyptian figures. Since I feel ever more intimidated and dare not approach a girl, I amuse myself by examining all the drawings with meticulous attention.

In a remote part of one of these galleries I find a highly singular series. In a number of small frames I see drawings, miniatures, photographs. They portray colorful birds with the most brilliant plumage, birds with *lively* eyes. At times, *there are only halves of birds*. Sometimes they portray images of bizarre, monstrous, almost *amorphous* beings, like so many *aerolites*. In the corner of each drawing there is a note. *The girl such and such, aged . . . brought forth this fetus in the year such and such*; and other notes of this kind.

The thought came to me that that kind of drawing is certainly not made to inspire ideas of love.

Another reflection is this: there really does exist only one newspaper in the world, and it's *Le Siècle*, capable of being stupid enough to open a house of prostitution and at the same time put inside it a kind of museum of medicine. In fact, I tell myself suddenly, it was *Le Siècle* that financed the speculation of this brothel, and the museum of medicine can be explained by its mania for *progress, science, and the spread of enlightenment*. Then I reflect that modern stupidity and arrogance have their mysterious usefulness, and that often, by virtue of a spiritual mechanics, what was done for ill turns into good.

I admire in myself the rightness of my philosophical spirit.

But among all those beings there is one who has lived. He is a monster born in the house, who stands perpetually on a pedestal. Although he's alive, he is part of the museum. He's not ugly. His face is even pleasing, very burnished, of an Oriental color. In him there is a lot of pink and green. He is hunkered down, but in a bizarre and contorted position. In addition there is something blackish wound several times around his body and his limbs, like a large snake. I ask him what it is and he replies saying that it is a monstrous appendage that starts from his head, something elastic like rubber, and so long, so long that if he wound it around his head like a horse's tail it would be too heavy and impossible to carry, and so he is obliged to wind it around his limbs, which after all produces a better effect. I chat for a long time with the monster. He informs me about his troubles and his pains. By that time he has been obliged to stay in that room for years, on that pedestal, for the curiosity of the public. But the main nuisance, for him, is dinnertime . . . because he is a living being, he has to dine with the girls of the house—staggering along with his rubber appendage as far as the dining room—and there he has to keep it wound around himself or rest it on a chair like a coil of rope, because if he let it drag along the floor, it would pull his head backward. Moreover he is obliged, he who is small and squat, to eat beside a tall, well-made girl. What's more he gives me all this information without bitterness. I dare not touch him—but I'm interested in him.

In that moment (this is no longer a dream) my wife makes a noise with a piece of furniture in her room and this wakes me up. I awake tired, enfeebled, with aching bones, my back, legs and sides all painful. I presume I had been sleeping in the monster's contorted position.

This dream should be contemplated first of all as if it were a story. An amazing story. Perhaps the boldest of the nineteenth century. In comparison, Poe's *Extraordinary Tales* have an antiquated, timid ring, the narration reveals itself to be compliant with certain obligatory cadences and a certain high-flown use of adjectives. Instead Baudelaire's dream is austere and sinewy, the prose run through by nervous lurches and surges. To *interpret* this dream—in the sense of claiming to possess that "key" to the hieroglyphs that Baudelaire realized he did not have—would be most indelicate. A kind of metaphysical lack of tact. It would imply admitting the existence of a mind through which Baudelaire's mind could be read clearly. Luckily, the *communicatio idiomatum* between one mind and another does not admit of such promiscuity. Nor does it admit of the full promiscuity of the individual mind with itself, insofar as the unknown part is always dominant. But we can at least accompany Baudelaire's dream, going through it step-by-step. We can let it send out its numerous tentacles, filaments, and pseudopods; we can observe it as it captures other scraps of images, even disconnected ones, since in dream, what holds is the "legitimacy of the absurd and the incredible."

It's two or three o'clock in the morning and Baudelaire is walking the streets of Paris alone. He has some "personal business" to attend to. For him, every day brings its "contingent of fits of anger, quarrels, vexations, work and things to do." And that persecutory squad continues to operate even in the middle of the night. Then Baudelaire meets Castille (a novelist and good friend of his). Castille also has some business to attend to. Two men of letters going about their business through the night. Baudelaire tags along with his friend. At a certain point he gets out of the cab, but intending "not to make Castille wait too long." Just the time to offer a book to the madam of the brothel and "to screw, on finding himself there, one of the girls of the house." Castille's cab ought to mark the beginning and the end of the story. But this was to turn out to be too long and is interrupted by chance. Why does Baudelaire meet Castille? And why does he write his name in italics three times for no apparent reason? The rhetoric of dream often considers names to be more important than things. All the more so in a writer's dreams. This time the person *Castille* seems to be a mere prop for his name, which immediately evokes Spain (Castille) and a Spanish castle (*castillo*). Perhaps Castille is the guardian of the door of a *château en Espagne*. An old expression (it's already found in *Le Roman de la Rose*) which designates chimerical, impracticable projects. The origin of the expression is a matter of debate, but everything seems to indicate that it refers to properties that someone attributes to a foreign country still to be conquered, at the cost of blood. Getting into Castille's cab would then signify entering the chimera, moreover with the intention of going back to it as soon as business has been attended to.

As an expert in "castles in Spain," Baudelaire had no equal. Almost every letter to his mother, to Ancelle, or to various creditors, includes some evocation of "castles in Spain." In Baudelaire's case, these were often *novels*. A few months before, in October 1855, Baudelaire had written to his mother: "Probably, in *December*, the *Revue des Deux Mondes* will publish a novel of mine." But M. Buloz, the editor of the magazine, knew nothing about it. And above all *there was no novel.* Then we come across a subtlety: Baudelaire juxtaposes the news of the nonexistent novel, which he gives as almost certain, with true information, which he gives as dubious: "*Michel Lévy* will also publish (but when?) my book of Poems and my critical articles." Castille thus serves to introduce Baudelaire into a chimerical territory that was particularly dear and congenial to him. He introduces him to his novel, which Baudelaire will never write and yet which exists already in this account of his dream, compact and formless as an aerolite.

Now the time has come for Baudelaire to have the cab stop at the door of a "great house of prostitution." He alights and rings the bell, leaving Castille to wait in the cab. Baudelaire will forget about him. Yet Castille will remain in the cab in front of the huge brothel, an indelible witness to what was happening to Baudelaire. Castille is Baudelaire's quiescent mind. Closed inside the black box of the cab, he sits waiting silently, after having thrown his Ego into the chimera. In the meantime, Baudelaire wants to offer the madam a copy of Poe's *Extraordinary Tales,* which he has translated into French and prefaced. The book had only just come into the bookstores. Reconstructing the events of those days, it emerges that the copy offered to the madam of the "great house of prostitution" on Thursday night was the *first* that Baudelaire gave away. There was therefore something solemn and unavoidable about that nocturnal errand. Another striking thing is the haste with which Baudelaire, a consummate procrastinator, decided to act before the night was over. It really must have been a pressing *"duty."*

Baudelaire explores the *chimera of the brothel-museum.* That the place has great significance appears clear to the dreamer during the dream itself, which is also a *reflection* on that place, a reflection that the dreamer is even pleased with. But why should that place put thought to the test? This is revealed little by little.

Baudelaire shows up at the brothel on a nocturnal errand that is both a *"duty"* (emphasized by the italics) and a pleasure ("a chance to screw, on finding himself there, one of the girls of the house"—and the colloquial, offhand verb *baiser* used here by Baudelaire is its only occurrence in his writings). Up to this point there is no hint of the singularity of the place. One's attention is instead focused on the strange way the dreamer presents himself. There is the obscenity of the penis hanging out from his pants, as if the dreamer were presenting himself *as an exhibitionist* in a "great house of prostitution." An obscenity connected to the book that the dreamer wishes to offer to the madam ("it *turned out* to be an obscene book"). But here, too, we note an oddity: of Poe's short stories, which Baudelaire ought to have been holding, almost anything can be said except that they are *obscene*. So what book can this be? Baudelaire insists on the fact that it is a book of *his*: "a book of mine that has just come out." The dream is farsighted: we may plausibly suppose that it already saw *the* book as Baudelaire's *Les Fleurs du mal*, due to be published a year later and immediately confiscated and condemned for obscenity. No matter how much Baudelaire identified with Poe, to the point of confusing himself with him, *his* book would always remain that first and only collection of poems that bears his name.

Between the moment in which Baudelaire is in the cab with Castille and that in which he presents himself at the door of the great house of prostitution, time has run forward. This explains Baudelaire's surprise ("it *turned out* to be an obscene book"), as if the book had been transformed in his hand. Deep down within himself, in that part corresponding to *Les Fleurs du mal*, *he already knows* he has been defined, officially, as obscene: but the paradox is that he must present himself as such *even in a house of prostitution*. That house is certainly a place where obscenity is more easily accepted than elsewhere. But there, too, a punctilious code is in force, a part of which is, for example, that obscenity can be widely *portrayed* on the walls, as in fact Baudelaire was to realize shortly after, on observing the drawings hanging in the house itself: "Not all are obscene." But with respect to the obscenities portrayed, the dreamer knows he has found himself on a higher level, of direct and unjustifiable obscenity, even in the brothel: "I decide that it is indecent to present myself that way, even in a place of that kind." There is something comic about the situation, desperately comic: Baudelaire realizes that he is introducing indecency to a brothel. And this makes him feel no less ill at ease than had he found himself in a respectable salon. This feeling condenses the peculiarity of Baudelaire. To be indecent *in any case*, the vehicle of a disruptive element that evenhandedly unsettles both virtue and vice, as if they were irrelevant distinctions.

At this point we find ("In addition") that Baudelaire realizes he is *"barefoot."* His obscenity goes beyond sex. Sex can serve only to introduce it. That obscenity had to do with the *shame of existing*. For this there was no remedy. The bare feet: his mother had already attributed all her son's misfortunes to the lack of rubber soles. He rejected this, claiming to be an expert in stuffing shoes with straw or paper. But the shortcomings of this are evident just as soon as he steps into a puddle. And that's what happens to Baudelaire *in front of* the stairs that lead to the brothel. The dreamer's situation is compromised right from the start—and his attempt to make things right calls forth an eloquent oneiric paralogism: "I'll wash them before I get laid, and before leaving the house." From that point on, the dreamer's concern is focused solely on his feet: "I feel very sad and very intimidated; I'm afraid they will see my feet." In the way he presents himself in the brothel-museum Baudelaire is showing, as in an emblem, the chronic condition of his life: to be *too exposed*, to suffer from this—and also to face the suspicion that this excessive exposure is due to a toxic blend of exhibitionism and dereliction. And perhaps that's how it really was, thinks Baudelaire, but for a metaphysical reason, which he was to render explicit only in *My Heart Laid Bare*: because not only writing, attitude, makeup, dressing, prostitution, but the entire cosmic manifestation is about *exposing* oneself, imputable at least to *racolage passif*, the "passive soliciting" that one day was to enter triumphantly into the French legal lexicon. Immaterial of the way one appears, the mere fact of appearing is an invitation to prostitution. Baudelaire's fault would therefore be first and foremost that of corresponding *too literally* with the general state of the world, and with its chronic exposure to appearance. But a writer is precisely someone who knows how to take everything literally. So the sentence the dreamer is about to face on account of the way he presents himself is also confirmation of the clairvoyance of his thinking.

Until this moment, Baudelaire's gaze is concentrated on himself, on the embarrassment that his appearance causes him, making it impossible for him to camouflage himself among the various clients of the brothel. It is a reflection on his own life, which speaks through images. Baudelaire knows that for him *obscenity* and *malediction* tend to coincide. And this was precisely the original meaning of the *obscena dicta*: "apud antiquos omnes fere obscena dicta sunt, quae mali ominis habebantur"

("For the ancients, nearly everything that was considered to be a bad omen was said to be obscene") we read in Festus.

Around the dreamer we catch a glimpse of a scene that must have been well known to Baudelaire: girls chatting here and there with clients, an atmosphere at once shady and tense, furnishings and décor that seem to have seen it all: "like old cafés, the reading rooms of once upon a time, or squalid gambling dens." But the chimera has not yet fully revealed itself. And it continues to unfold through the architecture, an eminently oneiric medium. (The only dream told by Baudelaire in poetry, in *Rêve parisien*, is an architectural vision.) The brothel is composed, the dreamer discovers, of "immense, adjoining galleries," like an erotic Piranesi. The dreamer proceeds from one gallery to another—and already at this point nothing makes him any different from a visitor to the Salons. And as in the Salons, the exhibition was divided into sectors (military paintings, landscapes, portraits, etc.), so here, after a zone that we may presume to be a large one of obscene representations, Baudelaire begins to come across other genres—specifically "architectural drawings and Egyptian figures." The architectural drawings bear witness to the plunging of the vision *en abyme*: in the dream (which is already a representation) the dreamer observes a kind of architectural invasion, both extensive and intensive. First in the expansion of the spaces in the brothel; then in the representations that stud its walls. It's true that "there is no point as sharp as that of the Infinite," as Baudelaire would write one day. But it should be added that "infinity appears more profound when it is more restricted," hence framed (as Baudelaire remarked in parentheses).

As for the Egyptian figures, they count equally—and this was the case since the days of *The Magic Flute*—as theatrical decorations and an allusion to the mysterious character of the vision to which they belong. Within the dream, they hint at the nature of the dream itself, which presents itself, as Baudelaire was to say, like "an almost hieroglyphic language, the key to which I don't possess." And this is the decisive point: it is not a matter of Champollion's hieroglyphs, and therefore translatable into phonemes like any other alphabet, nor even of those of Athanasius Kircher, and therefore of images not susceptible to discursive clarification but nonetheless composed in strict, articulated order that not only has meaning but also is the secret meaning of all. Baudelaire finds himself in a further position, with one *bare foot* exposed (whereas the other one is shod). In fact, he has no doubts about the hieroglyphic nature of what appears before him, but he has no key, either phonetic or symbolic, with which to unlock its meaning. For centuries, since the first success of Horapollo's *Hieroglyphica*, one may say that European culture was divided between the poles of substitution (perceivable in the stubborn determination to decipher) and of analogy (perceivable in the search for correspondences, and hence for a symbolic chain that made it possible, by way of resemblance, to move from image to image, without ever abandoning the cosmic play of figures). On getting as far as Baudelaire and his nocturnal errand (and also on getting as far as our own times), both these paths show themselves to be inadequate. The dreamer enters the brothel-museum barefoot, owing to that constant alternation that is part of his condition, and recognizes a series of hieroglyphs. But he knows he does not have the key to them. At the same time, his "philosophical spirit" is vigilant, and it applies itself to the vision, to the point of extrapolating from it far-fetched conclusions about the course of the world. If we had to define the original condition of the thinking being in the period spanning the early Romantics and the present day, it would be hard to find a more exact image than that of Baudelaire, with his feet shod or bare in turn, as he makes his way through the galleries of the brothel-museum.

"Without the necessity to offer the book, I wouldn't have dared to go into a house of that kind." If Baudelaire felt *"the necessity"* (the word is underlined, like an unexpected resurrection of Ananke) to offer the *first* copy of his book to the madam of a great house of prostitution, this presupposes that their relationship was so close as to impose that gesture as a *"duty."* Apart from his mother, this madam is the only woman to whom Baudelaire takes the trouble to give a copy of the book immediately. His solicitude is not entirely surprising: we know that Baudelaire frequented all kinds of shady places far more than the salons to which his stepfather could easily have introduced him right from his adolescence.

Instead the one who seems surprised is Baudelaire himself. To have reached such a level of intimacy with the madam, he must have frequented her house assiduously. But now his view is that, without the need to offer the book, he would not have dared to go in. It is as if the book itself, writing itself, *authorized* him to enter the place of venal pleasure. All the theology of prostitution, which runs through *My Heart Laid Bare* and is the most important supplement to Joseph de Maistre attributable to Baudelaire, is concealed in this passage. The unspoken premise is that prostitution, even obscenity, belongs to literature even before it belongs to the brothel that Baudelaire enters. Perhaps that house is waiting for his book to certify its existence—and this would explain the haste and the feeling of *"necessity"* that makes Baudelaire dash there in the middle of the night.

The vicious circle is evident. The place of prostitution is so familiar that it demands the offer of the book. But only the offer of the book affords access to the place of prostitution. This is already a powerful vise in the form of a paralogism. Now, however, something is added. The new times produce a further complication: the brothel is also a museum, a museum of medicine, a place dedicated to the science of *health*— and financed by a newspaper characterized by its "mania for *progress, science, and the spread of enlightenment.*" How could this have happened? However did the times get to the point at which a phenomenon of this kind was not only plausible but secretly *right*? It's time to unfold the mystery of the century, which is also the mystery of *Le Siècle*. Founded in 1836 by Armand Dutacq, dubbed the "Napoleon of the press," *Le Siècle* was, together with Émile de Girardin's *La Presse*, one of the first examples of a cheap, high-circulation newspaper in the central years of Louis Philippe's reign, which witnessed the birth of the daily press in a form that since then has remained basically unchanged. The general public entered the stage for the first time.

Baudelaire was on good terms with Dutacq, a friend of Balzac and a bold entrepreneur ahead of his time who was to be dispossessed, over the years, of the numerous papers he founded or purchased. But his most successful paper, *Le Siècle*, soon became a subject of perverse attraction for Baudelaire: reading it prompted him to cultivate stupidity deliberately "to extract its quintessence." One day he wrote to Ancelle saying that he had devoted himself to this exercise "for twenty years in *Le Siècle.*"

We are at the dawning of the *bêtise*—and for the first time a writer felt the need to see it concentrated in a place, as would happen one day with Karl Kraus in Vienna with the *Neue Freie Presse* (and would be heard in the roaring of Bloy), while the epos of the *bêtise* would be celebrated in the vicissitudes of Bouvard and Pécuchet. *Le Siècle* had a dual vocation: it was the ideal paper of Bouvard and Pécuchet as it was of the apothecary Homais. Baudelaire described it like this: "There is a spirited newspaper where everyone knows and talks about everything, where every editor, universal and encyclopedic like the citizens of ancient Rome, can teach from time to time politics, religion, economics, the fine arts, philosophy, and literature." It is a majestic vision. We are dealing with a "vast monument to foolishness, leaning over the future like the tower of Pisa, and in which they work out the happiness of humankind." And it was precisely this aspiration *"to work for the people's happiness"* that irked Baudelaire most. Already he glimpsed swarms of "pettifoggers that will manage, like many others, to make themselves up for the courtroom, aping Robespierre and *declaiming*, they too, *solemn* things, but certainly with less purity than he; for grammar will soon be a thing no less forgotten than reason and, at the rate we are proceeding toward darkness, there is reason to hope that by the year 1900 we will have plunged into total blackness." The spread of enlightenment promoted daily by *Le Siècle* struck Baudelaire as a race into the darkness. Even though the word *progress* was still associated with fine sentiments and a certain insipid benevolence, it was really more like a bobsled course, where all you need is the initial thrust and then all you have to worry about is not getting thrown out. But how to explain that it was precisely *Le Siècle*, the champion of all propriety and decency, which had financed the great brothel through which Baudelaire was roaming? And above all, how had the paper associated it with a museum of medicine, as the dreamer was gradually discovering as he penetrated deeper into the immense galleries of the place? And this is not all: the connection between the brothel and the museum appears to be extremely close, because among the most important pieces in the collection are drawings of "certain bizarre, monstrous, almost *amorphous* beings, like so many *aerolites*"—which, according to the captions, were fetuses borne by some girls of the establishment. Nor were the dates of birth lacking. The hostesses of the house were obliged to offer pleasure, but at the same time they offered material for science. And science had chosen to show itself, with pedagogical intentions, in the great house of prostitution. An unprecedented union, and at first sight a shocking one.

At this point Baudelaire pulls himself together and observes, "The thought came to me that that kind of drawing is certainly not made to inspire ideas of love." Here the word that strikes us is *love*. In the brothel one would expect *pleasure*, if anything, whereas science, cropping up with its museum and its drawings, seems to prevent any idea of love. We are faced with something very odd, which the dreamer wishes to investigate. And in fact, already years before, Baudelaire had been bold enough to unite these two words in fantasizing about a "museum of love." In one of the central pages of the *Salon of 1846* we suddenly come across a brusque digression, which directly involves the reader: "Has it ever happened to you, as it has happened to me, to fall into a great melancholy after having spent long hours leafing through licentious prints? Have you ever wondered about the reason for the enchantment that one sometimes feels on sifting through these annals of licentiousness, buried in libraries or lost in dealers' portfolios, and sometimes also about the ill humor they give you?" The answer followed: "Seeing those drawings gave me access to immense slopes of reverie, more or less as an obscene book plunges us toward the mystic oceans of blue." Apparently, the annals of licentiousness could take one very far away. A few years later, this scene takes place: Baudelaire enters the brothel-museum to offer *an obscene book* and on the walls he finds those very drawings that he had spent a long time seeking in the corners of libraries and bookstores. In that place a boundless fantasy seems to come into being, but it is one that Baudelaire would have wished to end differently: "How many times, faced with these countless scraps of other people's feelings, have I found myself wishing that the poet, the inquiring spirit, and the philosopher might be offered the enjoyment of a museum of love, where everything would have its place, from the tenderness of Saint Theresa to the serious depravations of the centuries that were bored with everything. No doubt an immense gap separates the *Embarkation for Cythera* from the wretched colored prints one finds in the rooms occupied by the whores, hanging above a cracked vase and a wobbly table; but in a matter of such importance nothing must be overlooked." Baudelaire had adumbrated something very similar to the brothel-museum, ten years before, but now that, in dream, he was wandering around it, he must have noticed that it was something very different. The brothel-museum and the "museum of love" were almost identical, yet basically divergent and incompatible. But why? What did that combination of near-resemblance and radical difference imply?

To answer this question, the dream has to turn speculative. The sequence is the following: according to Baudelaire, the institution of a great brothel that is also a museum of medicine presupposes that we have reached a very high level, perhaps a dizzying one, of *bêtise*—and that this can be attributed to "only one newspaper in the world," and hence to *Le Siècle* (and by this, letting it be tacitly understood that only *a newspaper* could finance such an enterprise). The scientific aspect of the initiative would then be explained by the "mania for *progress*" that characterized the paper. But it is with the following sentence that Baudelaire makes a metaphysical moral leap: "Then I reflect that modern stupidity and foolishness have their own mysterious usefulness, and that often, by the action of a spiritual mechanics, that which was done for ill turns into good." Suddenly the tone has changed. The emphasis is of the cutting, oracular kind found only in Joseph de Maistre. And the entire sentence seems inspired by his coruscating vision of Providence. But it should be studied from close up, as befits the paralogisms of dream. What is it that was "done for ill"? The brothel or the museum of medicine? And what is the good in the interests of which the enterprise ends up by exploiting "modern stupidity and foolishness"? Is it the fact that the brothel, inasmuch as it is a museum, *also* becomes an element of the spread of enlightenment? Or is it that the museum of medicine is justified because it is nonetheless housed in a great brothel? If the spread of enlightenment coincided with good, the answer would be clear—and comical: we would be in the presence of the redemption of vice through the virtues of science, which would act as the enlightened extension of the brothel. But since Baudelaire considered the spread of enlightenment as a catalyst toward "total blackness," all doubts are permissible. And another hypothesis also looms: that this good is precisely the implacable blend of science and eros, given that both permit themselves to be *transformed into image*—and to reveal themselves. If the madam's house were only a scientific laboratory or a business for producing money by selling sex, Baudelaire would not throw himself into his bold speculation, which is both theological and metaphysical. But the house also has the capacity to portray itself—in the form of a museum. And this *passage to the image* could be the sign of something "that turns into good," almost as if it were the prelude to a new creation, aberrant but tremendously alive, like the eyes of the framed birds. This new world is made up of amorphous figures like *"aerolites"* and winds up in a being resembling certain undefined creatures of primordial times: "a monster born in the house," both a statue and a living being, to whom Baudelaire listens with interest and, one would say, with instant, invincible affection, albeit with a residue of fear: "I dare not touch him."

The dream leaves all these questions unanswered. And these are not unimportant doubts, because they are tantamount to an uncertainty about the workings of Providence. But the dreamer remains firmly convinced that his *vision* was *right*. So much so that Baudelaire congratulates himself on having had it. And he delivers it to us like a gift, in the same way as he went to offer his book to the madam of the house. That gift and those questions are still with us, in every moment and in every corner of the world.

The brothel-museum looked like a huge, boundless mnemotechnical edifice. Apparently, inside it opened up a network of interconnected *passages*, from which no exit could be seen. It was the landscape of the *new*, according to Benjamin, that pulsating neural system of lights and goods in which the phantasmagoria of Paris was condensed, while Paris itself, in its turn, was a miniature of the entire planet that would unfold from that moment until this very day and beyond. But here the first characteristic of those galleries is that of *used things*, consumed and worn out by use. That old air is the trace of the past. Time is perceived not merely through ruins or monuments, but through its corrosive action that sweeps over all things, even the new. Nature is tacitly abolished—and the panorama is composed solely of latter-day institutions: cafés, reading rooms, gambling dens. In an illustrated guide to Paris of 1852 (Baudelaire had his dream in 1856), Benjamin found the definition of *passage* as "a world in miniature." And a world where the interior and the exterior tend to swap roles: *"Passages* are an intermediate entity between the street and the interior." The *flâneur*—hence Baudelaire—"is as much at home among the façades of the buildings as the citizen within his four walls."

On looking around, Baudelaire took note of the population of the place. Prostitutes, mainly. Scattered pretty much everywhere, as if the brothel had no center. What were they doing? Chatting with various men. Among these we recognize some high school boys. Ecumenical in admitting desires, this place ensured that Baudelaire felt "very sad and very intimidated." The sadness might be due to that air of vague decrepitude in the galleries. But why "intimidated"? Certainly not because of a lack of familiarity with such places, but because of his feet. The damned bare feet that made him feel ridiculous, like an irksome reminder of nature. But the situation gets better: soon Baudelaire realizes that *one* of his feet is shod. Shortly after, both feet appear protected by shoes. Now Baudelaire can finally wander around those galleries, once more taking on his favorite role: the spectator. It was a little like the Louvre, where he scanned the walls while waiting for Caroline. And here, too, there seems to be a great exhibition; an anomalous Salon has been put together: "What strikes me is that the walls of these vast galleries are adorned with drawings of all kinds, framed." Drawings, the primordial form of art. "Make lines . . . many lines"—this was the only advice that the young Degas had heard from the lips of Ingres. In drawing there is everything. On examining some studies by Degas, Ingres was to add, with even greater exasperation, "Never draw from life." Draw only what lingers in the memory. It is the essential. Baudelaire goes on looking. Nothing pleased him more. It was his devotion, the only one he had always practiced: "the cult of images." He observes that, among those drawings, "not all are obscene." And by this he implies that obscene drawings were the norm. "There are also architectural drawings and Egyptian figures." Here we notice for the first time that the place is changing. The "architectural drawings" are already a foray into the abstract. But the drawings of "Egyptian figures" are especially disturbing. Wherever Egypt crops up, there is mystery. By Baudelaire's time, for over four centuries, every time a mystery loomed, one was plunged into Egypt. And basically this meant little more than the renewal of a sentiment dating from Plato's day, when the Greeks felt like ignorant children compared with the Egyptians. But now we can believe that, for Baudelaire, those drawings on the walls of the brothel were the first examples—a kind of primer—of that "almost hieroglyphic language" that beset him in his dream. A feeling that might serve to distract him, since he felt "ever more intimidated" and did not dare "approach a girl." So he amused himself by "examining all the drawings with meticulous attention." The obscene, the hieroglyphic, the architectonic. What Baudelaire was observing was something like a compendium of his work, of his life. And this act of contemplation distracted him from the nagging condition that made him feel "ever more intimidated," even though he was now wearing two perfectly normal shoes. Those "vast galleries" had something of the temple about them. The deeper he penetrated into them, the more they offered revelations and shocking sights: "In a remote part of one of these galleries I find a highly singular series. In a number of small frames I see drawings, miniatures, photographic proofs. They portray colorful birds with the most brilliant plumage, birds with *lively* eyes. At times, *there are only halves of birds.* Sometimes they portray images of bizarre, monstrous, almost *amorphous* beings, like so many *aerolites.* In the corner of each drawing there is a note. *The girl such and such, aged . . . brought forth this fetus in the year such and such*; and other notes of this kind." Here eros and art are joined by a new element: science. And this brings us back to the erotic origin, because the monsters shown in these drawings are the issue of the sexual unions of the whores in the house. And there's more: dates appear—and with them the story. All in "small frames": an important element, because the frame stands for disparity with regard to factual reality, entry into the realm of representation. But the frame is where life, pulsating life, appears in the guise of the *"lively* eyes" of certain birds. It is an all-embracing concatenation, from prostitution to taxonomy, a progression of forms that culminates in the amorphous, in other words in creatures that seem to have fallen from *another world ("aerolites").* There is something highly erudite and at the same time insane about all this. Baudelaire follows his train of thought: "In fact, I tell myself at one point, it was *Le Siècle* that financed the venture of this brothel, and the museum of medicine is explained by its mania for *progress, science, and the spread of enlightenment."* The basis of the venture is the brothel, an enormous house whose limits far exceed Baudelaire's grasp. Perhaps those galleries never end. And within this project of universal prostitution, which is the common ground and the premise of everything, on each of the walls there unfold works

of art, until art itself spills over into science. And it is not so much a science of the universal but of the *unicum*, in this case of unmentionable
monstrosities that seem to bear witness to another world and instead
have emerged from the wombs of the various girls who swarm throughout the house. There is something solemn and ominous about this succession of powers, chained one to another. And this is the moment when
Baudelaire's reasoning comes to a halt. By now he is on the verge of ut-
tering an esoteric axiom: "Then I reflect that modern stupidity and arrogance have their mysterious usefulness, and that often, by virtue of a
spiritual mechanics, what was done for ill turns into good." A large part
of Baudelaire's clandestine metaphysics is concealed in this sentence. All
that was *modern* was that venture "made for ill," in its unwitting pretensions to science and enlightenment, which however winds up by *turning
into good* if observed by an eye with the gift of the *right* vision. The modern was everything Baudelaire had come across: the faded couches and
the girls who talked with strangers, curious school kids, the obscene
drawings, the architecture, the Egyptian figures, the first photographs,
the tropical birds with the lively eyes, the dismembered bodies, the
meticulous texts with the names and dates, the amorphous fetuses. But
evidently that composition of elements, in its immense sadness, in its
capacity to disconcert and intimidate, in the end—"by virtue of a spiritual mechanics"—reveals that it guards the potentiality of something
else, something wholly different. These disparate elements were not unlike the ones that would come together, a few months later, in the poems
of *Les Fleurs du mal*—in fact, they were very much alike, a surprising out-
come. Baudelaire pauses in thought for a moment and says to himself,
"I admire in myself the rightness of my philosophical spirit."

In fact, the thought only just formulated in the dream had unman-
ageable consequences, because it implied that history was *not* an accidental succession of events, and was borne up by a "spiritual mechanics."
One might say that all of Baudelaire's work was an attempt to discover
this process and *put it into practice*. For this reason, too, when we read
Baudelaire we sometimes get the impression that he is following a thought
more than an occasional literary form, and by proceeding this way, he
lets fall, as if out of distraction or impatience, some penetrating verse or
some fragment of prose. And these should be considered as the sumptu-

ous remains of a vision that never manages to manifest itself in full. Or perhaps does not wish to.

Baudelaire lived in the midst of a world whose inner workings he disliked, indeed abhorred, even though he acknowledged their "mysterious usefulness." As if only at the cost of crossing those boundless regions of the *bêtise* was it possible to turn toward a good that other ages had not known. But how could that very mix of elements that Baudelaire had come across in the brothel-museum reveal themselves to be "good"—or at least the makings of "good"? Perhaps in those galleries, far more than when he visited the suffocating Salons, Baudelaire felt immersed in a congenial element—in that composite assemblage of artifice, in the blend of sex and science, of monsters in cabinets and shameless intimacy. There he was destined to breathe, forever. He would not have wished to escape into nature, whatever it might be. And after all, he had been the one to seek that house, in the night. He had come to deliver a gift: one of his books no less, as if the substance of that book were one of the specimens that those galleries seemed ready to accept. The past could never have given him such a landscape. And if it all presented itself like an "almost hieroglyphic language" to which Baudelaire realized he did not possess the key, it left him euphoric. Now it was no longer necessary to consider images as an enemy to be run through with the blade of significance, but as a messenger from the unknown, who was perhaps the last god to devote oneself to: *ágnostos theós*.

There is something incongruous, even hilarious, about the solemnity with which the dreamer approves his own metaphysics. But perhaps this is the crux of all Baudelaire. He could not substantiate his thought except in dream, precisely because only dream admitted and prescribed the "most monstrous paralogisms." In the waking state, his thought could issue only sporadically, with sudden and circumscribed eruptions on the page. In this way, little by little, Baudelaire's œuvre was composed.

The galleries of the brothel-museum were clearly laid out according to a criterion (almost in the manner of the Salons): they began with *representations* of the world (drawings, mostly obscene, but also architectural designs), Egyptian figures, miniatures, and photographs. Then they move on to drawings of inanimate exhibits (fetuses resembling aerolites, and bodies, sometimes mutilated, of birds). And among the birds, some had "*lively* eyes." The items seemed to be displayed by degrees, on a scale leading toward the living. In the end, Baudelaire encounters a *totally* living being: "a monster born in the house, who stands perpetually on a pedestal. Although he's alive, he is part of the museum." The living are born from the accumulation and stratification of the inanimate. It is the new nature. Baudelaire follows his train of thought: first the surprise of meeting a totally living being, then the recognition that this being belongs totally to the museum.

In that place, art glides over all, absorbing into itself equally the erotic traffic and the exposition of monstrosities. It is the *prima materia* that gathers all others into itself—impartial, boundless, all-embracing. And so Baudelaire, almost without noticing, came the point he had been aiming at right from the start. He found himself in front of a work that was a living being: someone, he thought immediately, who "has lived," and seemed fated to carry on living, crouched on a pedestal like a statue, forever *on show*. A monstrous being, especially because from his head there hung a large blackish serpent—made of rubber, one would have said. And the serpent was coiled several times around his body, as if his reptilian brain had extended from inside his head to reveal itself in that embarrassing way to make his life difficult, condemned as he was to bear a burden unknown to others. Who did that being resemble? Another young man, of radiant beauty, with a serpent coiled five times around his body, from the ankles to the head. It was Phanes-Chronos-Mithras. He, too, housed in a museum, in Mérida. He, too, standing on a pedestal. Of course, that young man had a healthy body, with graceful limbs, whereas the being crouched down in front of Baudelaire appeared rather shapeless; and he was alive, not a statue. Observing his face, with its vaguely Oriental complexion, you might say that it was "even pleasing." And the hue of his body was a delicate match of pink and green, the dress of the dawn when it advances "slowly over the deserted Seine."

Finally, Baudelaire met himself. The two conversed at length, with immediate familiarity. The being crouched on the pedestal, squat and burnished, talked above all of things about which the other was most expert: "troubles" and "sufferings." It was as if he had at last found the right person to talk to, one who could understand instantly, for example, his keenest torment, even though an apparently frivolous one: having to sit down every evening at dinner, he small and squat, beside one of the girls of the house, who was "tall and shapely." An aesthetic worry, certainly. But aren't these sometimes the most serious of all? Especially when humiliation is involved. To get to the dining room every evening, he had to climb down from the pedestal and stagger along for a stretch, owing to his long and heavy blackish tail. This was enough to embarrass

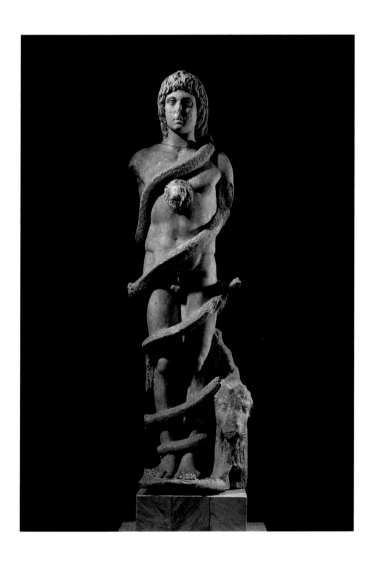

him and put him in a position of gauche defenselessness. Then, when he sat down, he couldn't even seat himself between two girls, because he always had to keep an empty chair beside him to arrange his tail on it, "like a coil of rope." Otherwise, its weight would have made him topple over backward. And his days were hard, too: "For years now he has been obliged to stay in that room, on that pedestal, for the curiosity of the public." The same thing had happened to Baudelaire, since he had decided to become an author and hence to sell himself, arousing the curiosity of the public. But how difficult it all was . . . And if one day he had succeeded, they would have judged him obscene, worthy only of being a guest in a house like the one where he had now met the monster. Perhaps standing on a pedestal, like him, with metrics and Racine as his pedestal.

In the epoch of *Le Siècle*, which endures to this day, Phanes still exists, but he is denied the honor of being a statue. Now he is someone who "has lived," a freak on show alongside images of other freaks, a "monster born in the house" (of prostitution), from which he has probably never gone out. He is no longer the one who bears up the world, but someone whom the world keeps imprisoned in the remotest part of himself. He is obliged to stand "perpetually on a pedestal," alongside the drawings of the girls' fetuses. The mercy of being a simulacrum has been denied him, but he must keep up the pose of one. He who is life perennial and recurrent, the mobile image of eternity, is subjected to various harassments and impediments, such as those he confided to Baudelaire. He who is the epitome of all *correspondances* is recognized and deciphered with difficulty. The majority would probably take him for one of the many freaks that surround him. Or pass him by with indifference, like any old piece of bric-a-brac scattered around the great brothel. And if someone recognizes him, as happened that time with Baudelaire, they speak of everyday sufferings and vexations rather than the secrets of the cosmos. As might happen between two old friends who meet again after years, melancholy and worn out, around a table in a café.

Exactly like Baudelaire, the monster would like to be decent in an indecent place. But this he cannot do, because of his long coiled tail, which is equivalent to Baudelaire's wet, bare feet. Both are doomed to be indecent creatures when it comes to indecency. This is what establishes the profound communion of their destiny. The monster would have liked to sit down civilly every evening, next to the girls of the brothel, after a long day having to sit motionless on his pedestal, exposed to the gaze of the visitors. But he could not do this—and would never be able to do it. Every time, he would have had to move in an awkward, clumsy way, dragging his tail behind him. And above all he would never have been able to sit normally with a woman beside him, because in some way he would have to arrange his coiled tail.

That being was accustomed to a kind of suffering and embarrassment that no one could understand better than Baudelaire. Had he not felt something similar when he showed up at the house with bare feet, his penis hanging out of his pants? The conversation proceeded, relaxed. The being crouched on the pedestal explained his difficulties "without bitterness." Baudelaire followed him with great empathy. They were immersed in these matters when Jeanne dispelled the vision. Baudelaire awoke with aching bones, as if a black serpent, coiled several times around his body, had clasped him at length, and almost crushed him. He felt "tired, enfeebled, worn out, [his] back, legs, and sides aching." He thought he had slept "in the contorted position of the monster." It seemed clear, now, why he had not wished to touch him. It would have been like touching himself. But why hadn't he dared? He had always felt keenly extraneous to himself, willing to look at himself as *an other*. And now he had finally met that *other*, and had been acquainted with "his troubles and sufferings." Discreet but sharing—and in the end keeping his distance—Baudelaire *took an interest in him*, and listened to himself.

V

THE FLEETING SENSE
OF MODERNITY

Baudelaire's manifest aversion to Ingres was first and foremost a rhetorical counterpoint to his enthusiasm for Delacroix. And it was also due to his dislike of Ingres's pompous proclamations in favor of the canonical triad Raphael-Greece-Nature. Baudelaire's thinking was too subtle and selective to be satisfied with that clumsy doctrine. But when he is faced with the paintings, one senses a brusque change of register. Baudelaire struggled to conceal the fact that he would have been the ideal critic for Ingres, the only one capable of dealing with his disconcerting originality. But Baudelaire, clear-sighted and mischievous, was playing a different game. So when it came to identifying "the painter of modern life," he had the choice fall upon an unknown devoid of any academic protection, a reporter of images who could not bear even to see his name in print: Constantin Guys. In one stroke, this move bypassed Delacroix, Ingres, and the Impressionism yet to come, and it led to the threshold of the new day in the form of a desire forever unfulfilled: a desire for futility, eros, lightness, and a life that might be adventurous and even a little shady.

The Painter of Modern Life, Baudelaire's supreme prose work, was conceived as a blatant provocation. In an epoch when the cult of genius was all the rage, where at every step people invoked Leonardo, Rubens, Titian—or Ideal Beauty or Nature—what was the artifice that Baudelaire fell back on in order to get in the mood, even to train himself mentally to talk about Guys? He leafed through a "series of fashionable prints that begin with the Revolution and end more or less with the Consulate." These were the enchanting images of Pierre de la Mésangère's "Journal des dames et des modes." To introduce us to the work of an artist whom he was to go as far as to present as *the* "painter of modern life," Baudelaire did not associate him with the Old Masters but with fashion plates. And plates from the Revolution at that. As if the Revolution had been first and foremost a good chance to change fashions and hairstyles a little faster than usual. Who in Baudelaire's time—and not only in France—would have had this kind of nerve, sardonically ending up by offering himself as a *feuilleton* for the daily paper of the solid bourgeoisie (*Le Figaro*, after numerous refusals on the part of other papers)? Obviously nobody. The great insolents who were on the verge of appearing (Rimbaud, Nietzsche, and Wilde, among others) would never have stooped to such idiosyncratic details, which belong to the most hidden stratum of sensibility. No one would have been as outrageously *aesthetic* as Baudelaire.

Now a reporter of images who sent his sketches daily to *The Illustrated London News* so that hasty xylographs could be made from them, a stenographer of the everyday scene, an illustrator (a degraded breed) was held up as an example, and preferred to Delacroix and Manet. A choice that is perplexing to this day. Various art historians have proved unable to make sense of this. What? An "enchanting lightweight" such as Guys, who struggled to find even a tiny niche in the manuals, preferred to the great Manet? Yet only two years after Baudelaire's essay, Manet was to show *Music in the Tuileries*, which looks like a diligent and sensational implementation of his suggestions—and encloses in its interior, like an inlay, a portrait of Baudelaire himself camouflaged among the crowd. Manet was Baudelaire's friend, and he had also joined the ranks of those who lent him money without expecting to get it back. But Baudelaire never wished to link the name of Guys with that of Manet. On the contrary, he reserved for Manet only these disquieting words of praise: *"You are but the first in the decrepitude of your art."* Like Guys, Baudelaire was impervious to any group spirit; even the school of the *refusés* would have struck him as too crowded, and perhaps even too devoted to "sanctified vegetables" in *plein air*.

Only with Guys, among the various people with whom he had dealings, did Baudelaire establish a rapport, a blend of admiration, complicity, and cautious friendship. Only with Guys would he go as far as to commission a few drawings, in a particularly distressing moment when, as usual, he was in debt. And seldom had he revealed such a sense of euphoria and pride as when he told Poulet-Malassis about what he had done: "I must add yet another folly. Despite my wretched condition, and your penury, I have bought and *commissioned* some superb drawings by Guys, for you and for me, without consulting you about it, but this must not alarm you. Since he does not know your name, if you're broke I'll pay for everything." Similarly, when Baudelaire had to give his mother a Christmas gift, it could only be a Guys (*Turkish Woman with Parasol*).

But the affinity is even more disturbing, because it extends to the line in drawings. If Baudelaire sketches the figure of a woman, sometimes with memorable incisiveness, one thinks immediately of a Guys.

Not only because occasionally the sketch is an explicit tribute, but also because Baudelaire *could not* draw any other way, as can be observed in certain of his sketches of female figures that date from some years before his encounter with Guys. Between them there was something that went beyond art: a subterranean and irrepressible communion of perceptions.

Vulgarité is a word introduced by Mme de Staël in 1800. We come across *Modernité* in Théophile Gautier, 1852. But in Chateaubriand's *Mémoires d'outre-tombe*, published in 1849, the two words are found juxtaposed in the same sentence, with regard to problems the author had had at the customs post in Württemberg: "The vulgarity, the modernity of customs and passports." As if the two words were fated to keep each other company. And before? Before there were vulgar people, but not vulgarity. And modern people, but not modernity. So how was it possible to think and feel without the help of these two potent categories, branches that we now know were somewhat slow to sprout?

Modernity: a word that emerges and rebounds between Gautier and Baudelaire in the space of a little more than ten years during the Second Empire, between 1852 and 1863. And this was always done with caution, with the awareness of introducing an alien notion into the language. Gautier, 1855: "Modernity. Does this noun exist? The sentiment it expresses is so recent that the word may very well not be in the dictionaries." Baudelaire, 1863: "He is looking for that something we shall be allowed to call *modernity*; since there isn't a better word to express the idea in question." But what was this idea that was so recent and feeble that it still had to become fixed in a word? What was modernity made of? The malicious Jean Rousseau immediately declared it was made up of *bibelots* and female bodies. Arthur Stevens responded to him in defense of Baudelaire, defined on the occasion for the first time as "he who is the inventor, I believe, of this word *modernity*." Through painting and frivolity, modernity burst into the dictionary. But it was destined to remain and spread, following progressive campaigns of conquest, accompanied by devastation. Soon no one would remember these frivolous and modest beginnings. In Baudelaire, however, the word remained enfolded as in a mist of perfume and face powder.

•

After the Congress of Vienna had given a semblance of order to the continent, in the European psyche there began to emerge a phenomenon of immense consequence: the past became available, ready to be put onstage. And *all* the past, not just a slice of it (the Greeks and the Romans), as had been the case until then. From Ossianic and druidic mists to Gothic shadows and the splendors of the Renaissance (and including what had been the chronicles of a few years before, which now already appeared as fragments *in costume*)—all came together to form a vast warehouse of stage properties, one that was dipped into first of all by melodrama and painting, but also by poetry and the novel. Then, with the age of Louis Philippe, the post-historic view of history extended beyond the stages and the Salons, finding its way into the *intérieur*. History was a sequence of dated scenes, which established themselves in the various rooms and corners of the home. Renaissance studies, Turkish niches, and rococo *boudoirs* all coexisted. Living in the *intérieur*: according to Benjamin, this was tantamount to allowing oneself to be trapped in a spider web "in which the events of universal history are dispersed, hanging like bodies of insects sucked dry." From then on, the mark of a single style that characterized an epoch began to disappear. Thereafter, the posthumous attempt was Art Nouveau, which enveloped the *rêverie* of universal history in the forests of the Carboniferous. Finally, history went back to appearing as a branch of natural history.

Together with time, space, too, no longer put up any resistance. By now Asia was not merely *turquerie* (or *chinoiserie*), but also a boundless expanse that encircled the world and where Indians devoted to repellent many-headed divinities were compared to the American Plains Indians, in whom Chateaubriand saw the precursors of the dandy. In becoming available, the past lost something of its extraneousness and gravity. From then on, a certain artificial character was to accompany this proliferation of appearances. We entered a new regime of the imagination, in which we still live.

For the Salon of 1855, "the works of all of Europe's artists were brought together solemnly in avenue Montaigne, as if for a sort of aesthetic council." Wandering through the rooms, Baudelaire felt obliged to recognize "the general tendency among artists to dress all their subjects in ancient costumes." But there was something new in respect to David, stubbornly faithful to ancient Rome and to no other epoch: "Today's painters, instead, while they choose subjects of a generic character, applicable to all epochs, insist on camouflaging them with medieval, Renaissance, or Oriental costumes." Here Baudelaire recognized the transformation of the past, in its totality, into a repertoire of ready-to-use scenes. It was a prodigious event, with intricate premises. One was the refusal to see what was circulating in the streets of the great city, because this risked being too novel. Artists interposed velvets, brocades, gauze, curtains, carpets, jerkins, muffs, Gothic arches, and balustrades to obstruct the visual field. In this way modernity was reduced to "the transitory, the fleeting, the contingent," the ephemeral and the ambiguous that Constantin Guys's sinewy, vibrant style tried to capture. And so it happened that the word *modernity*, unusual until then, came to stand out as the title of the fourth section of Baudelaire's essay on that same Guys who was ready to vanish into the crowd, retaining only the initial of his own surname, on that "solitary man gifted with an active imagination, forever journeying through *the great desert of men*" (these last words being a snippet from Chateaubriand).

Ever since the word *modern* invaded every nook and cranny, and then in its turn became an antique, it has been hard to realize the extent to which its origins were marginal and erotic. But it gets easier if we accept the challenge thrown down by Baudelaire: if you wish to recognize the modern, ask any "patient and meticulous" painter to tackle a portrait of a "courtesan of the present day." At a distance of one hundred and fifty years, after the advocates and execrators of modernity have filled bookshelf upon bookshelf, ever more rarely avoiding a deadly bigotry, the return to what might be described as *the Baudelaire test* is both refreshing and exhilarating.

To say the least it is strange that, precisely in the country where for almost two centuries a *dispute* had raged between Ancients and Moderns, it required so much circumspection to get to the point of pronouncing and defining the word *modernity*. What was it that loomed behind the term? Gautier gave himself away by writing "modern as a novel by Balzac," where "novel by Balzac" stood for the obsessive detail of everyday life in the big city. This was the all-enveloping event that was hard to accept. Balzac—a veritable prose prairie who names events, objects, procedures, and impressions *on the same level*—was himself a symptom (and not among the least alarming) of that modernity, rather than its theorist. So he could not be a confrere in the attempt to circumscribe the modern, as he himself was an intrusive manifestation of it. The incarnation of a demoniac "will to see all, and to forget nothing," Balzac was a "riot of details, all of which demand justice with the fury of a crowd infatuated with absolute equality. Inevitably, all justice will be violated; all harmonies destroyed, sacrificed; the slightest trifle, a usurper." These lines from Baudelaire, which do *not* refer to Balzac, are those that define him most accurately. There was something inordinate in Balzac, an "incorrigible and fatal monstrosity" that justified the convulsive aspect of his characters. All suffer equally from an excess of emphasis, of biological genius (because "everyone, in Balzac, even a concierge, is outstanding"). Every character is ready to explode; "all the characters are weapons loaded with will right up to the barrel." This rampant energy is so strong as to allow Balzac "to infallibly clothe pure banality in light and purple." This was his secret, and it would seem that he was the only one to possess it. Baudelaire added a rhetorical question: "Who else can do this?" Then he stopped, as if struck by something obvious: "But he who does not do this, to tell the truth, is not doing anything special." That phrase, "to tell the truth," is revealing. As if, suddenly, he had to make a point: not only Balzac, in his monstrosity, but every writer is obliged *at least* to clothe "pure banality" in light and purple.

But neither Gautier nor Baudelaire wanted to theorize about modernity too much. Baudelaire's aim was rather to extract its essence, isolate it like a chemical element, record its peculiarities, a constant nervous tremor that had always eaten away at and excited him. Not the legend of the centuries, but the legend of the instant, volatile, and precarious, with its timbre that could not be boiled down to any previous historical phase that was going to become the very stuff, the vast and obscure reservoir of sensations of *Les Fleurs du mal*. Baudelaire evoked this vicariously, when he wrote, with regard to Guys, that the characteristic of his drawing was a "*legendary* translation of external life."

And then came Rimbaud, the master of the intimidatory phrase. At the end of *A Season in Hell*, after a harsh and coruscating paragraph, these words blare out: "It is necessary to be absolutely modern." The reason why is not given. The modern blooms "without a reason," like the rose of Angelus Silesius. Countless people were to fall victim to this phrase: society ladies, who once they had breathed from the phial of the avant-garde could no longer do without it, in a long sequence of turbulent premieres and *vernissages*. And then there were all the middling artists and writers who would stop at nothing provided they lived up to the motto that had dazzled them.

If Baudelaire was the first to outline the *modern* in the most exciting way, he also had the honor of having been the first to strike a blow at the *avant-garde*, a word that for a few decades of the twentieth century was beguiling and that in the twenty-first century sounds like a bad joke. Baudelaire coolly observed that the term originated in the "French fondness for military metaphors"; a fondness typical of certain "spirits domestic by nature, Belgian spirits." It is not necessary to explain what the sobriquet *Belgian* implied as far as Baudelaire was concerned. As for the meaning of *domestic*, Baudelaire gives it elsewhere: "The Frenchman is a farmyard animal, so well trained that he doesn't dare climb over any palisade." It was a question of people "made for discipline, that is for uniformity," people "who don't know how to think except in society." They are the ones who talk incessantly of *veterans, recruits, penetrating the enemy's defenses, militant literature, flying the flag, entering the fray*. They are the ones, finally, who invented the "avant-garde literati." Thus the embarrassing origins of all avant-garde movements were revealed. And many Mme Verdurins would then do their utmost to conceal them.

There was something oppressive, cloying, about the petulant sociability of the Salons combed by Diderot. The way to avoid them was either to smash through the ceiling and flee toward Tiepolo's skies in Würzburg, or to open a side door that gave onto countless collections of drawings, some secret. Boucher alone, according to the artist himself, left around ten thousand. Then there was Watteau, the master of the three forms of charcoal drawing: red, black, and white. Or Greuze, with his masterful burnt sanguines. Or the exuberant Saint-Aubin, who was afflicted (according to Greuze) with a "priapism of drawing." Or Fragonard, who demanded that every one of his sketches be no less perfect than his paintings. According to Focillon, those years in Paris were unique be-

cause never before "had the great poets of drawing, art lovers no less
than artists, been so capable of combining tactile sensuality with the
intelligent divination that an art of that kind develops naturally in those
who know how to appreciate its beauty." Whereas the paintings tended
to be crowded by too many, often tedious elements, the drawings—with
their vast empty spaces—enhanced the details, down to a certain way
of tying ribbons in a handmaiden's hair, as in an admirable drawing
by Boucher made in 1740. It seems clear that by then the essential lay
only in those details. This is what Baudelaire meant when he claimed
that Guys was the painter of modern life par excellence (and the reference to Saint-Aubin was explicit). In perspective, this meant ousting
painting from its sovereign position and admitting that something no less

indispensable, in the marine realm of the image, had come from disreputable illustration or—an even greater scandal, this—from photography. Through Guys, Baudelaire evoked the cinema, with a potent charm. Guys was a harbinger of Max Ophuls rather than Manet. The subtle flavor of the present, its "essential quality of being present," began to demand a mysterious, opalescent surface, crossed by figures in motion. Even before it was invented, the cine-camera was the *rôdeur* that walked the streets of Paris.

The Goncourt brothers met Guys in Gavarni's home in April 1858, a few months before Baudelaire met him. For them he was "the one who drew for English ILLUSTRATION, the draftsman of the grand style and brilliant ink-wash brothel scenes." They found themselves in the presence of "a strange man, who has seen it all, who has lived through all kinds of adventures, frittering away his health in every clime and in every kind of love, a man who has emerged from the boarding houses of London, the castles of *fashion*, the green meadows of Germany, the massacres in Greece, the taverns of Paris, the editorial offices of the newspapers, the trenches of Sebastopol, mercury treatments, the plague, Oriental dogs, duels, whores, con men, debauchees, usury, poverty, gambling dens and slums, where as in a sea there swarm all those shipwrecked existences, all those nameless and bootless men, those submerged and terrible originals that never emerge on the surface of novels." This was clearly the man predestined for the role as the "painter of modern life," the celebrator of "equivocal beauty" in hundreds and hundreds of sketches of prostitutes of all kinds, from the lowest of the low to the high-class sort, who rode through the Bois de Boulogne in superb coaches or scrutinized the audience through opera glasses from their boxes at the theater. When he talked about painting, Guys couldn't even hide his extraneousness to the canons of the period. This happened to him also in the course of that soiree at Gavarni's, with the Goncourt brothers: "And now he talks to us about painting, about painters, about landscape artists, about those countless representations of nature without action, about the passion for fried foods: 'They never put gloves on; they never go to the *Italiens*! They don't like music, they don't like horses—because they don't have any. The sun, the countryside, and yet again fries!'"

If Baudelaire elected Guys as a model, it was also because, before Eduard Fuchs, he had come to a scandalous conclusion: illustrators tended to be more daring than the painters of their times. Free of the burden of the past, happily obscure, not held to justify what they did with respect to the old masters but only with respect to a customer determined not to lose money, saved from the humiliating rigmarole of the Salons, illustrators made their way through the realm of images without any need even to pronounce the word *art*. Thus, together with Horace

Vernet's *Incroyables et merveilleuses*, the fashion plates in La Mésangère's *Journal* set the stage for Ingres's supreme lead-point portraits: were it not for the intensity of her gaze, like that of an infanta by Velázquez, the portrait of Mlle Isabelle Guille might be an illustration in a fashion journal for children, just as the portrait of the Montagu sisters might be an example of the differences between English and continental fashions. The same happened with Guys: his countless *filles*, who welcome or wait for or entertain clients in houses of pleasure, or make their own amusements, blaze the trail for Toulouse-Lautrec's posters. Guys set his seal on a new genre of painting, comparable to the rustic scenes of the Flemings or the pastoral idylls of the gallant painters. It is "the variegated image of equivocal beauty" that finally finds its space, immense and closed, on the threshold of which two black-haired women are seated on the steps. Their facial features and hair styles are almost identical, their breasts bared, legs amply exposed and feet bare, enveloped in a wave of water green dresses. If one goes up those steps and penetrates the misty background of the place, there will also appear figures with a high charge of romantic seduction, such as the girl in a blue crinoline who stands out against the bold yellow background like one of those "living dolls whose infantile gaze reveals a sinister light."

·

Guys's sketches were soon to be found in large numbers in the most disparate places in Paris. You could buy them in packs of a dozen. Bought
one at a time, the price varied—according to the size—between fifty
centimes and one franc. A little investigation made it possible to find out
the sole source: a certain M. Picot, in the passage Véro-Dodat. The
subjects belonged to only four kinds: coaches, horsemen, soldiers, and
loose women (these last being the clear majority). It was as if, apart from
these four categories, there was nothing else worth the effort of observing. And without exception, they shared a distinguishing mark: instan-

taneousness, the imperturbable agility of line. The source of Guys's inspiration was very different from that of the caricaturists, such as his friend Gavarni or Daumier. Caricature abounds with meanings; it goes in search of character, of univocality in every line. Guys seemed wholly indifferent to meaning. For the most part his women displayed generic expressions, as if they used them only as much as necessary in order to carry out some tedious task. And it was hard to tell one from the other, if not for certain aspects of dress or hairstyle, or for the places where they were found, which ranged from the lowest hovels to sumptuous equipages. The most important thing was that these women were numerous and multipliable, samples of a quasi-industrial production of simulacra. Through Guys, Baudelaire glimpsed an impudent, insolent art, which addressed only the "daily metamorphosis of external things" and complied with "a rapid movement that obliges the artist to execute his work equally rapidly." This would have been an antidote to his saturnine, lethargic disposition. And in certain cases, as happens with some marvels—"À une passante" is the first example—the two tendencies could flow into and blend with each other.

Guys spent the last decades of his life like a walnut shell floating on the water. The researcher finds almost solely silence and emptiness. There seem to have been no exhibitions, affairs, quarrels, loves, or relatives. He had few friends, almost all of whom died before him. If the last of the survivors, Nadar, had not written a brief commemorative piece on Guys's death, we would know nothing of his last years, which he spent as a shut-in in a clinic after a carriage ran into him and broke his leg. In those he read the newspapers avidly, ignoring all else. When Manet made his portrait, Guys's hair was already white and his beard unkempt. His gaze was wary, proud, and distant. According to Baudelaire, at night he would rush into the city and wander around until the small hours. Then, when all were asleep, he would draw. About two thousand sketches remain. Baudelaire possessed dozens; Gautier, about sixty. No one wrote about Guys except Baudelaire, who made him the subject of the finest and most illuminating essay on any artist to appear in the nineteenth century.

Like a claustrophiliac Guys, Degas wandered about between the wings of the stage and the room where female ballet students practiced. Instead of Guys's *cocottes*, now there were young dancers. Obsession and repetition remained essential. In a letter from Naples dated 1886, Degas, under the weather, wrote, "I'm talking about a long time ago because, apart from my heart, it seems to me that everything in me is aging in proportion. And even this heart has something artificial about it. The ballerinas have stitched it up in a little pouch of pink silk, a rather faded pink silk, like their ballet pumps."

The Impressionists? "You need a natural life, I need an artificial one" was one of Degas's many *mots*, the product of mood swings and sudden fancies. But here there emerges a whole physiology, with all its incompatibilities. Degas abhorred the ideology of *plein air* and found something awkward about this kind of painter's claim to get closer to nature by setting up an easel in a meadow. (Manet, at least, when he did this, never took off his top hat.)

Degas was a city person; he needed a highly artificial filter in order *to see*. Such filters could be the stage lights or the artfully chosen accumulation of objects in his studio or even chance movements on the streets, which he scoured tenaciously (*Ambulare, postea laborare* was the motto he once coined). But he always needed something that distracted his gaze, which might delude or amuse him. A crease in a desolate psychic background, without any apparent reason. Degas took great pains to avoid talking about himself, obliging us to observe him in exactly the same way as he looked at the world: indirectly, surprising him while he talks about something else. So it can also happen that his words attain a kind of ulcerated pathos. Degas wrote to his friend Rouart to justify the fact that he wouldn't leave Paris, even though everyone went into the countryside: "It's not bad in the city, if you like it. And basically, as you know, I like it well enough. You have to keep on looking at everything, small boats and bigger ones, people moving about restlessly on the water and on land too. The movement of things and people distracts and even consoles, if one can be consoled when so unhappy. If the leaves in the trees didn't move, how sad the trees would be, and us too! There is a kind of tree in the garden next door that sways at a puff of wind. Well! Even if I'm in Paris in my less than clean studio, I think that tree is delightful . . ." That "kind of tree" was all of nature for Degas. He felt the same mistrust of nature as Baudelaire did, but without any need for theology or any reference to original sin. Degas had no need of Joseph de Maistre. Drawing was enough for him. His life was as "regulated as music paper." From morning until evening he worked in his studio. It seems that he was never tempted to put his foot in one of those *natural* traps that already afflicted his contemporaries and was to afflict even more those who came after him: instinct, sex, spontaneity, happiness, the noble savage, the new man. If he noticed a trace of all this he turned his back on it. One day a lady approached him and made the serious blunder of calling him "master." Then she said, "as if informing Degas of something about which he should have been sensible: 'My son paints and his is a painting of such *sincerity* with regard to nature . . .' 'How old is your son, madam?' 'He is almost fifteen.' 'So young and already sincere with regard to nature!' exclaimed Degas. 'Well, madam, he is a lost cause . . .'"

Degas: "a difficult man," in the sense of Hofmannsthal's character. For such a person the "malaise of life" is nothing new, and no "catastrophe" can take him by surprise. Whereas Manet tended to appear ecumenically human, instantly recognizable in his impulses and enthusiasms, Degas's psyche is shielded from the start by a carefully protected film of opacity. Everyone was obliged to admit that the essential part of his life occurred *in secret*. An impenetrable secret because it was devoid of ascertainable events. As for the rest, his daily routine was indistinguishable from that of a bourgeois. Respectability, regularity, taste in clothing, even the tendency to frequent chemists or engineers or inventors rather than artists or, worse still, men of letters—all of his traits conspired in that direction.

Degas often said that everything would be perfect if one could be left in peace without critics, without art dealers, without Salons, without journalists, and without literati. And there is reason to believe that he truly thought that way. To paint and rest the canvases against the wall. To go back to them after a few hours—or decades (as was the case with *Mlle Fiocre*). Not to let them leave the house—and, if they did, to find an excuse to get them back and retouch them. This was the rhythm that suited him. He abhorred those who claimed to *explain*. But he didn't even like those who merely expected to understand. Degas never declared what he intended to do. He held that the most important lesson had been given to him by Ingres, who, the only time they spoke, enjoined him to *make lines, lots and lots of lines*. There was not much more than this to say. Otherwise he slipped into that ciphered language of which he considered some maxims of Ingres to be shining examples. Talking with Blanche, Degas got to his feet and intoned:

"Form is not in the line, but within the line.

"Shade is not to be placed beside the line, but on the line.

"A reflection on the shading of the outline is unworthy of the majesty of art."

All of these were Ingres's maxims, solemnly repeated. Their meaning could remain a secret shared only *by painters*. Degas found talking about painting a torment. Yet he liked it. But the result was discouraging: "I am capable of finding the clearest and most correct words with which to explain what I mean, and I have talked about art with the most intelligent people, and they didn't understand me . . . but among people who understand there is no need for words: just go hmmm! oh! ah! and all has been said." A comical situation, in which only a few indistinct sounds guaranteed understanding. The torment occurred when others set out to discuss painting. Huysmans, for example, gave Degas the idea for a revealing phrase: "All these literati think they can play the art critic as if painting weren't the least accessible thing of all." Among the various forms of knowledge, painting was therefore the most remote and cryptic. Something like an esoteric truth, protected by a secret that cannot be betrayed simply because *there is no way* to betray it. But Degas would never have used the word *esoteric*. Another word employed by "literati."

Valéry expressed the hope that one day there might exist *"A Unified History of Things of the Spirit,"* which would replace every history of philosophy, art, literature, and the sciences. As always with his boldest visions, he went no farther than mentioning it. And, coquettishly, he hid it in a "Digression" that in its turn was part of the unrestrained digression that is *Degas Danse Dessin*. Of the "Unified History" he dreamed of he gave only one example: "In such an analogical history, Degas would stand between Beyle and Mérimée." A masterful coup de main aimed at bringing Degas back to his vocation as a "loner without remorse." Immediately after, Valéry offered a cameo of the "analogical history" that had flashed through his mind. Still on the subject of Degas, he wrote that "his drawing treats bodies with the same love and the same harshness with which Stendhal treats people's characters and motives." Since then, "analogical history" has not made much progress. It remains an ever-more-urgent *desideratum* in an intellectually debilitated epoch such as the present.

Nothing gets closer to muteness than the wisdom of the painter. And in order to conceal that silence, painting could present itself as Degas wished: "a wholly special discipline," made of "mysteries," provided with a "technical esotericism" (all terms used by Valéry). So, when it came to the word, either that discipline revealed itself to be protected by a jargon unknown to outsiders or it ended up by declaring itself, often with virulence, in imperious apothegms such as those of Ingres, which, however, always left a hint of vacuity—or of impenetrability. Something similar applied to Degas. "Drawing is not form, it is the way to see form" was one of his best known dicta. But if the young Valéry asked for some clarification, Degas would get furious. The more we move forward in the history of painting, the more we perceive its fundamental hostility to the word. Not only did the maxim *ut pictura poesis* no longer hold; painting did not accept that poetry was "painting that speaks," as Varchi had claimed. Closed in on itself, uninterested in providing a *libretto* (the name used in the Salons for the brief descriptions of the subjects of the paintings, the last, wretched remains of the lost iconological structure), painting got closer and closer to the self-sufficient and isolated condition of the ballerinas or ironers or women tirelessly washing themselves that Degas doggedly painted, as if hinting—in those absorbed figures, slaves of a fixed repertoire of movements—at a display of the relentless silence of his art, made solely of small gestures.

Yet here and there we come across, like drifting flotsam, certain phrases that give the impression of an approach to the "mysteries" of painting. Almost blind, "ever more savage, absolutist and unbearable," Degas seemed to have moved his eyes to his fingertips. "He fingered objects," and spoke of paintings in terms of touch. He would say of a painting, "It's flat like fine painting." A startling phrase, like a shard of a wisdom that otherwise remained silent. Valéry mentions this toward the end of *Degas Danse Dessin*, where, with sudden *sprezzatura*, he slips in a few oblique words that belong to that same wisdom, writing of Pascal that "he didn't know how to look, in other words to forget the names of the things we see."

In some ways Degas was similar to Monsieur Teste. In confirmation of this, he refused the dedication to his *La Soirée avec Monsieur Teste*. He said he was "fed up with poets." And then that young Valéry, with whom he liked to chat, had a serious defect: he wanted to understand everything. This was unacceptable to Degas. As for Valéry, he was enchanted when he first met Degas: in part he corresponded to the fiction of Monsieur Teste, and in part he contributed to its creation. Valéry acknowledged this on one occasion, talking with Edmond Jaloux: "One day Paul Valéry told me that the man who reminded him most of M. Teste was Degas . . . In his own way, Degas was just as isolated, just as unclassifiable as M. Teste was in his." At first, Valéry relished watching Degas in action: "Every Friday Degas, faithful, scintillating, unbearable, enlivens dinner at Monsieur Rouart's. He radiates subtlety, terror, merriment." His "essential feature" was "a kind of brutality of intellectual origin." And this allowed him to avoid "Mallarmé's cute little absurdities, which go on too long." On the other hand, Degas had other traits, including anti-Semitism.

Until Degas, custom reasonably located the subjects of a portrait in the center. In the same way, there was a tacit rule whereby every figure, even secondary ones, appeared *completely*. The visual field, with its arbitrary limitations, had to respect the intactness of the characters who came into the picture.

With Degas, this changed. Perhaps not even out of a conscious decision and certainly not to state some new principle. Rather, it was the result of a kind of gestural drift. When did he begin doing this? Not exactly from the start, as the figures in Degas's early portraits are in an irreproachably central position. But we already see a dramatic novelty in *The Bellelli Family*, a key painting, which the young Degas worked on for seven years. Originally titled *Family Portrait*—and hence referring

to something that is a nucleus par excellence—this painting develops around an empty space in the center. The father has his back to the painter, and the four figures are looking in different directions. All the figures seem to wish to exclude the others from their own visual field, as also happens in a portrait of the Bellelli sisters on their own. They are psychic entities determined not to come even close to one another. The mother's gaze is so fixed and absent as to make her seem blind. The two girls are recalcitrant: the one nearer the center avoids looking at the painter with mischievous determination, so much so as to invalidate her axial position. The other gives the artist a bored stare, as if to say, "When is this torment going to stop?" The father ignores the painter; above all *he has no gaze*. We know from various sources that the Bellelli family was riddled with acrimony, rancor, and fractiousness, an exemplary domestic hell. A southern Strindberg. Group portraits were usually commissioned to emphasize certain features: unity, solidarity, and harmony. Their origins lay in pride and vanity. Instead, Degas wanted to paint—and stubbornly perfected—the portrait of a family united by reciprocal aversions. But it's not the oddness of the spatial arrangement that hints at a psychological state. It is psychological tension used to attain a spatial revelation: *the absence of a center*. A center that can no longer

perform its symbolic function. Here the center is occupied by wallpaper and numerous frames, including that of a mirror. Elsewhere such things could take the form of a bunch of chrysanthemums, as in the portrait of Madame Valpinçon, as long as the figure was displaced from its canonical position. For almost fifty years, Degas was to carry on his covert struggle, his systematic sabotage of all centers.

A desolate plain, with depressions. Splashes of light from a turbulent sky. In the distance: smoke from a huge fire, with some flares. Even farther away, on a rise, the outline of a Gothic bell tower with constructions around it. In the foreground, a wide, dusty dirt road. Two tree trunks thrust thin, withered branches toward the sky. And then? Nine nude women. Three are dead or in their death throes. Two are moving away, but it seems that they are unable to run, as happens in dreams. Another two, clinging to one of the trees, are captured in the convulsive pose of those who are about to be shot and wish to protect themselves. One seems to have her wrist bound to the trunk. The other is stooping, and her long tawny hair is hanging down over her face, as if she wishes to hide it. Another woman is dragging herself through the dust. Of another again we see only her legs and buttocks: a horseman has seized her and is carrying her off, like a package. There is also a kind of ghost-woman, whom Degas has almost completely erased. But we can still make out her feet and a part of her leg. She was seen from the back and observed, perhaps paralyzed, as is borne out by a preparatory drawing.

But who dominates the scene? Three horsemen, in generic medieval costumes. One is turning back toward the women and is about to loose an arrow. The second is watching him. The third is already moving away, with a woman on the back of his horse. All act in concert, without any need to tell one another what needs to be done: eliminate the survivors and carry on.

The painting is mysterious—and terrifying. At the Salon of 1865 it was shown (without attracting any comment) with the title *Medieval War Scene*. No anecdote is illustrated here. The spectator ought to reconstruct it. What has led nine naked women (there are some clothes scattered around, but only for three of them) into open countryside, at the mercy of three impassive and impeccable horsemen? The women are now targets and nothing more. Some have already been hit (but no arrows or traces of blood can be seen on their bodies). Others—and it's impossible not to think this—will be shot at any moment.

Far more than in Goya's *The Third of May 1808*, far more than in Manet's *Execution of Maximilian* (which, divided into four pieces, was part of Degas's collection), this image portrays defenselessness and abuse. The tenuous, opaque color, almost like that of a fresco; the dull, pale light; the rare accentuations of color (the archer's yellow tunic, the woman's tawny hair hanging down, the red breeches worn by one of the horsemen)—all this confirms the irremediable coldness and silence of the event. It is the pure act of killing, intensified by the humiliation of the victims. A few seconds from now, there will be various bodies of naked women abandoned along the road and a cloud of dust settling. The horsemen? Vanished, forever.

Degas never said a word about this painting. Yet he always kept it close to him, in his studio. After the Salon, over fifty years would pass before it was again shown in public, in 1918, at the auction of the Degas collection, after the painter's death. The event marked the beginning of a strange story of confusion over the title. In the catalog, the painting was designated as *The Misfortunes of the City of Orléans*. Vain attempts were made to identify the episode that the painting was supposed to illustrate. It's plausible that Degas was referring to the bloody siege of Orléans by the English in 1428–1429. But the chronicles of the time offer nothing certain to go on. And the mystery, still total, of the subject of the painting also serves as an introduction to another esoteric zone, the one that concerns women in Degas—hence the predominant part of his œuvre.

Medieval War Scene is accompanied by various drawings of female nudes, rightly considered among Degas's finest. And also the most akin to Ingres as can be found. On observing them, and on observing the female figures in the painting, it appears evident that, for Degas, those figures constituted a kind of *repertoire of gestures*, which he dipped into on numerous subsequent occasions, above all for the intimate scenes, among tin tubs for bathing in and bathtubs. And that is not all; the repertoire also included two highly symbolic quotations. The woman bound to the tree in the *Medieval War Scene* is a link to Ingres's *Angelica*

chained to the rock, a painting that was a part of Degas's collection, together with a magnificent preparatory drawing (by Ingres) and an
equally magnificent copy of Angelica executed by Degas in 1855, hence
a decade before *Medieval War Scene*. And the woman dying in the dust,
on the right, refers back to David's *The Death of Joseph Bara*, which Degas
had copied in the Musée Calvet in Avignon, again in 1855—and it is an
incunabulum of neoclassical eros, in its hermaphroditic and fatal variant. With regard to the thirteen-year-old Bara, a revolutionary hero
slain by the cruel Vendeans, it is legitimate to wonder how he came to
die nude—and isolated against a background vibrant with painting, just
as it is inevitable to wonder the same thing about Degas's nine women.
Degas's female figures certainly do not refer to some Impressionistic *bonheur*. Their premise is mournful. All of them are descendants of the unknown women pierced by arrows one by one in *War Scene* and left lying
in the middle of an ordinary country road.

Medieval War Scene is borne up by a peculiar cruelty, unparalleled in
Degas's time. Either we do not perceive this at all (and this was the case
with his contemporaries—Halévy was the only one to allow that this

was a work of "disconcerting strangeness") or we can hardly avoid see-ing it as an adumbration of the new times. That this came about through medieval camouflage does no more than further emphasize the singu-larity of what is shown.

A war is going on—and this is proved by the city burning in the background—but the three horsemen are not dressed as warriors. They might be three gentlemen reconnoitering. The nine women are not ge-neric victims: they are all pretty, young, and totally defenseless—the way one would feel if found naked in open countryside. In their regard, the three horsemen are calmly determined: one is killing them, another is carrying one off. The two acts seem equivalent. These women are things that can be disposed of. We don't know why, and no justification is required. There is no trace of war's fury. The air is frozen, motion-less. No one will witness this; no one will ask why. What is being expe-rienced here is a new way of killing, for which a certain calm is necessary. The victims form a group but not yet a mass—and they can make no appeal for help, in the silence of the countryside. An image that is like a new kind of subject for meditation. We do not know if the horsemen are soldiers, criminals, or executioners.

The *Portrait of Mlle E.F.: Apropos of the Ballet "La Source"* (this was the title, already laden with ambiguity, with which the canvas was shown at the Salon of 1868) is the only painting we know of in which the landscape and the stage are superimposed to the point that they blend into each other without overlapping. Was this not the dream, for a great many years, of a West suspended between the opposition of Nature and Arti-fice? One that it had always tried to overcome? Degas took that step beyond. Like a dance step, which revealed itself in a vision that was ab-sorbed, silent, and fleeting, for it was never to be repeated, either in Degas or in others. Here, Mlle Eugénie Fiocre, a star of the Opéra, ad-mired by all of Paris during the Second Empire, is a Georgian princess, who appears at the center of a vaguely Orientalist scene. Melancholy, pensive, her gaze is fixed and lost before what may be a pool. Nearby are two young girls. And an unsaddled horse that is drinking, or at least lowering its muzzle toward the water. But is it real water? Or a reflecting surface spread out on a stage? In fact, almost half the painting is taken up by the reflection of the figures in that water, which is far too still, as if it were a mirror. Is it perhaps a mirror? Yet it's difficult to imagine a horse calmly drinking from a mirror. And behind the horse, the rocks and the ground are wholly natural, indistinguishable from certain studies of rocks drawn by Degas on his travels. How can we imagine them as papier-mâché? But there is one detail that doesn't fit. Beside the water, one of the two girls accompanying the princess is sitting on a white cloth. And that cloth extends into the liquid surface. If it were real water, it should be immersed. Instead, the girl's hand is resting on the cloth, which in its turn is resting on something more resistant: a mirror? The other girl's pose is also ambiguous, as she plays on what ought to be a one-stringed fiddle (that looks more like a lute), turned toward the rocks. But her ocher yellow dress, which hangs down to her feet, also ends up in the water—and yet again it is not immersed in it. Then we discover something that puzzles us even more: the princess Nouredda (Mlle Fiocre) has her feet in the water. But they really seem to be immersed, because a small ripple has formed in the water, a hint of a circle, as if the water has barely been disturbed.

Then, if we look up, we see that the pensive princess is supporting her head with one hand. Under her elbow, three large cushions are laid upon a boulder. Cushions that seem to have been transferred from a generically Oriental interior to this scene of intact nature. If we lower our gaze again toward the ground, alongside the water we see some stones, piled up irregularly. But then we see a row that seems made up of smaller stones arranged in a perfectly regular pattern. How is this possible? In fact, they are not stones, but the border of a carpet. Thus we pass from a real rock to a carpet bordering a pool that is presumably a mirror. It is a vortex from which we cannot escape. And there is something mocking about it. Indeed, if we did not know the title of the painting and Delibes's ballet, we wouldn't even pause to think about these details; perhaps we wouldn't even notice them and would take the whole thing as a generically exotic scene whose circumstances we know nothing about.

It would be plausible to consider it as representing a moment's pause in the wanderings of a caravan, which the three young women seem to have left. When Zola saw the painting at the Salon, he observed that it should have been titled *Stopover at a Pool*. But while we know the title, the questions proliferate. What are we looking at? Is it a moment of stasis in

the ballet (which in fact included the appearance of the princess leaning against a boulder)? Or are they three ballerinas from the same show, but captured during a break? And is the horse also *taking a break* to drink calmly from a mirror? Or are we in some remote Caucasian landscape in the suspended time of legend, where a princess, as in a previous existence, has taken on the features of Mlle Fiocre? So does the entire scene belong to the genre of *historical* painting? Even of a motionless and indeterminate history? There is no telling, because the two, incompatible, ways of interpreting what is going on in the painting are equally convincing. There are good arguments for each of them. But the general tone of the painting is such that it makes that opposition futile. Whether this is a pause on the stage of the Opéra in rue Le Peletier (and, nine years later, the ballet *La Source* was a part of the *morceaux choisis* picked for the inauguration of the Opéra Garnier) or a moment of repose for the cruel princess Nouredda, shortly before she throws herself into the dance, or whether it is a moment *like any other* swallowed up by time in a remote, legendary era, seems not to matter. It's as if those various moments coincided—or at least drew closer to one another like an image and its reflection in a mirror or in still, limpid water. But there is a kind of monogram that Degas made on the canvas, almost a hint that serves not to disentangle the enigma of the vision but to bring it closer to us: between the horse's forehooves we recognize two pink ballet pumps. These are the only trace that time has left, flowing from the Orient of legend to the stage of the Opéra. They are the artist's signature, and he vanishes after having brought about the fusion of what had always been separated: the pure artifice of the theatrical scene and pure nature welling up from a source. After all, this was the only *plein air* that suited M. Degas. Behind, the wings and the dressing rooms open up.

The stage is a perfectly uniform, flat surface scored by thin transverse lines: something not found in nature. The poses of the ballerinas form a restricted and rigid repertoire that can be shown only onstage. But what is it that looms behind the boards of the stage, trod only by the pumps of the ballerinas? The wings, the lights, the painted backdrops, in the Opéra in rue Le Peletier or in the Opéra Garnier or in many other theaters. But in Degas's paintings? There is a thickening of improbable colors—orange, emerald green, acid yellow, bright pink—that stand out amid the darkness of the auditorium. They form frayed marine masses that besiege the bodies of the ballerinas. We glimpse tree trunks, foliage, but soon we are lost in a varicolored luxuriance as if we were blazing a trail through a phosphorescent forest. This is nature that checks its billows, sending the billows as far as the feet and the shoulders of the ballerinas but no farther, so that the thin, angular bodies of the *petits rats* may not be submerged as they carry on with their grueling exercises. The commanding authority of geometrical gestures and the ebb and flow of blocks of vivid color—for Degas this was the totality to which, without any fear of monotony, he abandoned his painting, as certain Dutch artists did with cattle on the plain or as certain Byzantine artists did with saints' processions.

The fusion of nature and the stage is fulfilled in the subtlest, most provocative manner in the *Portrait of Mlle E.F.* The painting was a *unicum*, but the procedure did not remain an isolated case. On the contrary, it was destined one day to become the esoteric premise subtly applied by Degas in numerous paintings, pastels, and gouaches of ballerinas. Sometimes the staginess of the theatrical scene appears to be heightened: in *L'Étoile* of 1878 we can spot the divisions between the boards of the

stage; and the palms of the *Ballet at the Paris Opéra* of 1877 reveal the unmistakable frailty of the painted backdrops. But elsewhere Degas followed an opposite path: we start with the pure artifice of the scene
before penetrating deep nature, a nature that eluded the landscape artists working *en plein air.* (Degas would have liked them to be arrested by
the police for molestation in a public place.) In three fans dating from
the period 1878–1880 the procedure is taken to extremes. In all three
cases groups of ballerinas appear, but each time the nucleus of the figure
is a magmatic splash, jagged and unrestricted: one example is greenish;
the other two are impasted in pink and yellow. The more primordial
the form, the more delicate the chromatic amalgam. One would say
that the ballerinas emerge, perhaps for the last time, from the mass that
is expanding all over the fan. Their bodies still appear on the boards of

the stage (and in the wings we glimpse their faithful admirers with their top hats, as they observe them). But in the boldest of the fans (today in Switzerland, in a private collection) only the ballerinas' heads emerge from the billowy splash of color, like nymphs among the foliage, which in this case is also made up of the pink, clutching roots of three trees. Finally, in the Baltimore fan, the group of ballerinas seems to be fleeing, pursued by a wave as high as the sky, in which the intimation of all informal painting is condensed. To those (more than a few) who reproved him for ignoring nature, Degas could have replied by pointing to those three fans, epiphanies of a nature that was to nineteenth-century nature as prehistory is to history; a nature made of geological turmoil and boundless marshes, crossed by vast undulating surfaces, delicately disguised, whose interstices were strewn with the limbs of ballerinas, as if dance were an accidental and provisional blossoming of chaos.

In Degas's notebook 21 (1866), among addresses mostly of models (*cocottes*, probably), of suppliers and shops, abbreviated quotations and pencil sketches (it was the period of *Mlle Fiocre*—and there is also an abundance of horses and jockeys), we come across these verses, as if from a rococo song: "Piron plus gai que délicat / Sans nul préliminaire / Dit partout qu'un chat est un chat / Moi je dis le contraire / Souvent un seul mot / En dit beaucoup trop / Mais qu'une gaze fine / Sans cacher les traits / Voile les portraits . . . / Le reste se devine."
    Degas always avoided poetic declarations. If anything, like Ingres,

he issued decrees on drawing and color that could be understood only by his peers—that is, by other obsessive painters with a proclivity for silence. But here, hidden in his notebook between two profiles of horses, he allowed himself to enunciate something like a regulatory principle, and one with immense consequences: not just to avoid saying that "a cat is a cat" (with that tautology dear to Courbet, and fortunately belied by his painting), but even to say "the opposite." But what is the opposite of tautology? Evasion. This was the basis of painting according to Degas. But even when evading, it's necessary *to say*. And sometimes, indeed often, "a single word / already says too much." So evasion must retreat into omission. Or otherwise? What to do, if you spend most of your life painting in a studio? It suffices that "a thin gauze / without concealing the lines / may veil the portrait." This is the closest one can get to a definition of Degas's painting. Those who do not grasp, in all of his images, the "thin gauze" that envelops all (sprinkled with that powder storekeepers use for artificial flowers) simply cannot see Degas. It is this gauze that distinguishes him from the painter most similar to him, namely Manet. The secret did not lie in the "thin gauze" alone, but in the fact that the gauze acted "without concealing the lines." The *sureness* of line, for some years, was found in Degas more than any other. As a producer of lines, he was the only possible successor to Ingres. But for him the line had to be veiled by the imperceptible gauze, which safeguarded it from any claim to literality. Veiled and yet sharp: this was how Degas wanted the painted world. That is why he used to say that "nature is smooth." And this is why some of his portraits have an imperious but sealed presence; the figures suggest that something distressing has just happened but that they have no intention of revealing what it is. This is how things stand in the *Bellelli Family*, where unhappiness and resentment are palpable, coagulated in the stagnant air, as the two girls, glowering and cold, await the end of the sitting.

A girl's bedroom. Without luxuries, but tidy. There is an iron bed in the corner. The bedspread, in pale pink, is orderly and pulled tight. A long, striped bedside rug. A mirror with a gilt frame. Wallpaper patterned with little pink and green flowers. The lampshade is also decorated with little flowers. An upturned top hat on the bureau on the left. The bearded

man, leaning against the wall, has not just come in. Something has already happened. We understand this when we spot a corset thrown on
the floor. It is the only element of real disorder. And we immediately
link it with the sewing box lying open on the round table in the middle of
the room. One would say that someone has been rummaging through it.
The object is elegant; it shines in the light—in fact, its pink lining is the
luminous center of the painting. It could contain jewelry instead of
humble sewing equipment. Or something very intimate. A soft white silk
spills over the edge, and we don't know what it may be. A young woman
is sitting on the left with her back to the man. As if she wanted to keep it
forever turned, to him and the world. Her left shoulder is bared; her
white camisole has slipped down over her arm. But there is nothing to
indicate that violence has occurred. Her shoulder seems bowed under an
invisible burden—and perhaps that was enough to cause her camisole to
slip down. The bearded man is leaning against the door, impeccably
dressed. Perhaps he wants to exclude the possibility that the door might
ever open again. His legs are spread apart, his feet firmly planted on the
floor. His lean profile and small, staring eyes are like those of a criminal
Degas was to draw one day. The light enveloping the scene is warm, but
it is an unhealthy warmth. We can infer nothing certain regarding what
has happened. All we can sense is something diseased and desperate.

Only because we are dealing with Degas is it possible that a picture painted in 1868–1869 with the title *Interior* would be entitled *The Rape* by some of the artist's close friends forty years later. Why—in this scene with a bearded man leaning against a door, and a woman sitting with her back to him, both motionless, silent and distant in a room with a young woman's bed in the corner—should proof of a rape be evident? Even though the title was never used by Degas ("it isn't a part of his vocabulary," said Paul Poujaud, who knew him well), the extremely high tension of the painting and certain signs—especially the sewing box with the pink lining, wide open and almost eviscerated on the little table in the center of the room, under the clear light of the *abat-jour*—suggest that something sexual and unsaid has swept across the entire scene. That something happened only a few moments before, and probably something irreparable, is so obvious that on several occasions critics have attempted to interpret the painting as an illustration from a novel: at first with reference to Duranty, then to Zola's *Madeleine Férat*. Then Theodore Reff suggested a scene from *Thérèse Raquin* that offers some remarkable similarities: it is the night when the two lovers, who are also murderers, meet again after avoiding seeing each other for a year, out of caution. Zola had a flair for the explicit, and here he did not fail to show it. But Degas? He was almost the opposite of Zola, because, if anything, his flair was for evasion, though even his situations could be made to fit Zola. (Obviously the two men were not made to understand each other: during the years when they met in the Café Guerbois—the very years of *Thérèse Raquin* and *Interior*—they never ceased needling each other.) On this occasion, what unites Degas and Zola is the empty space between the two lovers. In Zola, it is occupied by the ghost of a drowned man. In Degas, by a splendid sewing box whose pink lining attracts the light. This is the center of the painting, its mysterious crux. But in that box there is no trace of the scene from *Thérèse Raquin*. And, almost a century and a half later, that box still guards its secret. What does it allude to? What has been searched for in it? Why is it so elegant (to the point that it reminds us of the magnificent overnight case used by Grace Kelly in *Rear Window*), in contrast with the room, which is modest? And what is that soft silk flowing over its edge? Degas did not want to let us know too much about what preceded the scene. What he painted is a violent silence. He leaves the details to act with their own irresistible means: the half light, the corset lying on the floor—Degas was to advise Gervex to introduce one in his *Rolla*, so that the superb body of the nude woman on the bed would not appear too clearly as that of a model, and the scandal at the Salon was caused precisely by that corset—the little pink and green flowers on the wallpaper and the *abat-jour*, the man's top hat lying on the bureau, the naked, bowed, oppressed shoulder of the young woman who is gazing into space, the staring eye of the bearded man leaning against the door. The light concentrates on the open sewing box, "a pink and black jewel" that someone has been rummaging in. Degas had said as much, in those verses jotted down in his notebook two years previously: "the rest is to be guessed."

Thirty years after painting it, Degas showed Paul Poujaud *Interior*, which was in his studio, turned toward the wall: "You know my genre painting, don't you?" A precious and sarcastic definition. *Interior* is a genre painting exactly as the *Medieval War Scene* is a historical painting. The definition should be scrupulously accepted, to be demolished from the inside. If we wish to stay very close to Degas, a real genre painter was James Tissot (and to him we may plausibly attribute the observations written on an envelope apropos of Degas's *Interior*, full of advice from a first-class expert on the subject, counsels that were almost always followed later). In many enchanting paintings, Tissot wanted every time to capture a fleeting *Stimmung*: a sulk, the emotion of a letter, the excitement at entering a ballroom, the melancholy of a bench. Or even just the fluttering of flags. They are all impeccable genre paintings, because their meaning, their vibration, appear already predetermined in a table of possibilities admitted and coordinated among themselves. The premise is that feelings are univocal and can be stated fully. With Degas, the opposite happens. *Interior*, his only "genre painting," grants no certainty. We do not know whether or to what extent the man is a criminal; nor whether or to what extent the young woman is innocent. We are faced with either a simple scene of hostility or a spat between lovers. What we are allowed to see, the painter sardonically implies, is always very little. The only certain element is the tremendous tension, among those flowers on the wallpaper, the shadows, the gleaming sewing box, the angle at which the woman's shoulder strap hangs, and the one formed by the man's legs. We are not given to know anything more. And in the end we cannot even say to which genre the painting belongs. Meanings are opaque, sentiments obscure, the whole thing could fall only into that all-enveloping, brooding, formless genre that is life itself.

As his contemporaries had already ironically remarked, Degas never tired of painting ballerinas and women ironing. But "No sensuality in the former, and no sentimentality in the latter." This was Mallarmé's definitive and enigmatic verdict. A voyeur without sensuousness and without pathos, Degas used ballerinas and ironers as an excuse to arrive at certain "delicate lines" and certain "exquisite or grotesque movements." The end result was the appearance of a "strangely new beauty," Mallarmé added. But he immediately retracted this, knowing that this crude term (*new*) would never have met with the painter's approval. And he almost apologized, feeling the need to assure the reader that Degas "would never use that word in his everyday conversation."

Unlike Ingres, Degas's rapport with females was not based on a primordial devotion. Nor, as with Baudelaire, did it plunge instantly into metaphysics. Degas spent the greatest part of his life drawing and painting the bodies of women and girls. He was dominated by a feeling in which attraction was secretly balanced with repulsion to the point that it reached an inaccessible point of indifference. His most perceptive contemporaries had already noticed this—and before any other, the eye of the critic par excellence Félix Fénéon: "Without ever verging on caricature, indeed showing the gravity of priesthood, M. Degas devotes to the female body an ancient animosity that resembles rancor." Something of that "ancient animosity" can be glimpsed in an entry in the diary kept by the eighteen-year-old Daniel Halévy, the son of Ludovic, dated May 27, 1891: "This morning Degas came to lunch. He talked about women with his customary horror. But he too has felt their bite! He too senses the soothing but demoralizing enchantment of women, an enchantment that enfeebles. And this is his complaint with regard to the perpetual tyranny they exercise. He is very friendly with Mme Jeanniot, a delightful person, and he often says to her: 'I must really love you to be able to forgive you for being as pretty as you are!' But why did he love her? Had she been a man would he have loved her? She is a fairly shallow person, she likes society and has no power of thought, no *wit*, none of the things that Degas likes. If he loves her, it's because she's a woman, and because she is good-looking. But all this is so subtle that he is unaware of it, I'm convinced of that."

His friends didn't dare say much more than this. And Degas himself always avoided the subject. On which there fell a blade of oblique and cruel light in the form of the words in a letter from Berthe Morisot to her sister, Edma: "As for your friend Degas, I definitely don't find his personality attractive; he is a witty man, and nothing more. Manet said something very amusing to me yesterday: 'He lacks spontaneity; he is incapable of loving a woman, or even to tell her so, or to do anything.'" It was 1869. Having abandoned historical subjects, Degas was already a painter of horses and jockeys at the track. Soon he would become the painter who more than any other could capture the covert spontaneity of feminine gestures.

He knew how a woman dries her toes; how she yawns as she irons; how she puts one foot out of the bathtub. But Degas did not know what it meant to wake up in bed with a woman. If this happened to him, he must have fled straightaway. None of his acquaintances was able to attribute a liaison to him, not even a fleeting one. It soon became standard practice to describe how Degas mistreated and tortured women in his pastels. People quoted the artist's cutting remarks about female animality. But this was a big mistake, a reaction of incomprehension and fear regarding the novelty of the poses that Degas drew and colored. His intimacy with women frightened people, as did his capacity to know them more than they did. We shall never discover anything precise about Degas's relationships with the *petits rats* of the dance. But his intention was certainly not to seduce them, as was common practice among the gentlemen in top hats who peeped behind the scenes of the Opéra. The great idler Boulanger-Cavé, who succeeded in doing nothing for a lifetime, except for a brief interval in which he served, inadequately, as a theatrical censor, probably hit the mark when he described Degas's indulgent attitude to the *petits rats*: "He finds them all enchanting, he treats them like his own daughters, he forgives them everything they do and laughs at everything they say." As for the little ballerinas, Cavé said, "They have for him . . . a genuine veneration, and even the least of the *petits rats* would give a great deal to please Degas." And, it would seem, Degas did not ask for anything more than a few sittings. Perhaps no letter of his sounds as affectionate as a note to Emma Dobigny, one of his favorites among the *petits rats*: "You've stopped coming to see me, little Dobigny. Yet I still haven't taken down my shingle and the door-plate still says: 'Hostelry,' and I have not yet retired from business. This evening I'll keep the shop open until half past six. Try to see if you can give me a couple of sittings."

The *petits rats* were girls between thirteen and fifteen years of age, part of the corps de ballet in rue Le Peletier (before the fire) and the Opéra Garnier. They could be, as the occasion demanded, coryphaei, butter-flies, flowers. They exited the stage tumultuously, like a "jaunty, jubilant little company, dressed in silks and satins, with low necklines, which dashed down the stairs" and broke up (still in rue Le Peletier) among "delightful old corridors with lots of nooks and crannies poorly lit by smoky lamps." The *petits rats* were eyed and watched over by two oppos-ing powers: suitors and families. The suitors were gentlemen in black frock coats and top hats, mostly with black or graying beards, occa-sionally leaning on canes or umbrellas. Often they were nobles or fake nobles—or officials, financiers, men with private incomes, or with something else that offered some guarantee of wealth. Some wore the ribbon of the Légion d'honneur. The families were represented by the mothers or, occasionally, aunts of the *petits rats*. Often concierges, they wore a solemn air and were conscious of their own dignity. Like impor-tant diplomats, they waited for the suitors—who, obviously, would never have declared themselves to be such, but were always ballet enthusi-asts—to come forward with some excuse and start up a conversation. The negotiations would begin. It was a matter of selling the little balle-rina on the best terms. A few jewels? To start with. Then there was an entire scale of possibilities. There was nothing to be gained by limiting the game at first. The more noncommittal one remained at the start, the farther one could go. In the end, the little girl could even become a marquise, maybe in Italy (which was something of a downgrading, but still a respectable result). Or otherwise they might become *cocottes* and give themselves over to "gallantry on a grand scale" (as a police report put it). And this was exactly what happened to Virginie and Pauline, two *petits rats* raised by Mme Cardinal.

There was one and only one poet of this world: Ludovic Halévy, a friend of Degas's since adolescence, an author who, in tandem with Meilhac, had reached the acme of operetta with his librettos for *La Belle Hélène*, *La Grande-duchesse de Gérolstein*, and *La Vie parisienne*. Offenbach and Meilhac-Halévy were the meteoric apogee of the Second Empire, in its mechanical and chattering madness. In 1870, Halévy published in installments a novel destined to rack up thirty-three editions in ten years: *La Famille Cardinal*, the epos of the *petits rats*. He noted in his diary, "A little violent, perhaps, but it is the truth. Here we find, just as I have seen them, the damsels of the Opéra . . . and their lady mothers or unmarried mothers." That violence, expressed with lucidity and precision, was close to that used by Flaubert in *Madame Bovary* or in *Bouvard and Pécuchet*.

A few years later, Halévy asked his closest friend, Degas, to illustrate a novel. Degas did not like the idea *in se* of illustrating books, but in this case he agreed. His images, if contrasted with the text, are of a piercing accuracy. If we push the term to its limits, one might say: of an indubitable *truth*. But Halévy did not approve them, for reasons never made clear. After that, Halévy looked for other, far less known illustrators. Perhaps, through Degas, he was frightened by himself. By that time he wanted to write only blander and more sentimental stories, such as *L'Abbé Constantin*. But Degas would not give him any rope. Sadly, Halévy noted his old friend's reaction in his diary: "Degas is indignant about *L'Abbé Constantin*, it would be better to say sickened. He is disgusted by all that virtue, that elegance. This morning he said some insulting things to me. I must always do things like [speak with] *Madame Cardinal*, small, spare things, satirical, skeptical, ironic, without heart, without emotion."

From 1870 onward Degas would devote about a third of his work to ballet. *La Famille Cardinal* remained the perennial allusion behind his paintings, pastels, and sculptures. Each of his ballerinas is a Pauline or Virginie Cardinal. The cold and strategic gaze of Mme Cardinal or the predatory looks of some habitué of the Opéra never left them. And the painter's gaze is an unwelcome third party in that scene of crowded solitude. This was the frame within which everything should be considered: a minor branch of prostitution, which united in itself the extremes of frivolity and sleaziness like no other specialty of the *vie parisienne.* "Without heart, without emotion."

It was not uncommon for a painter to marry one of his models. This happened to Renoir and Monet. Or otherwise they forged enduring relationships. Degas often used as models the *petits rats* he had met at the Opéra. This would seem to heighten the probability of sexual relations. But there is nothing to confirm this. If he had such relations, they must have been very secret, in a world where secrets did not last long. At home, Degas was always seen solely in the company of surly housekeepers. Yet an erotic aura enveloped all his female figures. And it did not matter if the bodies were attractive or squalid. Whether they were ballerinas or ironers or acrobats or music hall singers, they all belonged to a life that Degas hungered to draw. And drawing was everything for him. It involved every allusion becoming a line. But by remaining a line, it kept its mystery. The line has one great advantage: it does not speak. And only this satisfied Degas. Once he said to Forain that, at his funeral, he wanted no speeches. Then he corrected himself. He said, "On the contrary, yes, Forain, you will make one. You will say: he loved drawing very much."

The affinity between Ludovic Halévy and Degas was revealed as soon as they entered the Opéra. A few lines from Halévy's diary can be read as the draft for two, three, or four works by Degas: "I enter the foyer of the ballet. Not many people. M. Auber sitting on the plush bench, below the large mirror that reflects many pirouettes and many *entrechats* . . . On the steps of the stairs Mademoiselle Gauguin invites a most handsome young man to a performance scheduled to be held on the 17th in the hall of the École Lyrique . . . Two extremely pretty little coryphaei are stretched out on the red couch to the left of the fireplace, I approach, they are sleeping. Mademoiselle Baratte is holding on to the bar with one hand and, standing upright on her points, chats with M. X. I leave the foyer of the ballet, I wander around the corridors . . ."

But how did Degas's *petits rats* move, how did they speak? There was rioting in Paris. Ludovic Halévy went up boulevard Montmartre, empty and sinister. Then he left Meilhac and went into the Opéra. They were performing *Faust* to a full house. As Halévy passed through the wings, two *petits rats* stopped him: " 'How lucky you are, you can go and see the uprising.' A third ballerina came along and said to the other two: 'Come on, I've found a window on the third floor, you can see the rioting.' And all three vanished in their little Flemish peasant girl costumes, laughing like crazy, delighted by the idea that they could watch the uprising."

The Second Empire was the first epoch destined not to have its own style. Its name already condemned it to be no more than a repetition. A new and mysterious chemical element spreading through the air prevented anything from being taken entirely seriously. This was to arouse a subtle anguish in some, but in most people it inspired a rampant euphoria. That was the crazy device of operetta. Suddenly it seemed completely natural, even to the larger public, that everything could be accepted as parody. In the course of his day, the duc de Morny, the emperor's stepbrother, alternated high political functions, as an éminence grise and secret ruler, with those of a writer of light comedy, an activity to which he would obviously have liked to devote more time. And it was unclear which role was an extension of the other by different means. Nor which of the two, in the end, was more important to him.

And so the path was cleared for operetta. A tone of ecumenical mockery would have been justified years or even decades before. Yet the tone did not explode until then—and only then was it accepted without flinching. In 1865, "La femme à barbe," sung by Thérésa, "La Vénus aux carottes," sung by Silly, and the king's entry in *La Belle Hélène* were popular high spots of the year.

Not all, but much presented itself in the guise of operetta. Ludovic Halévy took note and then passed the outline to Offenbach. For example, the prince who would stamp his feet like a spoiled child. Ludovic Halévy's diary, January 21, 1866: "The Prince Imperial, a few days ago, asked for something that was refused him: *Oh! Is that so, well then, this means that when I go out I will not greet the people*." Even assassination attempts—the only unforeseen events that could interrupt the interminable parades of royal highnesses—resembled scenes from the operetta. One day Czar Alexander III, Bismarck, and their host, Napoleon III, had to review sixty thousand soldiers. They were followed by a "general staff of twenty princes and royal highnesses including the King of Prussia, the Grand Duke of Hessen, the Grand Duke and heir to the throne of Russia, etc." A young man fired a shot, hitting a horse in the head. "He was after me, he's an Italian," said Napoleon III to the czar. "No, he was after me, he's a Pole," said the czar. He was right: the youth was Polish. Ludovic Halévy noted this down—and they were lines typical of a piece by Meilhac and Halévy.

"He never says anything, and he always lies": this was an anonymous definition of Napoleon III. His was the reign of *demi-liberté* and the *demi-monde*, but only with some effort could the Second Empire be defined as a dictatorship, at least in the strict sense that the term took on a century later. On March 26, 1866, the Bouffes-Parisiens theater celebrated the fiftieth performance of Offenbach's *Orphée aux enfers*. "I do not feel oppressed in the slightest," Ludovic Halévy murmured a few days later; he was one of the authors of the *Orphée*, and his remark referred to a speech given by his friend Prevost-Paradol in which he talked of a "people governed and oppressed."

In 1886, at the eighth and last exhibition of Impressionism, Degas presented, "like an insulting adieu" (Huysmans observed), a certain number of pastels described thus in the catalog: "Series of female nudes bathing, washing, drying themselves, cleansing themselves or having their hair combed." There is a subtle sarcasm in this impassive wording, and Huysmans, who easily tended toward Grand Guignol, saw in it "a painstaking cruelty, a patient hatred." Both Huysmans and Fénéon (the most penetrating observers of the time) frenetically indulged in verbal acrobatics aimed at finding the words to equal the "horror" of Degas's women. A zealous effort that went beyond the mark. Observed a few decades later, Degas's women went back to appearing simply as exemplars of that rare zoological species that is the *ordinary woman*. Sometimes (indeed, often) attractive, sometimes not, always entangled in a prodigious chromatic spiderweb in their tin bathtubs, changing rooms, and the "dark rooms of a *hôtel meublé*" (Fénéon). Degas's models were not, through some perverse design on his part, more repugnant than those who posed during those same years for the painters of the Salons. In certain cases they were the same ones. But Degas did not make them take up a pose immediately; on the contrary, he asked them to roam around his studio in the nude. They would spend a long time wandering around the tin bathtub that guarded the studio like a totem, and finally the moment would come in which they would be caught making the right movement— the one that Degas, a man who according to Valéry was "entirely devoted to his inner ceremonies, to his deep prey" (whatever this "prey" may have been, for he never said a word about it) had been waiting for.

What shocked people about Degas was not the ungainly look of his female bodies, but something far more insidious: his complete abandonment of canonical poses. For centuries, painting had been accustomed to dipping into a fixed repertoire of poses, which admitted variations only within certain registers. This held for the Florentines of the Quattrocento as it did for the gallant painters of the rococo period. Every time, the painter had a range of possibilities to choose from. But he did not dare go beyond that. Degas's sabotage was concentrated on this point—and the effect was sensational. He stubbornly pursued the *intermediate* poses among the canonical ones, poses that have no meaning and are only functional, often unwitting, and often not perceived even by those who make them. Monologizing poses. Those nude bodies captured in the moments when they have yet to become so many Nudes, formalized in the sequence of Nudes in the history of art, from Praxiteles to Ingres and finally to Bouguereau. This held for the pastels of 1886 and for all the many women portrayed in intimacy. But an even more disorienting formula was the one Degas used for his ballerinas, where gesture attains the maximum of abstract tension, between a pole of strictly codified movement that does not correspond to any repertoire of elegant poses in painting (since the subject matter was the autonomous and self-sufficient code of ballet) and a pole of exhausted and abandoned physicality, following an exertion or between one exertion and another, or in any case dispersed in the bustling limbo that extends backstage to the dressing rooms and the rehearsal rooms.

Degas encountered the "terrible passion" of photography in the autumn of 1895. He had always needed a diversion for his evenings. For a certain period, he had spent those hours busying himself with engraving techniques, composing sonnets, and carving the knobs of walking sticks (the young Vollard supplied him with exotic woods in exchange for a few drawings: the start of his career as a great art merchant). Subse-

quently, wrote Daniel Halévy with the nonchalance of someone who cannot assess the import of what he is saying, Degas was seized by "a passionate anti-Semitism, and he was against the Louvre Museum; but these two passions were too real and they made him bitter."

And so, "this year he has taken to photography." He sought "the atmosphere of lamps or of the moon." Once he had tried to photograph the moon itself, but "it moved" too much. In photography, too, *plein air* was not for him. He was the master of the *black background*. ("My blacks were too excessive," he was to say one day, but that was where the novelty lay.) Before his lens the lace used to cover armchairs became a halluci-natory velarium, while the *intérieur* revealed itself to be animated by presences in the darkness, like crouching animals, which were frag-ments of mirrors, frames, and knickknacks barely grazed by the light.

When, on certain evenings, Degas decided to take a group photo-graph, everyone had to submit to "two hours of military obedience." With his "artist's ferocity" he imposed positions, shifted lamps, took girls by the nape of the neck and obliged them to bend it at a certain angle. Two minutes of posing followed. Then everyone said goodbye and Degas would go off "with his camera, proud as a little boy with his rifle." On looking at them today, it's difficult to believe that those photos were the result of a lengthy pose: whether it was Jacques-Émile Blanche chatting with his wife, Rose, or Jules Taschereau with a stranger, what we see is the instant of attention for a remark that no one has made, while the backs of their hands look like fans trembling in the darkness.

Two photographs condense the work of Degas the photographer into a talisman—as well as being the essence of those years. The first is the renowned portrait of Mallarmé and Renoir beside a mirror in which Degas's camera is reflected, while the photographer's head is en-veloped by a dazzling cloud, and indistinct female figures peep from a corner of the mirror. The entire image is a proliferation of moldings and

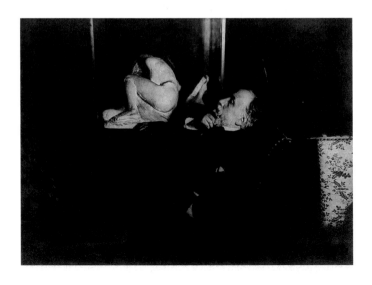

frames, as if to remind us that the frame counts for no less than the image it encloses, if for no other reason than the fact that it warns us that we are entering a metareality. Apropos of Degas, Vollard remarked, "Another of his worries was that they might change the frames of his works." It was to be the hatred of frames that marked the beginning of painting's death throes.

The second is a self-portrait of Degas alongside Bartholomé's little statue *Young Girl Weeping*. The light falls only on three points that stand out against the compact black: a fragment of a silken fabric with a floral pattern on the bottom right; then, toward the center, Degas's head as he brings his right hand up to his chin, as if following a thought (or an image), while the nape of his neck is leaning, almost horizontally, against the back of an armchair; finally, the naked and resplendent body of the sculpted girl, which seems suspended in the void on a level with Degas's gaze, like a phantasm that has just sprung from his eyes.

Degas helped Mallarmé to formulate a fundamental phrase on literature, which would have been lost in the hum of a soiree if Ludovic Halévy had not been in the habit of noting down what Degas said: "Degas had spent the evening with Mallarmé, who had outlined to him the following theory about words:

"Words, he said, can and must suffice unto themselves. They have their personal potential, their power, their individuality, their own existence. *They have enough strength to resist the aggression of ideas.*

"Degas confessed that this admirable phrase was his. But he assures me that he is merely summing up Mallarmé's ideas."

"To resist the aggression of ideas": there is no better passport for anyone desirous of crossing the threshold of all twentieth-century literature. And it is also significant that that phrase survived accidentally and indirectly—and was probably the fruit of two minds.

"We must discourage the fine arts": this celebrated *mot* of Degas's was also one of his most commendable and clear-sighted. As the end of the century loomed, Degas observed with steadily growing irritation the progressive aestheticization of everything. He felt that the world was on the verge of falling into the hands of a troop of interior decorators. In this he was of one mind with Karl Kraus, who, a few years later, was to declare that by then the world was divided between "those who use urns like chamber pots and those who use chamber pots like urns." The point that tormented him was this: the more widespread aesthetics grew, the less intense it became. The next century was opening up before Degas's eyes. A century in which everything, even massacres, would be subjected to the whim of some art director, while art—especially the ancient art of painting, the one that was most important to him—would become ever more inconsistent or might even dissolve.

In Madrid, fleeing from scandals in Paris that had made him "more famous than Garibaldi" (said Degas), Manet detested the food and showed no great love for the Spanish picturesque. But he had seen Velázquez in the Prado. Immediately, he wrote to Fantin-Latour about "Velázquez who, alone, is worth the journey." And straight off he defined him as "the painter's painter." But not in the sense that Velázquez was the greatest among painters. Manet meant something far more important: Velázquez was *painting itself*, the foundation from which every painter detaches himself, as best he can. And he went back to listing his marvels: "All the dwarfs; especially one, sitting face on, with his fists at his sides: a painting made specially for a true connoisseur." And the effect of that painting without qualifiers was fearsome for those that surrounded it, even for Titian: "A portrait of Charles V by Titian, which enjoys high renown, which must be deserved, and which would certainly have struck me as good elsewhere, here seems wooden to me."

In the hotel—the first European-style hotel to open in Madrid—Manet met Théodore Duret, who would one day become his biographer. Soon they were wandering around the city together; they would sit in the cafés on the calle de Sevilla, under the awnings hung between the houses to offer shade. And they would go "every day to linger for a long time in front of Velázquez's works in the Prado Museum."

The only one among his contemporaries, Manet participated to some extent in Velázquez's mysterious quality: that of embodying *painting itself*. This is why it grates so much when he is defined as an "impressionist." Every specification disturbs, because Manet aspired to be a painter in a *generic* sense. Degas's acid comment about him, reported by George

Moore, sounds much closer to the truth: "He is not an artist by inclination, but by force of circumstances. He is a galley slave chained to his oar."

Manet was won over when he realized that Velázquez's figures were
enveloped only in air. After having seen the portrait of Pablo, the jester
of Valladolid (who thought himself an actor), he wrote to Fantin-Latour,
"The background vanishes and the man, dressed all in a vivid black, is
surrounded only by air." There wasn't a place, a space in which to put
and imprison his figures, but a gray background, of a *"soft muddiness"*—as
the Goncourt brothers were to say—whose secret was guarded by Velázquez. That background sufficed for the most diverse figures, for in-
fantas and dwarfs, for ladies-in-waiting and jesters, and for a noblewoman
holding a fan, her eyes aware of everything. Indifferent as justice, she
accepts with gravity and nonchalance whatever appears before her.
Even a king—or King Philip IV. Patiently, and with the intense drive of
the imitator, Manet *wanted* that background. Before it stood a small boy
with a huge sword in his hands. Then a boy playing on a pipe. But that
gray was still too pearly and delicate. It seemed as if it had been passed
through a filter, whereas Velázquez's prodigy was the opposite: the filter
was absent. It seems there was no need for it.

George T. Robinson, the editor of the *Art Monthly Review*, asked Mallarmé to write a few pages on the Impressionists and Manet. In his
shaky and casual French, he invited Mallarmé to write simply: "Talk to
the public as you will talk to your friends—without too much discussion
but not too briefly." One day, Berthe Morisot, too, was to ask him to try
to write as he would for his cook, and Mallarmé replied, "But I wouldn't
write differently for my cook!"

Mallarmé obliged, handing in a masterful, crystal clear essay that
was rediscovered only a few years ago. As for the original French text, it
has been lost—an irony of fate. To understand Mallarmé's thinking on
the painters close to him, it is therefore necessary to reconstruct it from
an English version that the author said was "passable." But it's enough
to serve as an example of the almost aberrant clarity of his views and his
capacity to reveal and extricate the essential.

For Mallarmé—writing in 1876 for readers he assumed didn't even
know the term *Impressionists*—it all began around 1860, when from the

crowded rooms of the Salons, "a lasting light shone forth": Courbet. Attention turned next to certain paintings that were "disquieting to the
true and reflective critic," the work of a man who proved to be "persis-
tent in his reiteration, unique in his persistency": Manet. Then there
was an "enlightened amateur" who had understood those paintings even
before they existed and had then died "too soon to see these": Baudelaire, "our last great poet." With touching accuracy, Mallarmé fixed in
a few lines the points for a triangulation that made it possible to understand an entire epoch. Mr. Robinson could have had nothing to complain
about. And Manet could have seen himself recognized in his boldest and
most elusive aspect: that of a "genius" who is "singular because he abjures
singularity."

In trying to explain *plein air* to the English, Mallarmé defined it as
"that truism of tomorrow, that paradox of today." How better to resolve
the question? And a little later, discussing female beauty in relation to
painting, he remarked (in a striking aside) that painting "concerns itself
more about this flesh-pollen than any other human attraction." Of
course, no one would have been able to name that "pollen," if not Mallarmé about Manet. But the principle could be applied in various ways,
even among painters very close to him. Above all in Renoir, who had
solved the problem in a businesslike manner, as was his wont: "If God
had not created woman's flesh, I would never have been a painter."
(Carco's rendition, while Georges Duthuit phrased it rather more color-
fully: "If tits didn't exist, I wouldn't have painted.") The phrase was
repeated like a dictum, but we ought to remember that Renoir obliged
Madame Renoir to choose maids according to how their bodies *caught
the light*. A blend of sex, light, and air acted despotically within him and
enabled him to elude "that wind of the Revolution that has made everything barren." (Renoir was not exactly a progressive.) To a nuisance who
asked him how he managed to paint with hands deformed by arthritis,
Renoir, an old man by then, replied, "I paint with my p[rick]." The
source—an indubitable one—is his son Jean. Degas could not have
said anything like that. Not because he did not see, and no less keenly,
the "flesh-pollen," but because an invisible Jansenist lash stood between
him and every female body. So said Vollard, who knew him: "Degas's
so-called hatred of women is almost a commonplace. On the contrary,
no one loved women as much as he, but a kind of shame in which there

was also something like fear kept him at a distance from women; this 'Jansenist' side of his nature explains the cruelty he put into portraying women engaged in their intimate toilette."

As long as painting has a subject, it is tempted by the female breast. Manet dedicated two paintings to this, like a devotee. In this case, too, he was following in the footsteps of others, namely those of an old master and a friend he met occasionally in the Café Guerbois: Tintoretto and Renoir. In the Prado, Manet had seen Jacopo (or Domenico) Tintoretto's portrait of a courtesan, whose magnificent bosom is framed and caressed by her dress and all oscillates between mauve and gray. But he could not know the presumed parallel portrait of Veronica Franco: another courtesan and a celebrated author of Petrarchan sonnets. This time the breast

becomes above all the emergence of a pert nipple. Evidently literature complicates everything. All around, the play of mauve (or pink) and gray continues, a play that one day would also be favored by Manet, as soon as he wished to extol the female element, as in the portrait of *The Viennese*. Something similar, for the pink and gray, happened in Whistler, but for him this was always connected to a stubborn will to *produce elegance*, whereas for Manet that choice was like his way of breathing—and could be forgotten as soon as he turned his attention to something else.

As for Renoir, he never missed a chance to paint a breast. It was the very locus of his carnality. And he never forgot that he got started as a painter of roses on porcelain. Fénéon understood immediately that this was his esoteric doctrine: "If Renoir painted, it is above all because he loved youthful breasts and flowers and wanted to devote a cult to them.

On the contrary, for Cézanne, if painting had not existed before the world of appearances, he would never have noticed that women, apples and Mont Sainte-Victoire existed." Manet once tried, with his *Blonde Woman with Bare Breasts*, to outdo Renoir in the same obsession. The entire painting is concentrated in the outline of the Blonde's billowing breasts, and it's more complex, more majestic than similar portraits by Renoir, which were often merely variations of an enchanting series of Ninis. ("Whether it's Venus or Nini emerging from the bath, it's all the same to me," Renoir once said.) Parallel to the *Blonde* is the *Brunette with Bare Breasts*—it's uncertain which was painted first—as if Manet unwittingly wanted to compose together with Tintoretto a quartet of figureheads.

It is not right to say that Manet *imitated everything*, as Degas spitefully

maintained. But every so often he wanted to play someone else's game—
and beat him at it. A childish pretension, but painting (and literature) is
about this, too. He tried with Renoir, painting the Blonde and the Brunette with bare breasts. He tried with Degas, with a scene of the races at
Longchamp. (The result was less good, also because Manet was not familiar with horses.) He tried with Monet, when he painted *Argenteuil*, a
picture that scandalized many people because Manet had dared to
paint the Seine as if it were blue. Intolerable, said some. The more Manet imitated, the more he revealed himself. Even *The Balcony* was an imitation of Goya. But, instead of three generic *majas*, Manet introduced
Berthe Morisot into the painting, a hint of something extremely intimate and secret in his life. The mask can also be an excellent excuse for
saying words that otherwise might never have been said.

Mallarmé's article was intended to present Manet and the Impressionists as the royal road of art in a moment of crisis (the "present
crisis," an expression that would later appear in his *Crise de Vers* and has
never ceased to enrage people ever since). But his gaze was too perceptive not to grasp the radical flaw of Impressionism as a school: that of
being a sort of factory in which there worked an anonymous, tireless
group, ready to ensure that certain "light productions" might be "multiplied ad infinitum": meadows in bloom, little bridges, country roads,
gates, sheaves of corn, vases of flowers, beaches, pools, and jetties; in
short, everything you might come across "within an easy walk." There
were some specialists, however: no one could paint water like Monet.
But already with Sisley and Pissarro it becomes harder to establish the
basis of their excellence. The "thick shade of summer woods and the
green earth" in Pissarro? Clouds in Sisley? Maybe, but the point is no
longer obvious. It is as if Mallarmé had predicted, a century in advance,
the auction rooms of the late twentieth century, where the "light productions" of Impressionism would be presented in ordered phalanxes, a
few weeks apart, while in the intervals everything else expanded, down to
the lowest of the low, under the uninspiring name of Postimpressionism.

When painting crossed a certain safe zone, and looking at it challenged
people's habits and proprieties, there were cases of collective hallucination, which allowed the public, at least for a certain time, *not to see*. So for

decades there were periodic complaints about Ingres's insensitivity and ineptitude regarding color. And Ingres himself seemed to take part in the deceit, missing no opportunity to belittle the importance of color with respect to the sanctity of drawing. Today, anyone seeing one of his pictures, surrounded by those of some of his contemporaries, is immediately smitten by the varicolored harshness of those tones—be they the sky behind Thetis's torso, the ermine on Mlle Rivière's arm, the shawl hanging from Mme Duvauçay's shoulder, or the silks of Baroness Rothschild. Here are colors that had never existed before and would never be found again. And perhaps it was their uniqueness that kept them from being recognized.

A parallel case of incomprehension, but this time owing to a tangle of sexual and social reasons, as well as pictorial manner, occurred when Manet's *Olympia* was shown in room M of the Salon in May 1865. There was no lack of nudes around. Mostly aquatic, they were covered with allusive foam (there were four concomitant versions of the Birth of Venus in 1863). But only around Manet's courtesan "the crowd swarmed as in the morgue," wrote a reporter at the time. Many viewers laughed. They found something comical about her cold gaze, her petite and perhaps malevolent body. And they didn't stop at laughter: Olympia was described as a female gorilla, her left hand was compared to a toad, her flesh struck some as decomposed, her skin cadaverous. Above all, people harped on about one point: Olympia was dirty, she needed a revitalizing bath, and her body was lined with sooty streaks. It wasn't only the most narrow-minded journalists who wrote such things. Even Gautier could not manage to conceal his embarrassment. For him, that "frail model stretched out on a drape" was inexplicable. And he, too, found her *dirty*. "The tone of the flesh is dirty, the form nonexistent." Aubert summed up a widespread opinion when he wrote that Olympia was *shapeless, lewd, dirty*. And no one intended to pay any attention to the delightful cashmere shawl—a clear tribute to Ingres—upon which Olympia's flesh rested.

The most elegant among the critics was Thoré, who barely mentioned *Olympia*—Manet "has had all of Paris run here to see this strange woman, her splendid bouquet of flowers, her black serving woman and her black cat"—limiting himself to deprecating, with sound arguments, the *Christ Mocked by the Soldiers* that Manet had ordered to be hung immediately above his courtesan, to dubious effect. For Thoré, that poorly executed Christ was proof that Manet always needed to follow in someone's footsteps: first Velázquez, now Van Dyck. Degas's view of Manet was not very different: "He has never done anything else but imitate." But if *Olympia* was an imitation of anybody, it was the Titian of the *Venus of Urbino*—and precisely that reference appeared offensive. From an airy Renaissance portico we have plunged into a cramped erotic bedroom. Manet's most famous painting was his most eloquent negation of *plein air*.

But what set Olympia apart from the multitudes of nude women whose images were hung on the same walls of the Salon during the decade 1860–1870, scandalizing no one? With names such as Amymone, Europa, Venus, and Phryne, they were protected by mythology or ancient history. Whereas Olympia flaunted a name that already thirty years earlier Parent-Duchâtelet, the austere taxonomist of Parisian prostitution, had included (in the variant Olympe) among those most used by "superior class" prostitutes, together with Armida, Zulma, Amanda, Zélie, Sidonie, Flore, Balzamine, Aspasie, Delphine, and Fanny. But there were paintings of nameless women, too: Jules-Joseph Lefebvre's *Reclining Woman* is an anonymous subject stretched out on a kind of couch covered by a cloth. Nor are names provided in Courbet's *Woman with Parrot* or in the numerous *baigneuses*—including *Japanese Woman in the Bath*, by James Tissot—that abounded in those years. So it took more than an ambiguous name to create a scandal around Olympia. Her very essence was shocking. She looks straight at the observer, but it's uncertain whether she sees him. She is neither complacent nor complaisant; she is neither languid nor dreamy. Above all she is not surprised. She knows that nothing is more normal than the parade of eyes looking at her. Are they clients or visitors to the Salon or, one day, to the Louvre and a triumphant retrospective? It makes no big difference. Confined in a claustrophobic bedroom, Olympia knows she is in the window. And she doesn't want to give up her frivolous whims, which allow her to elude the defenselessness of one who is completely naked: a *hibiscus* at her ear, a velvet ribbon around her neck, a gold bracelet on her wrist, her oriental slippers. Her head is as if it were glued to her body. Even if she is not "empty," as Valéry supposed, still "a strand of black velvet isolates her from the essence of her being." The scandal of Olympia lies above all in the opacity of her expression. Is it too much to attribute to her that "ironic acceptance of existence" of which Flaubert had written in a letter a few years earlier? Olympia is not ironic. If anything, she is terribly serious—and absent. Irony is concentrated only in the hump of the cat's back. But there is the equanimity of her gaze, which does not change whether it falls on a cupboard or a new client. What is wholly missing is complicity with the world. And the black serving woman is staring, almost worried, at her mistress, who is staring at what lies beyond the picture.

The reason why *Olympia* caused such a scandal has yet to be identified. After all, remember, it was already accepted, with enthusiasm or resignation, that the *demi-mondaines* were the dominant, omnipresent figures in the Paris of those years (and Olympia could have been accused, at most, of not belonging exactly to the *haute bicherie parisienne*, like the model Victorine Meurent). Yet something must have stirred up the crowds, who reacted as one, a blend of derision and intense curiosity. Perhaps the reason lay in something bluish, dazzling. Perhaps it had to do with the light: *Olympia* was the first photo taken with a flash to shine in painting, as if for a moment Weegee's lens had superimposed itself over Manet's eye.

Manet loathed being defined as an "Impressionist." He strongly disapproved of a tendency among his painter friends to take pleasure in being *refusés*. Manet wanted the Salon and the honors of the Salon. He had them only once—and (not by chance) for one of his worst paintings, *The Good Beer*. He, too, wanted what the honor the Salon often brought: he had no objections when, one day, he was able to wear the ribbon of the Légion d'honneur, but above all he wanted his studio to draw the society crowd or, even better, the *demi-monde*. They chatted, and he painted. Nothing could disturb him.

He was delighted the time Méry Laurent came into his studio, like any other visitor. She had superb tawny hair, and Manet surprised her as she was admiring a painting that few understood: *The Laundry*. Méry was a neighbor who lived in the rue de Rome, as did Mallarmé. At that time she was the kept woman of an English dentist (Napoleon III's dentist, we should add), just as Mme Sabatier, Baudelaire's "too gay" lover, was the kept woman of a Dutch businessman. This was the cosmopolitanism of the *demi-monde*. Soon it would be possible to observe this scene: Méry waving a handkerchief from the window when Doctor Evans disappeared, and then Manet appearing. This went on for a long time, even after Méry and Manet bumped into the dentist on the stairs one day when he came back to pick up a notebook.

Zola on Manet: "The artist confessed to me that he loved society and found secret pleasures in the scented and luminous delights of the soirees." One of those soirees was the masked ball held at the Opéra in rue Le Peletier on March 20, 1873. Manet must have loved that ball and found many "secret pleasures" in it, as for months he let it spread over his "mental canvas" (Mallarmé's expression), in the guise of a rather small rectangular canvas (sixty by seventy-three centimeters). Often, when his society friends dropped by the studio in rue Amsterdam, he would ask them to sit for him. Manet was pursuing a bold plan to place in the space of a few centimeters twenty-four gentlemen, almost all bearded or at least with mustaches and all with top hats, interspersed with rare female figures in fancy dress, because, Mallarmé observed, "a modern

crowd . . . could not be painted without the few clear notes that bring it to life." Manet was still working on this painting when the Opéra burned down in a fire. Those "gentlemen, serious as notaries and gloomy as undertakers," who wandered around "for hours in search of an intrigue"—as Texier had described the foyer in his *Tableau de Paris*—did not know that they had been summoned to render a final homage to the place. Nor did Manet.

Mallarmé wrote that the painting was "crucial to the painter's œuvre." In it we see a "culminating point" where "various previous attempts" converge; and see (he added at the end of a detailed description) that little painting as no less than "a total vision of the contemporary world." Why such insistent praise for a painting that might have seemed anecdotal? Mallarmé saw something more in it. He saw that "group *formed almost exclusively by men*" and almost compacted in the "delightful range" of a single black material—"tailcoats and dominos, hats and the Venetian kind of domino known as the *bautta*, velvets, drapes, silks and satins"—as a single formless creature. The individuals no longer had a "repertoire of genuinely human postures" at their disposal. The very stuff of painting, gesture, is no longer there. There is no breathing space, only the buzz, the chatter, the billowy euphoria of a polycephalous being, anonymous, indeterminate, and rapacious in character. The twenty-four men are no more individual than the glints of light on their top hats. So what is it that keeps the whole composition in precarious equilibrium? Two lady's bootees, arranged at two diagonally opposed points: one blue, the other red. The blue one belongs to a budding Nana, of stunning fragrance, whose elbow has already been grasped by the hand of a gentleman in a top hat. But it is understood that it will not be easy to bridle that masquerader. The red bootee instead belongs to another young girl, of whom we are allowed to see only a part of her leg, in a white stocking. We note the strangeness of her position straightaway. Her bootee has straddled the balustrade of the balcony. Her leg is at an angle, as if this unknown masquerader were about to glide down over that black sea of top hats. This is the only true *gesture* in the scene, but it is one of such insolence and frivolity as to affect the whole: those red bootees, which a casual observer could easily miss, are the secret of the scene. Already ill, in his last, superb painting portraying a public place—the *Bar in the Folies-Bergère*—Manet was to return to that device

of the bootees suspended in the air. In the upper left corner, once more above a wavy surface of top hats, we see two bootees (light green this time) and the lower part of the legs of an unknown acrobat who is swinging on a trapeze. And that swinging motion is transmitted like a frisson to the entire painting.

The Masked Ball at the Opéra was refused for the Salon of 1874. Mallarmé remarked, "For an Academy (and with that I have named what here has unfortunately become an official huddle like any other) M. Manet is, from the standpoint of execution no less from that of the concept of his paintings, a danger." The perennial danger of the red bootee.

They met in the Louvre. She was copying from Veronese, he from Titian. She was a young middle-class girl from Passy, who was there with her sister, Edma, each with her own easel. He, as Banville described him, was "That smiling, that blond Manet / Who gave off charm / Cheerful, subtle, in short enchanting / With the beard of an Apollo." She, Berthe Morisot, in all probability fell in love with him right away. When she saw his first works, she wrote to Edma, "His paintings, as always, give the impression of wild fruits or even those that are a little unripe." She added, "They do not displease me in the least." She would taste that unripe flavor in her mouth for years, passing through the cruelest and most perverse forms of jealousy. While Berthe was dreaming of him, Manet up and left for Holland to get married. Then Edma, who lived in symbiosis with Berthe, decided to marry an old friend of Manet's, a naval officer, leaving her sister on her own. The intersections and coincidences began. Then, when Berthe had begun to see Manet more and more often, Alfred Stevens introduced the painter to a twenty-year-old Spanish girl, Eva Gonzalès, who wanted to become his pupil. So Berthe was eclipsed by this double, this happier version of herself: not just a Spanish-type beauty but a real Spanish woman; not just young but very young; not an aspiring talent but a certain one. Berthe's mother, who had observed like a clinician her daughter's profound infatuation for Manet, brought the lowest means to bear in order to distract her: "I went to return the books to Manet, whom I found ever more jubilant before the model Gonzalès . . . Manet didn't budge from his stool. He inquired after you and I replied that I would tell you of his coldness. At this moment you are not in his thoughts, Mlle G[onzalès] has all the virtues, all the graces; she is a refined woman . . . There was no one at last Wednesday's soiree at Stevens' home, except M. Degas." Degas was another witness to Berthe's tormented love. Loath to discuss his feelings, he made Berthe a gift of a fan on which he had painted a group of Spanish dancers and musicians and right in the middle of them he put Alfred de Musset, an untrustworthy man par excellence. Meanwhile, there were other incidents. As the Salon of 1870 drew nearer, Berthe was as usual anxious about the painting she wished to present: a portrait of her mother reading to her pregnant sister. One day, Manet showed up at the Morisots' home. He said he thought the painting was good. Then he began to retouch it. Laughing and telling jokes all the while, he corrected the skirt, the bust, the head, and the background, unable to stop. Berthe was furious. But in the end she agreed to present at the Salon the painting Manet had transformed into something else. The painting was well received. Then war broke out. Berthe turned thirty in a state of profound melancholy. Not long afterward, she would find herself posing for a splendid portrait by Manet, with violets, which stand for constancy. Her love was undiminished. Manet urged Berthe to marry his brother Eugène, a good man. And only that way would

they be able to carry on seeing each other. Berthe took time to think it over. She wrote, "My situation is unbearable from every point of view." In the end she went along with it. Now she would be called Madame Manet. Degas asked to make a portrait of her husband as his wedding present. Eugène never looked anyone straight in the eye, and that's how Degas painted him. Then Manet came along. He wanted to paint another portrait of Berthe. He used various elements from previous portraits: the predominance of black, the uneven locks of her hair, the ribbon around her neck, and her sinewy fingers well in evidence. And, like a talisman, there was the fan. But now her pose was nervous, unsure of what would happen next. This is the only *portrait in movement*, a snapshot, in effect, that has come down to us from Manet. The sharpest impression is that her pose is defensive. But how had that gesture come about? Perhaps it would have been blocked in the position of another, memorable portrait where the fan was raised as far as to conceal the face completely. Never had Manet gotten so close to the spirit of Guys. But not even Guys had dared such an audacious pose, one that denies the very essence of the portrait. Berthe's pose is frivolous, elegant, mysterious,

as if she wanted to transform the fan into a mask. And at the same time it is an act of self-effacement. It is no simple negation of the portrait, though, because her dark eyes still show through the slats of the fan—piercingly so. Casual spectators, we are witnessing the exchange of a coded message between the woman in the portrait and the painter. And the message is farewell.

This recalls something Valéry wrote about the other portrait of Berthe Morisot, painted by Manet in 1872, in which she is shown wearing a black hat and violets in her décolleté. In this, Valéry noted first of all "the *Black*, absolute black . . . the black that belonged only to Manet." Then he focused on the "vague fixity" of Berthe's eyes, which suggested "profound distraction." He saw in her expression a "je ne sais quoi of something rather tragic." This expression was the one, when she hid her face behind the fan, that Berthe had suppressed, forever. All that remained was her *"presence of absence,"* as Valéry put it. Screened by the fan, Berthe was "comfortably, dangerously silent" once again.

From Boulogne, in midsummer 1868, Manet wrote a letter to Fantin-Latour. Adopting his usual light, playful, brazen tone, he begins with Degas: "I, who have no one to talk to here, envy the fact that you can converse with the great aesthete Degas on the unsuitability of an art within the reach of the poor classes." Then follows some chitchat about painting. Finally Berthe Morisot appears: "I am of your opinion: the misses Morisot are enchanting. It's a shame they're not men." Then he returns to Degas: "Tell Degas to write to me. Judging by what Duranty tells me, it seems that he is becoming the painter of high-life." Degas and Berthe Morisot were to be Manet's most secret, most enduring bonds. A pity that Berthe was not a man. At least, they could have taken a few trips alone together.

A few months after his father's death, Manet married Suzanne Leenhoff, a rather plump Dutch blonde. Suzanne had come into the Manet home ten years before, as piano teacher to the young Édouard and Eugène. At the wedding, Suzanne showed up with a much younger brother, Léon Koëlla. As now seems clear from many clues, that eleven-year-old boy was instead Suzanne's son by Auguste Manet, Édouard's father and a civil court judge who often dealt with cases of dubious paternity (and who died of syphilis, just as his son Édouard was to do). At home, Léon called Suzanne "godmother"; outside, he introduced himself as her brother. And he called Édouard "godfather." Manet painted this unrecognized half-brother in seventeen canvases. Only Berthe Morisot and Victorine Meurent were portrayed as frequently. In his will, Manet stated clearly that his wife, Suzanne, would have to consider Léon as his heir. Many posthumous decisions about Manet's œuvre— mostly regrettable, such as the dismemberment of *The Execution of Maximilian*—were taken in mutual agreement by Suzanne and Léon. Léon always claimed he did not know the "family secret" that surrounded him. But he did not complain about it, because he maintained that his presumptive sister and his presumptive godfather had "coddled and spoiled him," pandering to all his whims. At Suzanne's funeral, in 1906, Léon still described himself, in the notes of condolence, as her brother. Subsequently, he married and started up a business trading in rabbits, poultry, and fishing tackle. He died in 1927. Just as Degas was to pay his brother's debts to the last (and doing so obsessed him for ten years or so), so Manet protected his father's secret to the very end. It was the father's and son's way of being upper middle class: to make the family impenetrable. And it was also a way to hide a part of their most painful feelings in a remote underground room.

There is reason to believe that Manet was attracted to Berthe Morisot no less than Berthe was attracted to him. But in his life there was that underground room to protect and hide. In the meantime, Suzanne grew fatter and fatter, and Berthe Morisot's mother wrote to her daughter that Manet stayed at home "making a portrait of his wife and struggling to turn the monster into something slim and attractive!"

The story of Berthe Morisot and Édouard Manet is an *Éducation sentimentale* that was not written, only painted. As heartrending as Flaubert's use of the imperfect tense, the story runs through a series of paintings where Berthe's name often does not appear: *The Balcony*, *Repose*—the titles of paintings often cited as among Manet's finest works. But it takes no effort—if we also pay attention to the *subject*, as was once the

custom—to recognize those paintings as chapters in a single story of a smothered love that could live only in the form of painting.

After Victorine Meurent, the model for *Olympia* and *Déjeuner sur l'herbe*, vanished in America, Manet felt lost. For a long time, whenever he had problems with his models, he had reassured himself by saying, "I have Victorine." For him she had been a street singer; for him she had disguised herself as an *espada*; for him she had taken part, nude, in a picnic; for him she had been Olympia; for him she had posed with a parrot. She always had the look of one who doesn't bat an eyelash. Neither ugly nor beautiful, deadpan, cold, Victorine was pure impassive neutrality, willing to accept everything on the same level.

But now Manet had something else in mind: a painting with three figures on a balcony, another subject inspired by Goya. And at least one of the figures had to have a certain Hispanic ardor. Manet thought of Berthe Morisot, of her pallor and incurably somber, too-penetrating gaze. Not to mention her face: dramatic, intelligent, and unsettling in a way that did not really befit a woman. Alongside her, the other two characters look like extras, whereas Berthe's gaze, so different from Olympia's, and her unchecked melancholy, leave a glimpse of the black background behind Manet's "blonde clarity," as Zola called it. Thus *The Balcony* was born, with the splendid brilliant green railing and the fan clutched in Berthe's hand as she looks toward a precise point, absorbed and desolate, with large irises that obscure the cornea. And what is running before her eyes is certainly not the spectacle of the street, but that of her life, which opens—and closes—under the mark of Manet.

It's hard to think of another painting in which there is such a gap between two of the three characters—insipid next to insignificant—and the third figure, Berthe Morisot, nominally their equal but who draws all the attention to herself, whose scorching and imperious intensity annuls the other figures. Fanny Claus, the violinist, and her friend Guillemet, with his vacuous, self-important expression, might be outlines traced on a wall, which are erased in a moment and leave no memory. Berthe is a psychic precipice. Seldom has a painting captured the immense difference in pressure between one person and another. Not only in themselves, but also in how they are seen. It is as if they have been plunged into the thoughts—or how else can we call them?—of Berthe as she poses and of Manet as he paints. Madame Morisot, her daughter's chaperone, embroidered in a corner. She wrote in a letter that during those days Manet had the "air of a madman."

There are eleven portraits of Berthe. She is the opposite of Victorine. Every time, her expression is vibrant, overloaded with meaning. Every time, she must be masked, dispersed. Every time, a chapter of a novel emerges through her, but through the silencing and suppressing of the previous and successive chapters. Only through Berthe is it possible to glimpse the dark, tormented, extreme side of Manet—this "enthusiastic, flexible and theatrical" man who loved to present himself as

lighthearted, enamored of all the most obvious things in life and wanting no complications, because he had a certainty he revealed when he chose it as the motto printed on his letterhead: "Everything happens."

On two occasions Manet painted a woman with black hair, parted in the middle, sitting almost slumped on a dark-colored couch wearing a flowing white dress from which emerges one foot shod with a light black shoe. One is holding a fan in her left hand, the other in the right. At a distance of years, they seem to correspond to each other. The first was Jeanne Duval, in her condition as an "aging beauty transformed into an invalid" by paresis. The second was Berthe Morisot. These are two highly psychic portraits. Stasis laden with tension, Jeanne's small, incongruous head, "like an idol or a doll" (Fénéon), is lost in the white and gray of her dress and of the curtain behind the couch, while her face has a motionless, distant, closed expression. If we did not know that it was Jeanne, no one would think of Baudelaire's enigmatic mistress (and some have doubted that it is she). On looking at her, Fénéon—always accurate, always cruel—thought of a poem in the *Épaves* that calls up an "old infanta," ground down and worn out by her *"caravanes insensées,"*

while around her "billows the immense and paradoxical expanse of a summer dress with broad white and violet stripes."

Berthe's gaze is too penetrating and melancholy, as if she had been surprised in solitude—or as if she had forgotten she was posing for a portrait. Behind her head, a triptych by Kuniyoshi suggests a whirl of figures, more like an informal painting or a Turner seascape than a set of lean Japanese profiles. In the portrait of Zola we can also see a Japanese print on the wall. But there it is a hint at the tastes of the day. Here it serves to set Berthe's face against a background of chaos. Both portraits are dominated by the presence of something dramatic and unspoken: in the two female figures, but indirectly in Baudelaire and Manet, their lovers are *en titre* or on the canvas.

Even though they did as much as possible to hide and ignore it, Manet and Berthe Morisot gave away their complicity. And nothing gave it away like Manet's gift to Berthe of a tiny canvas composed of three elements: a posy of violets (which bear comparison with those of Dürer), a closed fan, and a white sheet on which we read, "To Mlle Berthe [Mo]risot / E. Manet." Years later, when Berthe was resigned to dispel, with a great

effort, her melancholy in the pretense of a dubious domestic happiness, almost out of defiance she decided to paint a picture in which it was possible to perceive her physiological closeness to Manet, the most scandalous kind of all. Thus we find ourselves faced with two variations on the theme of the *woman before the mirror*, painted at a distance of two years, first by Manet, then by Berthe Morisot—and *almost* attributable to the

same hand: a dual example of "silver and blonde" painting, as Huysmans was to say, thrown onto the canvas with supreme *sprezzatura* and foamy brushstrokes, varying only in the tonality of the background, from light blue to water green. The model for *Woman Before the Mirror* might be Morisot but neither of the two mirrors reveals her face.

Manet wanted to close the novelistic sequence of portraits of Berthe with a fragrant and adolescent image of her—or at least one that was far younger than she was when she looked out over the balcony six years before. Yet he wanted her to look troubled, as if awaiting decay. That portrait has a sinister twin, which Manet painted at the beginning of that same year, when Berthe was in mourning for her father's death—and

very few people must have seen it. It remained in Manet's studio until his death. And at the subsequent sale it was bought, not by chance, by Degas.

Accustomed to portraying women of an unimpaired impassiveness, such as Victorine, here Manet plunges to the extreme opposite and paints what can be defined as the *first Expressionist portrait*. Berthe is not even recognizable: devastated, emaciated, a prey to the awful ugliness of grief, which the painter inflexibly captures. Her face is besieged by a compact black mass, of the same tonality as her big stunned eyes. Perhaps no one knew it—except the painter and the model—but this is the portrait that lets itself be read in transparency behind the last, enchanting, airy watercolor with the fan. Sentimental education, for Berthe, was over. Upon Manet's death, nine years later, she was to write to her sister that, for her, on that day, an "entire past of youth and work" had sunk. She added, "as you will understand, I feel shattered."

"He was greater than we thought," said Degas on Manet's death. No one more than he had reason to think so. For years, they had observed and checked each other, sometimes clashing, careful to avoid saying how much they admired each other, especially when one was in the other's presence. But Degas had rightly spoken in the plural. Because Manet had had the fault of seeming too normal. According to Baudelaire, he was "a very loyal man, very simple, who did his utmost to be reasonable but unfortunately was tainted with Romanticism from birth." Many people easily persuaded themselves that they understood him. Manet loved success, parties, the old masters, women. And all in an immediate and childish manner. His solid physique emanated vitality; he showed himself to be cheerful, touchy, sensitive, and witty for reasons that always seemed evident. But as soon as we look at his paintings, everything becomes far more obscure and disturbing. Zola, who had defended and celebrated him with memorable energy, once confessed that he had always found him *disconcerting*. And as time went by, Manet would show himself to be more and more disconcerting, a little like Velázquez.

The moment of greatest closeness between Manet and Degas occurred when Manet asked Degas to give him back the two books by Baudelaire that he had lent him, promising him that he would soon return them again.

Four cavaliers escorted Berthe Morisot to her grave: Renoir, Monet, Degas, and Mallarmé. No painter had so much honor in death and so little honor in life. Different in every way, those cavaliers shared feelings of affection and profound esteem for Berthe. One year after her death, they wanted to organize a retrospective, which might give her some of the glory that had not been granted to her in life. Her death certificate, like her marriage certificate, stated that she had "no profession."

Almost four hundred canvases, pastels, drawings, and watercolors flowed into the Durand-Ruel gallery. And for three days the four cavaliers argued about how to arrange them. Degas failed to impose his idea of putting the maximum emphasis on the drawings. Renoir was bent on setting an ottoman in the middle of the gallery so that visitors would be at their ease. Mallarmé wrote the introduction to the catalog. He wanted to evoke, in the transcendental prose of the *Divagations*, a "thoroughbred figure, in life, and one of absolute personal elegance." And he recalled a young friend—perhaps Valéry himself?—who had said to him one day, "Next to Madame Manet I feel coarse and brutish." *Madame Manet*: Mallarmé, too, with his dizzying delicacy, had felt the need to make that name ring out, superimposing it upon that of the woman who had married Manet's *brother*. The day before her death, Berthe Morisot left a note for her daughter Julie that began with the words "Je t'aime mourante," and she did not forget to entrust her with a task: "You will tell M. Degas that, if he founds a museum, he must choose a Manet."

Degas cultivated and worshipped pure pathos. But he found it where others did not look for it. When someone suggested that he read some novel of the moment, in rejecting the offer, "he loved to quote the words with which the abbé Prévost expresses Des Grieux's love for Manon Lescaut. He sees her for the first time at a staging post, leaning against a wall as she waits for her coach to leave. That simple gaze determines his entire life, and the narrator has him say: 'I advanced toward the sovereign of my heart.' Those words had an absolute value for him and he would repeat them often." And Daniel Halévy added a valuable observation: "Repetition, which in many people is a sign of weakness and becomes loose talk, is a different thing altogether when it comes from the lips of a solitary man who bases his life on personal certainties." This last is the soberest definition, and perhaps also the most accurate, ever attempted with regard to Degas.

Yet Prévost was as far as you can get from Degas and his "choleric rigor." Degas had found the pathos congenial to him in a writer whose death called forth this comment by the journalist Collé: "He wrote solely to make money and never thought of his fame. He was an unhappy man who always lived in the most shameful dissipation. In the mornings he would cobble together a page in his bed, with a streetwalker on his left and a desk on his right, and he would send that sheet to his printer, who immediately paid him one louis: for the rest of the day he drank; that was his normal life: he never revised anything nor did he correct anything." Collé acknowledged "the beauty of Prévost's imagination, which was a little dark," but thought that his "utter negligence" would mean that nothing would remain of his writings.

In the brief, heady days of the operetta, Paris was stirred by a new spirit: the spirit of Meilhac and Halévy, where every word was accompanied by the perpetual motion of Offenbach's music. It was a spirit that originated in Mérimée (with the *Théâtre de Clara Gazul*), but with the two librettists, it had taken on a captivating rhythm: "a nimble spirit, stripped of commonplaces and stock sentiments," endowed with an "intentional dryness," elastic, scathing, intolerant of the "verbal sentimentalism of a previous epoch" (as Proust was to describe it). This spirit governed "a kind of conversation that rejects all that is fine-sounding and expressions of elevated sentiments." In a kind of final surge, it would become the *Guermantes spirit*, and ensure that the duchess "displayed a sort of elegance, when she was with a poet or a musician, in talking solely of the dishes they were eating or the card game they would play." In an intermediate phase of that evolution we come across Degas, the least sentimental painter of the age and the one richest in pathos. The Halévy spirit safeguarded him, just as it was protective of him to go to the Halévy home every Thursday for dinner (and for lunch two or three times a week). For Degas, whose relatives were scattered between New Orleans and Naples, this was the closest thing to a family. He knew that there he would not find flowers on the table or tiresome children. And that they would dine at a decent hour. Then he would sit down, and if in the course of an evening he could not resist coming out with some caustic quip, it would then echo around Paris. This, too, was a ramification of the "Meilhac-Halévy spirit."

During the Second Empire, the duc de Morny was said to be behind all kinds of plots, but he was also considered one of the wittiest of men. He wanted to meet the young Ludovic Halévy to show him the outline of a *vaudeville*: *M. Choufleury restera chez lui*. Halévy was understandably overawed at their first meeting. But he realized that not even Morny was entirely at his ease. He was suffering like anyone else who has submitted a manuscript to a stranger. That was the start of what was probably a perfect relationship, without misunderstandings, without resentments, which was interrupted too soon following Morny's sudden death in 1865. For five years, only two people had direct access to Morny: the secretary-general Valette and Halévy. Whether it was a question of running a war or the possible censorship of a nasty line about blondes in one of Sardou's plays, Halévy was in the know. Following Morny's death, Halévy resigned his post. He was no longer having fun.

How did Degas become violently anti-Semitic? How did he get to the point, during the Dreyfus affair, of breaking off his relationship with the Halévys, the most agreeable and talented Jewish family in Paris, over whose table he presided every Thursday evening? Degas's housekeeper-cook, Zoé, used to read him a few pages at lunchtime, usually from the novels of Dumas. And one day she started to read him Drumont's venomous articles in *La Libre Parole*. According to Pauline, Degas's favorite model, the scene unfolded like this: Sitting by the window, Zoé would read with "a rapid and monotonous diction." Degas listened to her "with an attentive expression, occasionally approving with a nod of his head." These were other stories of plots, intrigues, machinations, and crimes. This time, however, they had nothing to do with Richelieu or Milady, but with a formless and pervasive entity, and one that was at the same time easily noticeable: the Jews. Naïve, stubborn, and utterly confused,

Degas believed it all, just as he had believed in the tales of *The Three Musketeers*. Perhaps he needed to congeal in one name all his irritation at the new world that was proliferating around him. He thought, like many others, that behind those annoying novelties (including "modern comforts," an expression that "drove him up the wall") there was a single, malevolent will at work: that of the Jews. There was something puerile and ferocious in Degas as soon as he sallied forth from the walls of painting. Then he would become a man like other men, ready to be swept away by the gusts of opinion. Even when Captain Dreyfus was cleared, the arguments of anti-Semitism did not strike Degas as incongruous or groundless, but as those of a party that had been unjustly defeated, which would now merely hone its weapons in preparation for revenge. The rehabilitation of Dreyfus was only one of the thousands of wrongs perpetrated by the Jews. Yet again, it was necessary to close ranks. So in December 1898, he subscribed to the fund to help the widow and orphan of the suicide Colonel Henry, implying that the blame for his death was to be attributed to the Dreyfusards. He gave twenty francs, as did the art dealer Durand-Ruel. And three francs were given by his young friend Paul Valéry, who had already published *La Soirée avec Monsieur Teste*.

Delacroix, Degas: for decades looked after and watched over by a housekeeper. Jenny, from Brittany, for Delacroix; Zoé, from Oise, a former schoolmistress ("particularly expert in mythology," as her niece was to say one day, with comical seriousness), for Degas. They were the key figures at the artists' sides, the ones with the most power, and the only ones who stayed with them until the end. Surly, tenacious in their dislikes. Strict administrators. Jealous of their prerogatives. Jenny had permission to eavesdrop, so that Delacroix had no need to recount his conversations. They looked visitors up and down and took pleasure in denying access to those they held to be untimely. Their masters were known to be difficult. In their own way, Jenny and Zoé wanted to be no less so. Every woman was an enemy—and the models were troublesome little animals, as far as Zoé was concerned. Jenny denied access to the studio to a mistress she did not like, Mme Dalton. When Degas, shortly before his death, insisted on giving one of his sketches to the delightful Hortense Valpinçon—"You are a little brioche," he had told her when he was drawing her—Zoé, who was listening as she pretended to clean some glasses, said to her, "Take it, madame, it still looks like you." Degas talked about "his problems with Zoé, who demands blue aprons because her master spends money on paintings by Ingres." Valéry recalled that the boiled veal and the macaroni she served up were "strictly tasteless."

Zoé carried on looking after Degas right until the last, devastating years. Almost blind, she continued reading to her almost-blind master. A long time before, in response to a group of friends (including Manet) who had permitted themselves a few insinuating questions about Degas and women, the lady who had preceded Zoé, a certain Clothilde, had dared to say that her master *was not a man*. In what kind of tone was that ominous remark made? One thinks inevitably of Françoise in the *Recherche* and some of her oracular statements about the *boeuf en gelée* or certain friends of Marcel's. But there's no point in insisting on this. In the end, as Degas used to mutter, "painting is private life."

Degas's old age was harrowing—a lengthy, prolonged desolation. Almost blind, but still ruddy and vigorous, shielded by an imposing white beard, like "a grubby Prospero," he launched into mad wanderings through the streets of Paris. He walked for the sake of walking. By now unkempt, like a tramp, he went along with little steps, apparently confident. His acquaintances watched him anxiously, convinced that he risked being run over at every step. But they were wrong. Degas made his way swiftly, almost as if his blindness, as long as he ignored it, protected him. Every so often he would stop "as if to say something important." To Daniel Halévy: "I sleep, and very well too . . . eight or ten hours a night . . . Sleep and my legs, that's what I have left."

After having lived there for fifteen years, Degas had to leave his house on three floors in rue Victor-Massé. The entire block was about to be demolished. He moved to a rather uncomfortable apartment on boulevard de Clichy, where he was never to paint. He left his things packed, his paintings propped up against the walls. By then he spent his time taking endless walks through Paris. He took less and less care with his appearance. With a shiny old cape and his uncombed beard, he looked more and more like a "poor old man." According to Vollard, he resembled a portrait of the Italian school that had walked out of its frame. A noble expression, a devastated look. Vollard recalled, "Now Degas spent his days wandering around Paris, aimlessly; and his steps always took him back to his demolished home. Once the last rubble had been removed, they had laid down a row of planks along the sidewalk. And you could see an old man looking at the empty lot through the gaps in the fence . . ." When war broke out, he didn't seem to notice. Once, in 1915, he suddenly stopped walking and asked Daniel Halévy's mother: "And the war? Is it over yet or not?"

Daniel Halévy's last visit to Degas, who was ill with bronchitis: "A bare room, new, without a past," in the apartment on boulevard de Clichy. Degas was lying down, motionless. He lived in that house as if passing through. He uttered a few benevolent words. There was no conversation. Already three years previously, Halévy had noted his "semi-absence that presages death." Now "at a certain point his niece goes up to him and plumps up his pillow. Her arm is covered by a light, short sleeve. Suddenly, Degas grasps it, with surprising strength. He draws her left arm toward the light coming in from the window and looks at it with impassioned attention. How many women's arms he has looked at that way, spying on them—so to speak—in his studio. I thought his strength was spent and yet he is still at work."

After Degas's death, when everything was put on sale in May 1918—the collection and his works, those he showed and those he didn't—his friends were shocked by a sad revelation. They saw in the cascade of pastels and drawings of his final manner "a kind of dogged ugliness, squalor, which surprises and saddens." This was what Daniel Halévy wrote—and certainly his judgment was marred by a certain awkward *pruderie*. But that feeling also helped him finally to say something about Degas that he had not dared utter before then: that his whole life, from 1870 on, had been an "unconfessed catastrophe." Since childhood, Halévy had listened, noted, admired, and worshipped Degas. More than anyone else, he had grasped the sound of Degas's "fine voice," especially when it was "intimate and sorrowful"—and certainly Valéry would not have surpassed him. But now, before the sense of decay exuded by that indiscriminate exhibition of all that Degas's hand had drawn, Halévy found himself led almost perforce to use a different tone: "I admit that in this work there is destruction, catastrophe, and to explain this I invoke the malady of life that starting from 1870 began to run through Degas's work, preventing him from undertaking long projects, and obliging him to pursue fragments, work always wrested from shadows." Tough, clear words that give us a glimpse of that "lugubrious gravity of the flesh" that is so frightening in Degas's last works. And they can be understood in a converse sense, because it is precisely the latency of an "unconfessed catastrophe" that seems to preserve, as if in balsamic bandages, the fragrance of those drawings. Following those words, rather like someone who takes courage after having done something foolish, Halévy further compounded his statements with words that skillfully suggested the "malady of life" in all French art of those years, leaving it devoid of any cult of *bonheur*: "Yes, there is a catastrophe in this œuvre, as in the history of all French art since 1870. But in this catastrophe no one was greater than Degas, no one has drawn such magnificent results from his own desperation."

VI

THE VIOLENCE
OF CHILDHOOD

For Baudelaire, poetry was not a commando of life, as Rimbaud sometimes seemed to imply. Nor was it something unbreathable, above all for itself, as Mallarmé sometimes seemed to suggest. For Baudelaire, poetry occupied more or less the same place it had always occupied, as for Horace or Racine. Formal innovations did not appeal to him. With him, perhaps for the last time, the Alexandrine was the universal medium. One day, Aleksander Wat showed Czesław Miłosz a poem by Baudelaire along with a sixteenth-century sonnet, without saying who the authors were. "It was hard to guess," recalled Miłosz. All this does not explain—and makes it more difficult to explain—why his words were a little more penetrating than those of others, more prone to lodge themselves in the meanders of memory, simply by virtue of their power over sensibility, to which we may add—a decisive element, this—that those words came from someone who could say of himself, "I have spent my whole life learning how to construct sentences."

In a passage of his "letter of the seer," Rimbaud concealed the most perfidious and unexpected objection to Baudelaire: that he supposedly "lived in an excessively artistic milieu." It was a hint at that spider's web in which Baudelaire had been entangled all his life, between writing for magazines, cafés, theaters, and ateliers. Something that smothered, poisoned—and maybe it had some relationship with the fact that in Baudelaire, "the much lauded form is parochial." Because "inventing the unknown demands new forms." This was the watershed from which the plunge toward the avant-garde was to begin. And the wording chosen by the implacable adolescent judge is so accurate that it's almost impossible not to be tempted to agree with him. But, at a distance of over a century, Baudelaire's threadbare and perhaps even a little "parochial" forms have withstood the assault of time far better than that embarrassing poem, "Accroupissements," which Rimbaud included along with the "letter of the seer" by way of an example of his new poetic practice.

Baudelaire concealed within himself an age-old exhaustion, but his every element was *well made*. Laforgue instantly recognized this: "There is never anything scoundrelly about him, never a false turn to the expressions with which he clothes himself—he is always courteous in the presence of ugliness. He behaves well." Rimbaud was driven by an insuppressible, raw energy, but behind him he dragged a dead weight of filth, stridency, the inheritance of a wretched, acrimonious life.

The outworn question of where the gods had wound up was dealt with several times in France after the Revolution, but it never touched, or even came close to, the vibrant tone of Hölderlin and the integral presence of those things called up by his words. In Paris everything tended to take on a *cabotin* tone. The act about the pagan gods was a part of the other numbers that a poet kept in his repertoire. The opening chord came from the most important of the *cabotins*, Alfred de Musset, who in *Rolla* said:

> Regrettez-vous le temps où le ciel sur la terre
> Marchait et respirait dans un peuple de dieux;
> Où Vénus Astarté, fille de l'onde amère,
> Secouait, vierge encore, les larmes de sa mère . . . ?

Note first of all the tone of nostalgic memory ("Regrettez-vous le temps"), which was to be revisited by Baudelaire ("I love the memory of those nude epochs"), who nonetheless abhorred Musset, whom he considered an overgrown adolescent—and Rimbaud was to multiply that loathing by "fourteen times." In addition, the erotic tendency of the picture: of all the gods the first to appear is an Asiatic Aphrodite ("Vénus Astarté"), which gives us a glimpse of hierodules and temple prostitution. Finally the apocopated form ("Astarté") that was to spread years after (with *Le Parnasse contemporain*), to produce various Ariadnés, Europés, and Aphrodités. (Rimbaud, too, like a diligent and insolent pupil, was to write this way.) As long as you were different, everything was fine—and you might as well start off with the spelling. Then the current branched out until it reached the young Marcel Proust, whose friend Bloch explained to him that all the wonders of Racine were condensed in one line: "The daughter of Minos and Pasiphaé."

How did the adolescent Rimbaud behave with the gods? He was a fifteen-year-old from Charleville—a city he declared "of all provincial cities the most idiotic"—when he decided to make his entrance on the literary scene. The form he chose was a typical one: a letter from an unknown offering some of his poems for publication. The addressee: Théodore de Banville, old enough to have been Baudelaire's first literary companion, and new enough to be the promoter of the only attractive enterprise for a poet wishing to make his debut: *Le Parnasse contemporain*.

Rimbaud's opening gambit reveals a cold, precise strategy: First, choose the right target. Second, lie: "I am seventeen," he wrote in his opening line, when he was still five months shy of his sixteenth birthday. Then show deference ("Cher Maître" repeated three times in a few lines), while adding ready praise to generic devotion, something that writers grasp immediately: "The fact is that in you I love, with the greatest candor, a descendant of Ronsard, a brother of our masters of 1830, a true Romantic, a true poet." These words suffice to establish complicity. And what is literary life if not a chain of complicities? Rimbaud already knew this perfectly well, as if his wild being had forever been a depository of the age-old wisdom of the Republic of Letters. But Rimbaud also knew that it was up to him to make *his* tone heard, the one that would set him apart from all others. And nothing came easier to him. That tone, which presupposes a perennial air of defiance, is already noticeable in the rhythm of his first sentence: "We are in the months of love; I am seventeen years old." Who else would have had the nerve to introduce himself like this? And above all, who else would have had the nerve to insert that semicolon where he did? But Rimbaud was a master at alternating impertinence and the gestures of submission. After having made his declaration of faith ("because the poet is a Parnassian—enamored of ideal beauty"), he also managed to add, "It's silly [*bête*], isn't it, but why not?"

In a few lines, Rimbaud composed a gem of rhetoric. But the ordeal, for the new poet, lies in the first poems. Which to choose? Here, too, his vision was strategic, shrewd, and a portent of what was to come: three compositions, different in length and register. "Sensation"—eight verses—is a harbinger of Rimbaudian intoxication, destined for vast future development. The sureness of tone is immediately evident ("Par les soirs bleus d'été, j'irai dans les sentiers . . . Je laisserai le vent baigner ma tête nue"), whereas the most penetrating verse already suggests utter detachment ("Je ne parlerai pas, je ne penserai rien") of which he would perhaps think again one day, even though the harshness is mitigated by the verse that follows: "Mais l'amour infini me montera dans l'âme," because one knows that "l'amour" is sufficient to liquidate any awkwardness. But this is immediately followed by a none-too-reassuring reference to the nomadic vocation: "Et j'irai loin, bien loin comme un bohémien." And in fact Rimbaud was to go very far.

The second poem ("Ophélie") is a masterful exercise in the Romantic manner. It serves to show that, if the occasion demanded, that register, too, could be perfectly controlled.

The third poem ("Credo in unam," subsequently retitled "Soleil et chair") has the function of an ideological manifesto. It was necessary to make Banville—and, behind him, the sparse Parnassian tribe—understand the new poet's *stance* with respect to the ancient gods. A decisive question, it would seem. And here Rimbaud gives another demonstration of his shrewdness, by juxtaposing, from start to finish, tributes to his elders (in the form of imitated verses, borrowed vocabulary, and maxims calculated to win easy praise) and swift stylistic surges that give a glimpse of the person who is writing and what he has in store: something that goes well beyond, indeed overwhelms, the *Parnasse*. What is Rimbaudian about Rimbaud (in the sense of Fraenkel's *Plautinisches im Plautus*) comes onstage for the first time here. We can see this in the fourth verse, which is copied from Chénier: "Que la terre est nubile et brûle d'être mère," which is transformed into "Que la terre est nubile et déborde de sang."

That earth "overflowing with blood" is already Rimbaud. And it is an earth that appears for the first time. Not even Baudelaire had dared such harshness.

Shortly after:

Je regrette les temps de l'antique jeunesse,
Des satyres lascifs, des faunes animaux,

This is a revisitation of the nostalgic *frissons* of Musset and Baude-laire, making it even clearer that it is a question of erotic rather than theological nostalgia. And in matters erotic, Rimbaud is at once so sure in naming and so firm of gesture that these "satyres lascifs" are any-thing but vague:

Dieux qui mordaient d'amour l'écorce des rameaux
Et dans les nénufars baisaient la Nymphe blonde!

The blond nymph who permits herself this *baiser* (a verb that can mean either "kissing" or "screwing") in a pool overrun by lotus flowers begins to have a hallucinatory presence. There follows a predictably neo-pagan passage, where the fifteen-year-old still wants to reassure, show what he can do. Yet already, there stand out some verses that, taken in isolation, mean something more. Above all "le pur ruissellement de la vie infinite." That "pure flowing of infinite life," with its intimation of an overwhelming superabundance, is the true, nameless, multiform divinity to which Rimbaud would always be devoted. It was also the only one.

The verses that follow contain the new ideology: the gods have disappeared ("plus de dieux! plus de dieux!"), man has become king ("l'Homme est Roi"), but at the cost of losing the capacity to feel ("les yeux fermés et les oreilles closes"). Yet there is still a salvation—and it is the usual "Mais l'Amour, voilà la grande Foi!" A blend of enlightened democratism (Hugo, Michelet) and scorn for what the world has re-duced itself to (Baudelaire). Thus far, Rimbaud is like a politician sug-gesting an honorable compromise between divergent outlooks (humanity that liberates itself and humanity that impoverishes itself). But he soon gets tired of this sensible mediation and explodes anew:

Chair, Marbre, Fleur, Vénus, c'est en toi que je crois!

Those three initial nouns, complete with far more intense capitals than that of the threadbare *Amour* and followed by the name of the goddess, pave the way for Mallarmé. An impatience is making its way, a will to tighten up form. Deprecatory verses on the ugliness of modern bodies follow; verses that add nothing new, largely because they culminate in a Baudelairean whiplash:

> La Femme ne sait plus même être Courtisane!

Thus we come to the third part, where Rimbaud hazards a conclusion. And if ancient times were to return? If man, who by now "has played all the roles" and is "tired of breaking idols," were to discover a new life? It would be Aphrodite of "the rosy navel where snowed the foam" to grant man "sacred Redemption." A frivolous and solemn scenario, erotic and humanitarian. Would this be the solution? By this point Rimbaud already shows he has no fear of fateful platitudes—the ones that go far and soon become advertising slogans:

> —Le Monde a soif d'amour: tu viendras l'apaiser.

Of course, Baudelaire would have had himself whipped rather than write such a conceited and vacuous line. But Rimbaud doesn't bother. When he wanted to be, he was the ablest of copywriters. And he instantly moved on, wedging into the verse a formula that seems like a Vedic snippet:

> . . . La Pensée,
> La cavale longtemps, si longtemps oppressée

Thought seen as a mare overburdened for a long time (maybe for centuries and centuries), which lunges forward again, erupting *from the brow* of man like Poseidon's horses from the rock: this is a dazzling vision, one the reader almost doesn't have time to grasp, because the verse presses on and immediately falls back on more customary images. But only for a little. On looking up toward the vault of the heavens, what do we see?

> Un Pasteur mène-t-il cet immense troupeau
> De mondes cheminant dans l'horreur de l'espace?

Here, too, the novelty stands out above all when the verses are isolated from the context. Then we notice only aphasia before the cosmic horror. And this is pure Rimbaud—a Rimbaud in the manner of Pascal.

The fourth and final part is a sequence of Alexandrine cameos, where parade Ariadne, Theseus, Europa, Zeus-bull, Leda, Zeus-swan, Aphrodite, Hercules, Selene, and Endymion: skillful, at times virtuoso examples of how the ancient stories have always been waiting to be retold. But in the closing verses the tension increases—and the fifteen-year-old Rimbaud takes his leave with images still waiting to be probed. It all begins with the distant murmuring of waters:

> C'est la Nymphe qui rêve, un coude sur son vase,
> Au beau jeune homme blanc que son onde a pressé.

We have often wondered about the origin of the image of Melancholy leaning on her elbow and meditating. This image found its last variant in the hallucinatory young girl who appeared to Baudelaire at the far end of the deserted corridor in his boarding school (in the debut poem sent to Sainte-Beuve, the perfect counterpart to "Credo in unam," sent by Rimbaud to Banville). Now the point of origin is shown to us: it is the Nymph, who has just drowned Ila, the young friend of Hercules, and is already dreaming of him. So Melancholy would be the first murderous lover. Her elbow rests on the vase from which water eternally runs; from which she herself runs. From which the water that has submerged Ila runs. These are two mysterious and elliptic verses, where the crime is only hinted at. It is no longer another Alexandrine cameo, but an obscure, haunting mythic event. And it ushers in the final verses. Here the talk is of a "breeze of love" that "has passed in the night." Suddenly, as before at the Nymph's fountainhead, we are introduced to the "sacred woods" and to "the horror of the great trees." And we barely manage to pause and wonder: Why *horror*? Can it be that this forest is like the heavenly desert, where the Shepherd led his astral flock? We shall not know this—but immediately, in the middle of the forest, we discover something that might also terrify. In the depths, statues are hidden:

Majestueusement debout, les sombres Marbres,
Les Dieux, au front desquels le Bouvreuil fait son nid,
—Les Dieux écoutent l'Homme et le Monde infini!

Now we know where the gods have ended up. They are statues hidden in the forest, perforated by robins' nests. And from there, as always, they observe us, they listen to us. Even though man flaunts an improper capital letter and declares himself to be one who scorns "ancient yokes," as well as "free of all fear," the gods, in their stony silence, continue to follow him, indifferent to cults, devotions, and curses. The gods can appear or disappear from human sight, according to the places where they settle. But they always *are*—and they watch.

There is something in Rimbaud that goes to the head: his commentators immediately become overexcited, bombastic, as if prodded by an invisible goad. Thus accuracy wound up taking refuge with a reader like Sergio Solmi, discreet and subdued, but ready to grasp already in Rimbaud's first poems the signs of a "mad childish rebellion," which was also a "negation of the world, both physiological and metaphysical." Solmi lovingly auscultated, verse by verse, the first shots at poetry and did not withdraw when the form obliged him to recognize not only that "the predominant note, in this Rimbaud of the early days, is insincerity," but that this paradoxically confirmed "Rivière's disconcerting statement about a fundamental 'innocence' and 'purity' in Rimbaud." Tortuous tunnels, with no exit. But those who study Rimbaud have to get used to living in them. In him the violence of childhood resounds as never before: a state that arouses fear, and the first to be buried. Rimbaud instead always remained one of those "seven-year-old poets" to whom he dedicated one of his first poems. This explains the worldly-wise, bold, and expert tone with which the fifteen-year-old Rimbaud addressed Banville. After all, he already had eight years' experience of life as a poet. At first he was a sullen little boy, of whom no one, least of all his mother, could decipher "his soul . . . devoted to repugnant things." Then he would close himself up in the "cool of the latrines." To think. He played with the ragamuffin kids of his neighborhood, who talked "with the meekness of idiots." But above all "he constructed novels."

About what? "About life / In the great desert, where the light of abducted Freedom shines / Forests, suns, shores, savannahs!" A landscape and a portent to which he would hold, unswervingly. A burning thread united the imaginary novel of the "seven-year-old poet" with *A Season in Hell, Illuminations,* and Africa. The correspondences are revealed so clearly that no explanations are required. The tonality already declared itself:

Vertige, écroulements, déroutes et pitié!

Especially vertigo and debacles, in word and deed.

Together with the "novel," eros. This appeared in the guise of a little girl recognizable by her "dark, mad eyes" and her "calico dresses"; a "little brute" of eight years, "the daughter of the workers who lived next door." Shaking her braids, she would leap on the little poet. Then she would hurl him to the ground. And the vanquished little boy "would bite her buttocks / Because she never wore any knickers." Then they would hit each other. In the end the "seven-year-old poet" would retreat, "aching from punches and kicks," and "take back to his room the flavor of her flesh." Literature had lived until then without knowing any of this. No previous writer, not even Baudelaire, had dared to describe scenes of this kind. And one may wonder how letters managed to do without them, such is the intrusiveness and indubitability of those feelings, perhaps already known to and left unsaid by many. Now a wild adolescent from the Ardennes talked about them with the same confidence with which for centuries others had woven amoebean chants.

What happens in the first Rimbaud (in Charleville, between fifteen and seventeen years of age)? A "massacre of meanings" from which nothing could survive "if not . . . the vibration, the dazzlement of pure appearances." The quotation is from Solmi, writing with the precise boldness that only the timid can handle so well. That ferocious and abstract scenario presents itself when one is born in a land loath to accept civilization, and not merely visiting it. This was the Ardennes of Rimbaud's day.

But is it possible to reconstruct a story within this "dazzlement of pure appearances" that might also be the last stop of poetry? Solmi tried to do this in a few lines, with a felicitous touch, by identifying various phases in the process whereby those appearances were elaborated. In the first phase, "detached from their historical cohesion, which made them only machines of coercion and torture, in the subjects of the poet's violence, they once more become inoffensive and enchanting as in the remote Eden of childhood." This explains the perverse, euphoric grace of some of Rimbaud's first poems. Thus those appearances by then dissociated from oppressive meanings "shine through in darting flashes that are ever more intense and enduring." In only one case (in "Le bateau ivre") do they "come to blend into an integral vision." What can follow at that point? The attempt to "deliberately release such appearances, by now more like apparitions, and to organize them into a system of visionary objectivity"—these were to be the *Illuminations*. With a few touches of the critic-poet, Solmi reconstructed the sequence of tremors in the seismic graph that was Rimbaud before Africa.

Raised by an embittered and miserly mother, Rimbaud was a handsome boy with a talent for Latin composition. Was this enough to sustain the unconditional resentment of the adolescent poet? Yet Rivière's observation sounds exact: "Rimbaud rejects everything en bloc: he rises up against the human condition, or better: against the physical and astronomical condition of the Universe." There is something strident, comical in the pretensions of the youngster from Charleville. An even more amazing fact is that precisely *that* stridency is present in his first poems. The themes are miserable, stifling. The fury that inspires them has something disproportionate, overwhelming about it. He is merciless with the old people who frequent the town library. They are ugly, and their principal defect is that they remain seated. Even the poor in church disgust him. He dwells on their "long yellow fingers," on the "grimy" exposed breasts of the "soup eaters." The children in church are "dirty brats that befoul the columns." (Everything that appertains to the church in general is filthy.) The lyrical tension increases only with the image of a little boy motionless in front of the window, who allows the "slender, terrible and bewitching fingers" of two women to delve into his "heavy hair" and remove his lice.

"Le bateau ivre," is the inaugural ceremony of a literature that has cast off its moorings. An announcement and a demonstration are under way.

"Au fond de l'Inconnu pour trouver du *nouveau!*": the wish with which Baudelaire had sealed *Les Fleurs du mal* is now a note in a ship's log. The boat sails without a crew because monologizing solitude and cold delirium are enough to pilot it.

Among the first results: like trash from the deck, all forms of historical exoticism are swept away—that of Flaubert, but also that of Chateaubriand. History is a negligible accident. Now all one can do is escape from one geological era to another. Quaternary, Tertiary, Carboniferous—this is the landscape. But what waters are plied by the ship? First, earthly and Amazonian; subsequently, celestial and sidereal. To finish in a "puddle / Black and cold" where "A little boy crouches full of sadness" watching the tiny craft he has just launched. He is the "seven-year-old poet" on his return from an adventure.

It took a rootless Romanian such as Benjamin Fondane, educated in the school of Chestov, to see in the voice that speaks throughout *A Season in Hell* the timbre closest to that of the "bad clerk" whose monologue is Dostoevsky's *Notes from the Underground.* Of course, the clerk is subtle and venomous, while Rimbaud is insolent and a ruffian. The clerk's images are wretched; those of Rimbaud, fiery. But they both dip into the same depths. And they share certain strange tendencies. The clerk launches into a discourse about the "putrid snow." Rimbaud says, "I stretched out in the mud." This is mud that in the cities suddenly struck him as "red and black"—and this was one of the many optical transformations out of which he wove the *Illuminations.* When the clerk confesses, "The more I became aware of good and of all those 'beautiful and sublime' things, the deeper I sank into my mud and the more inclined I was to put down roots in it," Rimbaud knew what the other was talking about and felt less bored than he did on listening to the diatribes of the Parisian poets. *Notes from the Underground* dates from 1864; *A Season in Hell,* from 1873. Two delirious voices, unknown to each other. The grating, piercing, brazen tone of Dostoevsky's clerk announces entry into an indecorous new continent of literature that Rimbaud was to cross like a prince of the blood—and obviously of "bad blood."

•

"Aden is the crater of an extinct volcano filled with sea sand. So you see nothing and touch nothing but lava and sand, which cannot produce even the smallest vegetable." And again: "Here there are no trees, not even withered ones, not a blade of grass, not a particle of soil, not a drop of fresh water." Is this nature? Certainly no less so than the idyllic valleys so often described over the centuries. Among all the places of his wanderings, Rimbaud seemed attracted to Aden, "a place where one does not stay except out of necessity." He stayed there longer than he planned to, and there he returned. And he also got to the point of giving reasons why it was better for him to stay there than elsewhere: "Since I earn a living here, and since every man is a slave to this wretched fate, Aden is as good as anywhere else; in fact, Aden is better than any other place; it's a place where I am unknown, where I am completely forgotten and where I should start from scratch!"

Like Bouvard and Pécuchet rolled into one, Rimbaud stubbornly insisted on asking his relatives—from Aden but from Cyprus, too—to send him only *manuals* on all kinds of disciplines: carpentry, metallurgy, urban and agricultural hydraulics, naval architecture, mineralogy, telegraphy, trigonometry, topography, geodesics, hydrography, meteorology, industrial chemistry. He was also eager for "catalogs from factories producing physical toys, pyrotechnics, prestidigitation, mechanical models and miniature constructions, etc." To justify his request, he once wrote, "Without these books, I would lack a quantity of information indispensable to me. I would be like a blind man; and the absence of these things would do me great harm." But this heartfelt appeal does not manage to conceal the disproportion between the books requested and their possible use. Working from seven in the morning until five in the afternoon in a place where "one year is like five elsewhere," it seems difficult that Rimbaud could have gone into such disparate studies in any depth. And what purpose could treatises on prestidigitation and pyrotechnics serve in Aden or Harar?

The long, insistent lists of requests to his relatives never included a work of literature. Apart from the treatises and manuals, Rimbaud asked only for a Quran (with a French text on the facing page—or even without one). Yet on several occasions he reiterated, among the atrocities of the place, the total absence of reading matter. ("Newspapers don't arrive, there are no libraries.") The act of reading seems to have remained essential for Rimbaud, provided it was completely detached from literature.

Even though Rimbaud did his best to ignore them, his talents as a prose writer occasionally erupt in his letters from Africa. Without warning, like a hallucination no less intense than those that stud *Les Illuminations*, one day he called up in a few lines a map of adventurers, merchants, fugitives, and tribal chiefs, scattered across immense spaces, each captured in a pose, like waxworks or characters out of Raymond Roussel:

The King [*Roy*, in the archaic manner: this was Menelik] has returned to Entotto and the splendid court is reformed, with Ato Petros as master of ceremonies.

Antonelli is laid up with syphilis at Lit-Marefia—Traversi is hunting hippopotamus on the Hawache—M. Appenzeller is repairing the bridge, they say—Borrelli is with the king of Djimma—M. Zimmermann is awaiting your arrival—Antoine Brémond is nursing his newborn babies in Alin Amba—Bidault is wandering around taking photographs of the mountains of Harar—the dyer of hides Stéphane is lying in the drain in front of our door, etc., etc.

The mere phonic impact of the names (Appenzeller with Alin Amba, Ato Petros with Bidault, Zimmermann with Entotto), the mobility of the temporal forms, swinging between telegraphic contraction and heroic-comic gesticulation, suffice to make the vision stand out as if in a shadow theater. This is the stuff of the world of those who have lost their bearings—and camouflaged among them, we also recognize Rimbaud, who signed himself on the occasion "a French trader in Harar."

To the French consul at Massaua, Rimbaud appeared like this: "tall, thin, gray eyes, almost blond but slim mustache." His documents did not inspire trust, and the consul asked his colleague in Aden to make a check on this "individual with a rather louche air." One week later the same consul was to write an enthusiastic letter of recommendation for Rimbaud, whom he now defined as a "very respectable Frenchman." Something must have convinced him in the meantime. At that time Rimbaud was thirty-three and said that his hair was "completely gray." This marked the final stage in the transformation of the adolescent poet who had gotten off the train like a meteor in the Gare du Nord into an extra in a Peter Lorre movie set in some unspecified Asian location.

In Aden and Harar, Rimbaud could think he had cut all ties with France. Except one: military service, the first evidence of subjection to society. It was his only worry, and he regularly left traces of this in his letters to his family. One month after his right leg was amputated, in Marseilles, his mother let him know that the authorities considered him a deserter. (*Insoumis* was the technical term, the most suitable one for him.) Had he remained in France, in all probability he would have ended up in prison. Without a leg, in jail for disobedience. This was the final prospect of his relations with the country of his native tongue.

Six days after the amputation in the Hôpital de la Conception in Marseilles, Rimbaud wished to write only one letter, addressed to the governor of Harar, Ras Mekonen. He assured the ras that, in the space of a few months, he would return to those places "to carry on trading as before." It was the sign of an imperious calling, which urged him to return with a wooden leg to that country where he had been accustomed to throwing himself every day into "races through the mountains, horseback rides, walks, deserts, rivers and seas."

But he made his reasons clear to his sister, Isabelle: "I shall die where destiny throws me. I hope to return where I was. There I have friends I have known for ten years, who will have compassion for me, with them I shall find work, I shall live as I can. I shall always live down there, while in France, apart from you. I have neither friends nor acquaintances or others." Replying to him, Isabelle spoke of an acquaintance of hers without a leg, whom she often saw moving around confidently. And she added: "I have heard it said that, wooden leg or not, he is the most tireless dancer at the country fairs."

The account of Rimbaud's *edifying life* is based on his sister Isabelle's letter to their mother of October 28, 1891. Rimbaud had agreed to speak with a priest. Isabelle wrote, "He who is about to die at my side is no longer a poor unhappy outcast: he is a just man, a saint, a martyr, one of the elect!" From the seed of these words there would bloom a luxuriant literary hagiography. But the celestial aura of the event has obscured a detail in his sister's account. After the priest's visit, Isabelle, moved, approached her dying brother, who asked her if she had faith. But another exchange followed: "He also told me with bitterness: 'Yes, they say they believe, they pretend to be converted, but it is because they want people to read what they write, it is speculation!' I hesitated, then I said: 'Ah no, they would earn more money by blaspheming.'" If proof were required, then this would show that Rimbaud thought to the last not only about literature, but about the literary life. But it is also the proof that Isabelle, so sound in her sanctimony, had anticipated the development of every avant-garde of the twentieth century. In that moment alone, she shared her brother's scathing spirit. And she came up to the mark.

At one time, everything that the imagination and trade could offer was presented in the form of Universal Expositions. It was a perpetual updating of the psyche, a growing catalog of its elements. For this reason the Crystal Palace terrified Dostoevsky. Under its transparent ceilings were housed, as in a greenhouse, an overwhelming blossoming of simulacra.

In this, too, Rimbaud wanted to go against the flow with regard to time. He did not want to be just a spectator but an object in the Exposition. And he made this known by following the only path available: in one of his letters to his family (which were so many monologues). Always maintaining a practical tone, like a merchant: "I'm sorry I won't be able to take a trip to the Exposition this year, but my income is far too low to permit this and besides, here I am absolutely alone, and, if I left, my business would disappear completely. So it will be for another time; and perhaps on that occasion I shall be able to show the products of this country and, perhaps, show myself, because I believe that a fellow must have an extremely bizarre air after a long sojourn in countries like this one." Having disembarked from his drunken boat, Rimbaud had succeeded in becoming one of those savages who escorted him from the banks. If the fortunes of his œuvre have gone well beyond the region of the poets, it is also because, in the end, Rimbaud succeeded in his intention: *to exhibit himself,* like an ethnographic specimen captured in the forest.

VII

KAMCHATKA

Sainte-Beuve hovered over Parisian literary life like an authoritative and malevolent uncle. Baudelaire and a few others called him Uncle Beuve. A certain deference was obligatory as was the expectation of, or sometimes the demand for, some critical blessing on his part, which could be of vital importance. But this was seldom granted, especially to writers of great talent. Sainte-Beuve got rattled and became evasive as soon as he suspected certain of his contemporaries of greatness. This happened regularly: with Stendhal, with Balzac, with Baudelaire, and with Flaubert. He mentioned them only to belittle them. And sometimes he barely mentioned them at all (Baudelaire was the cruelest case) or avoided them altogether (as happened with Nerval). In those same years, he was indulgent and scrupulous with many mediocre writers. Yet Sainte-Beuve's elusive and disparaging words went farther, even with those writers he ostentatiously ignored, and his words are of more help in understanding them than anything written by their first devotees. Subsequently, Sainte-Beuve's sidestepping became the main argument for sidestepping Sainte-Beuve's own work, a posthumous vendetta of the harshest sort, which made *Port-Royal* one of the least read great books in French literature.

But Sainte-Beuve did not ooze venom only for writers who were younger than he or his contemporaries. Even with regard to masters he ostensibly venerated, such as Chateaubriand, he was lethally venomous, and sometimes he could not manage to conceal this. His course on *Chateaubriand et son groupe littéraire sous l'Empire* teems with defamatory *asides*, whispered in a corner by an old friend of Mme Récamier's who willingly let everyone suspect that Chateaubriand had a detailed knowledge of the secrets and tricks of the house, some of which he practiced himself to please the Enchanter and his lady.

Once more Baudelaire wrote to Sainte-Beuve, daring to ask for a review. As always, in vain. In the postscript, he added that a few days before, heading toward rue Montparnasse, where Sainte-Beuve lived, he had passed in front of a gingerbread shop—and had been struck by the "conviction that he [Sainte-Beuve] must have liked gingerbread." He followed with a detailed explanation of how to eat it (with wine, as a dessert, or also in the English manner, with butter and jam). Then the conclusion: "I hope you have not taken this piece of gingerbread, coated with angelica, for a naughty boy's joke and that you have eaten it with simplicity . . . Warmest greetings. Wish me well. I am in a great crisis."

About Baudelaire, Sainte-Beuve's feelings first of all betrayed a certain fear. The great critic, whose task it was to show every Monday, with calm affability—albeit invariably with some drops of concealed venom—the correct attitude toward matters of literature and the world, realized that Baudelaire had gone *too far*. That he had crossed the barriers of civilized society and had by now settled in some remote territory, forest, or steppe.

Sainte-Beuve vowed not to talk about Baudelaire—or even about Poe, that sinister alter ego of his, even though his editor had judged Poe to be suitable material for him. For a critic-judge of Sainte-Beuve's ilk, the decision *not* to write about a contemporary was a political act of great consequence. But at times the critic was obliged to express himself fitfully and circuitously, condensing in a few stray lines all that he was loath to discuss in depth.

On more than one occasion Sainte-Beuve, with the agility of a monkey, avoided writing an article about Baudelaire. When he finally decided to do so, he took such a roundabout approach that no one could have suspected him. On Monday, January 20, 1862, instead of dealing with a single author, as was his custom, he published an article titled "Des prochaines élections à l'Académie," a current affairs piece on a subject that was always a delicate one. This seldom happened, and all the ladies or illustrious officials whom Sainte-Beuve imagined savoring his words every Monday must have felt a mild *frisson* on picking up their copy of *Le Constitutionnel* that day. Sainte-Beuve's arguments were, as always, clear and seamlessly written. But an attentive eye would have spotted, right from the first lines, that this was a discourse on various levels of which most readers would have done well not to notice. And yet again Sainte-Beuve would humor them in their wish not to know, thanks to his tone of "decent liberty," which implied a firm resolve to round off any rough edges. Yet the topic was fraught with risk. It was not so much a matter, as Sainte-Beuve claimed, of proposing a new procedure for the selection of candidates for the Académie, but of insinuating a sharp, peremptory judgment on what the Académie was in itself. And this, since Richelieu's day, was tantamount to making a judgment on the state of health of the literary world. A master of reticence, Sainte-Beuve was also a master of the sudden, piercing thrust. So, after having described the academicians with affectionate irony as figures devoted to "perfect idleness" and relieved of any menial task because they were held only to "correspond directly" with the sovereign, Sainte-Beuve dared to write, "The Académie, in the persons of various important members, is, in effect, very much afraid." Let's remove the padding. What remains? That the Académie is *very much afraid.* But who could threaten it? Perhaps politics, ever oppressive and intrusive? No, there is something even more worrisome: "the fear of the literary *Bohème.*" At this point the prudent Sainte-Beuve realizes that he has gone over the score. And he immediately circumscribes the statement. But, notoriously, toning down statements often ends up making them even more emphatic. And that is what happens here: "Nonetheless it is a good thing not to exaggerate its extent, to know where it begins and ends [for a moment, *Bohème* returns to its geographical connotation]. A discussion of the names considered suspect would be useful [suspect? whom? and regarding what?]. It is necessary to avoid, by dint of being on one's guard against the *Bohème*, to abstain from all current, vital literature." Prudent now, and on his guard, he ends by referring to the zone from which the danger is coming: "current, vital literature." But who are we talking about? Why should the Forty Immortals, protected as they often are by their noble birth and impregnable social position, be *afraid* of a certain literature of shady origin? Sainte-Beuve immediately avoids answering questions that he himself has raised and cuts things short, as if frightened by what he has done. By way of an excuse, he says that the public ("which must always be taken more or less into account") has not yet reached the point in which it "imperiously imposes one of those choices whereby renowned fame almost assumes the right to do violence to the naturally conservative spirit." It is an irresistibly slippery downward slope: with every word of apology and mitigation for what he has just said, Sainte-Beuve makes his situation worse. There is nothing else he can do but cut things short. And so he moves on to the examination of the candidates for M. Scribe's position: a list made up of three lines of names now forgotten, at the end of which we read, "M. Baudelaire." For the other vacant position, that of Lacordaire, there was only one candidate: the Prince de Broglie. (And Sainte-Beuve was later to explain the reasons for this undisturbed solitude: the duke was someone who "has made the effort to be born"—and by this he implied that all other efforts in his life would have been superfluous.) Brief portraits of the candidates follow, all imbued with a lethal *bonheur*. Praise of the critic Cuvillier-Fleury, as soon as it goes into specifics, becomes sardonic: "He is a man of true merit, learned, conscientious, who applies himself." And immediately after: "Sometimes he is ingenious, but after much sweat. He is more estimable than agreeable. It is never necessary to dare him to make a gaffe because he does this by himself, even without being asked to." Few can match Sainte-Beuve in the art of debunking with what seems like praise.

At the tail end of the list, it is Baudelaire's turn. Since the other candidates were presented by Sainte-Beuve as highly respectable—even though, for different reasons, they have nothing much to qualify them— Baudelaire appears to be the only one to whom Sainte-Beuve's initial argument about the perils of the "literary *Bohème*" and the fears that it aroused may apply. Not to mention the fact that, for Baudelaire, who was certainly not a bohemian but "a dandy lost in the *bohème*," according to Gautier's definition, it already sounded humiliating to be considered in such a light.

But Sainte-Beuve was only at the beginning of the humiliations he felt obliged to inflict upon the oldest of his young friends. How was it that Baudelaire had so much as entertained the idea of presenting his candidature for the Académie? Sainte-Beuve answers his own question:

"At first one wondered if M. Baudelaire, in applying, wished to make an epigram, to mock the Académie; unless his intention was to let the Académie know in this way that the time was ripe for welcoming into its ranks that poet and writer so distinguished and so able in all genres of writing who is Théophile Gautier, his master." One humiliation heaped upon another: to make it understood that Baudelaire's candidature was in itself an affront, and hence conceivable only as a joke; and even as such, comprehensible only if understood as an allusion to a better writer than Baudelaire, one who was his master (just to keep things in the right proportion). But there's more. Baudelaire is not only minor, but nonexistent: "It was necessary to make known, to spell out M. Baudelaire's name, to more than one member of the Académie, who was completely unaware of his existence." For no previous candidate had Sainte-Beuve felt obliged to produce such a certificate of nonexistence. Moreover, he knew Baudelaire well enough to understand how sensitive he was about the way in which his name was liable to be mispronounced. This time, too, Sainte-Beuve made sure he wounded at least twice with the same blow. There follow some lines of measured appreciation for *Les Fleurs du mal*, in which, however, the emphasis is on the generous efforts that, one is led to suppose, Sainte-Beuve had to make in order to illustrate the work: "It is not as easy as one might think to prove to certain political academicians and men of state that in *Les Fleurs du mal* there are some passages that are truly remarkable for talent and art." This is the highest praise that Sainte-Beuve would allow himself. But here, too, he does not hold back from betrayal, giving us the very words he might have uttered to the face of some impassive, incredulous, and bored academician absorbed with some problem of state: "As you can see, my dear friend, we have done everything possible."

One might think that, once his judgment of *Les Fleurs du mal* had been handed down—and once he had defined as "gems" two prose pieces in *Le Spleen de Paris*—Sainte-Beuve no longer felt bound to justify his lukewarm attitude toward Baudelaire himself. But Sainte-Beuve was not just a shrewd voyager in the baser waters of literary life. He was also a great writer, and at times, even in the most stifling contexts, he managed to shrug off all his fears and scruples to say some tremendously precise, definitive words, which erupt in the middle of his argument. It had been hard enough to make sclerotic academicians understand the singular beauties of some of Baudelaire's poems. But it would have been even harder to introduce them to the *locus* of Baudelaire. "All in all," Sainte-Beuve continues, "M. Baudelaire has found a way to construct, at the extremities of a strip of land held to be uninhabitable and beyond the confines of known Romanticism, a bizarre pavilion, a folly, highly decorated, highly tormented, but graceful and mysterious, where people read the books of Edgar Allan Poe, where they recite exquisite sonnets, intoxicate themselves with hashish to ponder about it afterward, where they take opium and thousands of other abominable drugs in cups of the finest porcelain. This singular folly, with its marquetry inlays, of a planned and composite originality, which for some time has drawn the eye toward the extreme point of the Romantic Kamchatka, I call *Baudelaire's folly.* The author is content to have done something impossible, in a place where it was thought that no one could go." This passage is the foundation of all that can be said and has been said about Baudelaire. It cannot be replaced with any other description; it should be observed in every detail, as if one were wandering around that solitary folly, which stands out against a desolate landscape. It does not appear that Sainte-Beuve had particular geographical or ethnographic interests. For him, Kamchatka must have been one of those names that appeared in *Le Magasin Pittoresque* along with some exotic drawing. But his choice of place for the transposition of Baudelaire into an image could not have been more apt. Of course, Kamchatka is a slender strip of land (to signify that Baudelaire, too, is more like a pointed extremity than a vast rustling forest), but behind him there extends the immensity of Asia, which supports him. But to what does that boundless steppe and taiga correspond? To "known Romanticism," which borders on civilized eighteenth-century Europe to become, little by little, ever more "uninhabitable" before finally extending, as if in a final lunge, to that Kamchatka pierced by one hundred and twenty volcanoes, which would be the place "beyond the confines" of Romanticism itself. And there stands a folly that contains a blend of the *horror vacui* of primitive ornamentation and the sobriety of the products of perfect civilization (the exquisite porcelain). A place that is "highly decorated, highly tormented, but graceful and mysterious": a quadrilateral of words that delimit the *locus* of Baudelaire, where the pleasure of ornament is united with self-inflicted torture, where mystery cannot forgo being frivolous and erotic seduction opens the doors of mystery. In the middle of a desert inhabited only by shamanic presences, what meets the eye, like a mirage, is a Folly, a name that stands not only for that which has always eluded psychic habitation and rational control—and this is the real reason for that "fear of the *Bohème*," which was rather a fear of Kamchatka—but also for certain enchanting *maisons de plaisance*, pavilions devoted to idleness and pleasure. Since the days of the Régence up to Bagatelle, which the count of Artois had built in two months, like a dream, to win a bet with the very young Marie Antoinette, such constructions dotted the outskirts of Paris. Later absorbed into the metropolis, they often became the residences of the supreme *demi-mondaines*. Ambiguous and mad, uninhabitable and sensual, Baudelaire's folly was a self-sufficient, sovereign place, which would have been pointless to introduce to the *academicians*. They could never have understood it. Then, little by little, like successive waves of nomads who made their camps in it, there grew up around that folly the essence of that which was to appear since then under the name of *literature*.

As soon as he had finished the memorable lines on Kamchatka, Sainte-Beuve felt the need to fall back on the triple cross, as if afraid that he had exposed himself too much. And the sound of this falling back grates more than ever. "At this point, and after having explained as well as possible to somewhat amazed and esteemed colleagues all these exotica, these piquant flavors, these refinements, could they then see them as qualifications for the Académie, and could the author have perhaps been able to convince himself of this?" A brusque return to the initial argument: Baudelaire's entire œuvre is a curiosity that the author had thought to propose to the Académie only in jest. And Sainte-Beuve wants his colleagues to be completely convinced that this is what he thinks, too. But the high point of the gibe, which Sainte-Beuve inflicts simultaneously on Baudelaire and his colleagues, and on himself, comes immediately after, in a few words as heartfelt as a peroration in favor of a young man accused of some reckless behavior: "Certainly, M. Baudelaire loses nothing by being seen [in person], and whereas one expects to find a strange, eccentric man, one finds oneself in the presence of a courteous, respectful, exemplary candidate, a good boy, refined in speech and entirely classical in form." At this point the curtain is drawn, and the "good boy," Baudelaire, withdraws again to his folly in Kamchatka.

•

Whoever set foot in that outpost in the Far East where Sainte-Beuve situated Baudelaire, and which from the outside retained a certain frivolity and disquieting beauty, could find many surprises, of a kind that Sainte-Beuve was determined to avoid. Bringing to bear his gift of foreknowledge, Nerval could *see* it, in one of those proliferating deliria that he experienced in Doctor Blanche's clinic. One night, he felt "closed up in a kind of Oriental folly. I examined all the corners and saw that it was octagonal. A couch reigned around the walls, and it seemed to me that these were made of a thick glass, beyond which I could see the gleaming of treasures, shawls, and tapestries. A landscape illuminated by the moon appeared to me through the grille of the door, and I thought I could see the outlines of tree trunks and rocks. I had already spent time down there in another life, and I thought I could recognize the grottoes of Ellora. Gradually, a bluish light penetrated the folly and brought forth bizarre images. Then I thought that I found myself in a huge charnel-house where universal history was written in strokes of blood." Such visions were not suited to Sainte-Beuve.

The "folly" in Kamchatka was rather a city, traversed by streets that were rivulets and creases, subdivided into inlays, pierced by alleyways and courtyards, distinguished by a character that was indubitably "graceful and mysterious": Paris. No one had crossed that city so wisely and congenially, like some saturnine guardian; no one had made it breathe in his prose and poetry as Baudelaire had done.

Sainte-Beuve. Flaubert. Baudelaire: a triangle of high-tension power lines. Flaubert published *Salammbô*. Sainte-Beuve devoted three articles to it that, albeit with all due respect, demolished it. Furious, Flaubert replied. Baudelaire read *Salammbô* and Sainte-Beuve's article. He knew that *Salammbô* was an unmitigated disaster. But he still felt more on the side of Flaubert than that of the "great man," who did not know how to "study the crime in his own heart," but "believes he can study it only in the hearts of others." And so he wrote to Sainte-Beuve: "I have reread the article on *Salammbô* and the reply to it. Our excellent friend is decidedly in the right when he earnestly defends his dream. You are right to make him understand, laughing, that sometimes it is imprudent to be too earnest; but perhaps, at certain points, you laughed a bit too much." Here the razor is in the air. To say to Sainte-Beuve, the master of quiet suggestion and euphemism, that he has "laughed a bit too much," to the detriment of good manners, at a novel by Flaubert, while letting so many lesser writers off the hook in his *causeries*, was tantamount to letting him know that someone had recognized something in Sainte-Beuve's behavior that he would have done anything to conceal: malevolence, especially toward those who might be suspected of greatness.

Without a doubt, Sainte-Beuve touched the apex of his tongue-in-cheek insolence when *Salammbô* came along. She, the virgin priestess holding her little ebony lyre; she, made paler by the moon; she, of whom Flaubert said that "something of the gods enveloped her in a subtle vapor" and that "her gaze seemed to look far into the distance, beyond earthly space," was immediately defined by Sainte-Beuve, as if he had seen her since she was a child in the house of friends as, "a sentimental Elvira with one foot in the Sacré-Coeur." But Salammbô, heartsick, walked majestically into the toga party, because the brutal mercenaries had, it would seem, killed the sacred fishes of the Barca family.

The divine is recognizable by its bearing, Virgil had us understand. Flaubert wants us to remember this and he also wishes to sound a first erotic chord when he describes Salammbô's arms, adorned with diamonds, that "emerged naked from her sleeveless tunic, starred with red flowers against a black background." But here is how the disrespectful Sainte-Beuve describes the same scene: "So she goes down into the midst of the Barbarians, her gait measured and also a little awkward on account of some kind of golden chainlet she drags between her feet, followed by a retinue of beardless and effeminate priests singing in shrill voices a hymn to the goddess, and she herself deplores the loss of her sacred fishes." Nothing like that "some kind of golden chainlet" hindering her movements could detract all solemnity from the condemnation of the slaughter of the sacred fishes, which Salammbô instantly evokes by name, in vain: "Siv! Sivan! Tammouz, Eloul, Tischri, Schebar!" After decades of book reviewing, Sainte-Beuve wanted to show, with a minimum of effort, and almost without the reader's noticing it, how one could

produce the most dismal anticlimax. But Flaubert certainly noticed—
and perhaps he roared.

At the start of his three-part review of *Salammbô*, Sainte-Beuve set
himself a question that must have occurred to many others: Why had
Flaubert, after the triumph of scandal and style that was *Madame Bovary*,
not kept to the same path, the path of modern stories about everyday
life? And even the most banal of stories, since he had shown that he was
capable of dealing masterfully even with "the most hackneyed, the most
prostituted, the hurdy-gurdy's most threadbare tune" (here Baudelaire
is talking), namely adultery? Might it be that "he felt humiliated by the
fact of being too much read" (a good example of *persiflage*)?

Now, not only did Flaubert avoid going on in the direction of *Madame Bovary*, but he sought the exact opposite, calculated geometrically.
And the compass pointed to Carthage. He fled from the present world,
which is oppressive because too much is known about it, because in every detail, in every triviality, it reiterates its triviality, in order to seek
another that was totally absent, buried, whose traces were minimal and
not even held worthy of being set alongside the glories of the past, but
bloomed and faded all at once like a rare tropical flower, which can also
occur when no one is looking. Flaubert was looking for a world sealed
by absence. Carthage lent itself to his purpose. No texts of Punic civilization remained, either poetry or chronicles. Archaeological finds were
still very few. One could doubt everything, even the location of Carthage. But finally there, one would have breathed an air extraneous to
Greco-Roman civilization, in fact hostile to it. And then, within that
world, one day there, broke out an obscure and sordid war—between
the Carthaginians and their mercenaries—of which Polybius had written that "as far as we know there had been no other that had plunged so
deep into barbarism and impiety." A people wiped out and an *"inexpia-
ble"* war: this was the "new subject, strange, distant, savage, almost inaccessible," which had attracted him. And the reason was all too clear.

Flaubert ensconced himself like a sovereign in that void of the word.
He would name all, even the least of the Carthaginian *bibelots*, with inflexible consistency, like a new Adam. He would even strip the names of
their Greek versions in order to reconstruct the sound and the spelling
in languages he knew nothing about. That world was the precise opposite of Monsieur Homais's pharmacy. "I was definitely not born to write

modern things," he was to complain one day in a letter. But now, with his Carthage, the ancient world was at his complete disposal, sheer and isolated, glittering in its magnificent costume jewelry, which also included garnets "formed by the urine of lynxes." Obviously, Sainte-Beuve would not fail to mention these, and Flaubert retorted that he had found them in Theophrastus.

Perhaps in this "dream" (as Baudelaire called it) of the most laborious execution, Flaubert pushed to the unbridled parody of itself the *resurrectionist* drive that had emerged several times before him, from Chateaubriand to Michelet. And yet he did not manage to get as far from Madame Bovary as he would have wished. In fact, when they are alone, Madame Bovary and Salammbô have similar psychical gestures. Verbs in the imperfect tense, melancholy. Madame Bovary: "How sad she was on Sundays, when the hour of Vespers struck! Dully attentive, she listened to each stroke of the cracked bell. A cat on the roof, moving slowly, arched its back under the pale rays of the sun. The wind, on the main road, blew up clouds of dust. In the far distance, a dog was howling: and, at regular intervals, the bell continued its monotonous pealing that faded away in the fields." Salammbô: "Almost always she would crouch in the back of her apartment, holding her bent left leg between her hands, her mouth half open, her chin lowered, her gaze fixed . . . Finally, wearied by her thoughts, she would get up and, dragging her little sandals whose soles slapped at every step against her heels, she would roam aimlessly through the immense, silent room. The amethysts and topazes on the ceiling made spots of light tremble here and there, and Salammbô, without ceasing to walk, would turn her head a little to see them."

The modest objects that surround Emma are an excellent springboard for reverie; while around her, Salammbô sees reverie realized. A terrible encumbrance. Emma's dreams expand, driven on by long waves of images; whereas those of Salammbô clash every time against some scented furnishings or a ceiling studded with gems. In the end, Emma Bovary was to appear as "truly great," at least in the eyes of Baudelaire, who went so far as to add that "despite the author's systematic harshness," Emma managed to "take part in the dual nature of calculation and reverie that constitutes the perfect being." Whereas Salammbô was always to remain a temple puppet, unceasingly subjected to the attentions of someone who decked her out, made her up, dressed and undressed her.

It was true, as Flaubert realized with regret, that he had been unable to show anything else. He should have devoted another hundred pages only to Salammbô, "since one never sins for *too much*, but for *not enough*." Then, perhaps, he might have been able to present her as she appeared to him: "a maniac, a kind of Santa Teresa." On this point, Flaubert really felt in trouble. He knew that Salammbô had eluded his grasp ("I am not sure of her reality"), and to justify himself, he found the most disarming excuse and confided it to the least ingenuous of his correspondents, Sainte-Beuve: "Neither I, nor you, or any other, none of the Ancients and none of the Moderns can understand Oriental woman, since it is impossible to frequent her."

But what are the fragments of *Salammbô* that "will remain"? Perhaps not the ones pointed out by Sainte-Beuve in his review, which make one think a little of Chateaubriand when he abandoned himself to his number on the moon for Mme de Cambremer. Fine passages, but written by a Flaubert who had already assumed a pose and wished to test the rumble of his voice. Memorable, instead, are certain foreshortened, dazzling visions. Here Salammbô and her guide ride through the night toward Matho's camp: "Every so often a piece of half-burnt wall appeared at the side of the road. The roofs of the shacks had fallen in and, inside, there could be seen shards of pottery, scraps of clothing, utensils of all kinds and other broken, unrecognizable things. Often a man clad in rags, his face yellowish and with blazing eyes, would emerge from those ruins. But immediately he would run away or disappear down a hole. Salammbô and her guide did not stop."

The most effective point in the long letter Flaubert sent to Sainte-Beuve about *Salammbô* is not to be found among the multitude of arguments made in self-defense, but in an observation strategically placed toward the end, after an armistice seems to have been declared. Here Flaubert responds to an admonition that Sainte-Beuve would never have said outright, but knew very well how to insinuate to his respectable readers, who had supported him for years: Might it not be that a novel such as *Salammbô* could *do harm*, might it not perhaps be *dangerous*, with the disclosure of all those perversions—and above all that certain "hint of sadistic imagination"? Sainte-Beuve says no more than this, but

Flaubert understood the perfidious implication perfectly and replied in sovereign terms, which could be engraved on the threshold of all subsequent literature: "Besides, my example will find very little following. So where does the danger lie? The Lecontes de Lisle and the Baudelaires are less to be feared than the Nadauds and the Clairvilles [two mediocre writers now forgotten] in this pleasant land of France where the superficial is a good quality and where the banal, the facile, and the foolish are always applauded, adopted, adored. There is no risk of corrupting anyone when one aspires to greatness." The entire, long letter converges and erupts in this last sentence, which alone would have been enough.

Sainte-Beuve complained that Flaubert (in *Madame Bovary*) and Stendhal (in *The Charterhouse of Parma*) could find no place, among their characters, for a figure of good, genuine, and noble sentiments. In *Madame Bovary* he claimed to have found the rudiments of such a character only in little Justin, an apprentice to Monsieur Homais. But this character was all but "imperceptible." So he came to a serious conclusion: in *Madame Bovary*, "goodness is too lacking." His judgment of *Charterhouse* was even sharper and more offhand. How can you expect the imposition of good sentiments in a novel that "from start to finish (if we exclude the beginning) is no more than a lively Italian masquerade"? And at this point Sainte-Beuve could no longer restrain himself, and he vented his resentment, which had more to do with the defense of morality than literature: "On finishing this book, I need to reread a simple, compact novel of a good and generous human nature [when Sainte-Beuve refers to "good and generous human nature," it is always to elude the pointed barb of some writer who intimidates and disturbs him], where aunts are not infatuated with nephews, where coadjutors are not libertines and hypocrites as Retz might have been in youth, and far less witty; where poisonings, deceit, anonymous letters, and all baseness are not ordinary methods accepted with indifference; where, with the pretext of being simple and shunning effect, I am not hurled into incredible complications and thousands of labyrinths more frightful and more tortuous than those of ancient Crete." (A mark of Sainte-Beuve's greatness: even when he argues poorly, he allows his true feeling to emerge—in this case, fear.)

Years later, Chekhov's first critics said pretty much the same thing: Why, in his short stories and plays, do we never come across someone of good and heroic sentiments? One can almost see the weary and re-signed expression with which Chekhov, talking with Bunin, responded to these observations. Where could he find such characters around him? And his gaze ran over the vastness of the shady and delirious Russia that surrounded him.

A few more years later and those objections would crystallize in the Soviet concept of the *positive character*, so the wretchedness and shame of the times were revealed. But the premise should be shifted farther back, to the by-now-forgotten Sainte-Beuve. Obviously he had nothing in common with the inquisitorial *animus* of the Soviets, yet he was the first to be alarmed by a certain sectarianism and bias in art (in Stendhal and Flaubert, and in Balzac and Baudelaire). But Sainte-Beuve formulated his thesis more shrewdly, as if art had to offer a statistically reliable im-age of the surroundings: "The truth, moreover, if one seeks nothing else, is not entirely and necessarily on the side of evil, on the side of hu-man stupidity and perversion. In these provincial lives, where people encounter much harassment, persecution, vain ambitions and pinpricks, there are also fine and good souls, still innocent, better preserved than elsewhere and more decent." With these arguments, by now sociological rather than literary, Sainte-Beuve tried to gain acceptance for a concept incompatible with literature itself, which is always made with exclusions no less than inclusions and which casts upon the world an oblique, cut-ting blade of light, careless of that which it abandons to obscurity, be-cause its challenge is to make everything breathe, down to even the most desolate and unrelated detail.

Sainte-Beuve halted before no obstacle in the art of understanding, but beyond a certain threshold, his foremost concern was to conceal, or at least to render inconspicuous, what he had understood. In Restoration France, two extreme minds had been at work, both virtually ignored and diametrically opposed, to such a point that no one would have dared ut-ter their names in the same breath: Stendhal and Joseph de Maistre—no one except Sainte-Beuve, who was determined not to grant too much importance to either one or the other, because he was well aware of how

dangerous they were, because of the intransigent purity of their qualities. But he could not refrain from adding, confining his observation in
a note to make it even more marginal (but it's well known that some notes
end up being more striking than the text), the hidden trait that linked
Stendhal and Joseph de Maistre, one that nobody before then had even
remotely perceived: "I would not like to make improbable comparisons;
but I find it impossible not to note that Beyle, in a lighter order of ideas,
does no more than direct at the French people the same kind of re-
proaches as those leveled at them by Count Joseph de Maistre. Both have
this in common, that they say some very harsh things to Parisians, even
very impertinent things, and that they attach great importance to what
Paris thinks." In the very moment in which he established an unshake-
able connection between Stendhal, who claimed to be a disciple of Ca-
banis and Destutt de Tracy, both abhorred by de Maistre, and the
theologian inquisitor who cast any form of the modern spirit into hell,
Sainte-Beuve could not resist adding his drop of venom in order to para-
lyze and petrify the overheated minds he was talking about. Basically
they were two emigrants, who kept on dreaming of Paris precisely because they knew they were excluded from it. And for his part, Sainte-
Beuve far preferred the position of someone who lurked inside Paris, like
him, weaving his web in a corner of Montparnasse.

Cioran was the one who identified the strongest link between Joseph de
Maistre and Baudelaire. And this did not lie so much in a submerged
ordo (to which Baudelaire referred only by way of reaction, while he continued to sail through the murky waters of the modern), or in confessional
devotion, which he considered "lacking in warmth" even in Joseph de
Maistre, and which in Baudelaire was acute but sporadic and often
mixed with incompatible gestures. Something else united them: the
"incomparable art of provocation in which Baudelaire would distinguish himself almost as much as de Maistre." In fact, de Maistre wrote
something that sounds like the perfect epigraph for *My Heart Laid Bare*:
"That which we believe to be true needs to be said, and said boldly;
even though it may cost me dear, I would like to discover a truth made
to shake all humankind: I would tell them this to their faces, point-
blank." There were few examples of that "tell them this to their faces,

point-blank" attitude around Baudelaire. Unbridled rhetoric also served to round off the rough edges. And the *flou* of the sentiments continued to expand, without meeting serious obstacles. Only obliquely and briefly had Benjamin Constant (in *De l'esprit de conquête*) and Chateaubriand (in certain parts of *Memoirs from Beyond the Grave*) dared to venture in the direction of such audacity, an audacity that came naturally to Baudelaire no less than did a certain wavelike motion of verse. And it is precisely the alternation between those two tempos—the *prestissimo* of provocation and the *sforzato* of the Alexandrine—that separates him from all those who came before him and those who were to follow him.

Writers should never send letters to the authorities, because their letters are invariably filed, though often unread. The archive is the most constant and formidable mark of power. So, immediately after the end of the Second Empire, from the papers of the imperial family there emerged a secret note sent by Sainte-Beuve on March 31, 1856, to the cabinet of Napoleon III. This note contains these words, which should have done away with any illusion that one can rely on intellectuals, even before the word became a noun: "Until today literature has always been left to itself, and this was an ill thing for letters and society alike. Under the Restoration literature was still kept at bay by certain doctrines and some kind of principles; under the eighteen-year reign of Louis-Philippe there was nothing left to restrain it and the desire for gain, along with the need to cause a stir, has produced many works that have contributed to the dissolution of public powers and ideas." Hence, Sainte-Beuve suggested, it was now necessary for the government, through the Société des Gens de Lettres, to step in and "propose a moral direction for works of the intellect, indicating which themes should be dealt with and passing all this in the form of assistance granted to needy authors." In short, here Sainte-Beuve presented his credentials like the first of all Zhdanovs. The note was discovered a few months after Sainte-Beuve's death, immediately after the end of the Second Empire. Everybody knew that a certain festering pusillanimity lay deep in Sainte-Beuve's nature. But for some, including Baudelaire, the name Sainte-Beuve was synonymous with literature itself. On learning of the critic's death, Flaubert wrote to Du Camp, "With whom shall we talk about literature, from now on?" He wasn't wrong. But evidently literature was associated, by virtue of an ancient curse, with a certain tendency to voluntary servitude.

It was up to the "bad boy" Barbey d'Aurevilly to give Sainte-Beuve the hardest time of his life. Without mincing words, he declared that Sainte-Beuve was in the habit of saying, in conversation, the opposite of what he wrote: "In his books, M. Sainte-Beuve, whose talk is the opposite of what he writes, fawns on M. Cousin, whom he demolishes in conversation! But one day the truth will out. M. Sainte-Beuve is waiting for M. Cousin's death before going, according to his wont, to spit on his grave."

Barbey d'Aurevilly had at one and the same time the moves of the swordsman and the hooligan: as irritating as could be for Sainte-Beuve, and an attitude most apt to wound the master of caution and expediency. And it is precisely on this point that Barbey's attack reaches the acme of comic ferocity: in his view Sainte-Beuve was incurably "circumspect, a consequence of his refinement, and entangles and bedaubs his talent with reservations, allusions, prudent or perfidious insinuations, with treacherous precautions of false modesty. He invented the *perhaps*, the *it seems to me*, the *one might say*, the *if I may be permitted to observe*, and so on, abominable expressions which are the smallpox of his style . . ." Attacking a writer's style is a real low blow, from which it is difficult to recover. But Barbey d'Aurevilly was not content with this—and instantly, with the peremptory tone that Bloy would inherit, he forges ahead with flaming sword: "He does not possess the essential qualities. As a critic he does not possess dispassionateness, conscience, justice. He is always halfway between infatuation and resentment . . . He is merely a nervous system clad in literary *amour propre*, but a soul, no! What does he care about such things, for that matter! He does not believe in the soul!"

In a very weak article for *La Revue de Paris*, Anatole France had just declared that "all singularity in style must be rejected." And this in support of the argument that Stendhal *wrote badly*. Proust had not seen France for more than twenty years, more or less since he had asked him for, and obtained, the first signature for the "Manifesto of the Intellectuals" in favor of Dreyfus. But France was still the man whom Proust had transformed into Bergotte. And it was to him that he dedicated the exemplar on Japan paper of *Swann's Way*, describing him as "the first Master, the greatest, the most beloved." But by now we are in 1920. Proust had just become aware that he had witnessed an "unexpected event" in his head. He put it like this: "A stranger has ensconced himself in my brain." The stranger was death. It was necessary to redouble the haste, the speed, the incisiveness of his words. It was necessary to take advantage of the intervals in which the visitor was still absent. Those words of France, the old master of the supremely urbane tone, who had uttered a doctrine that ran contrary to literature itself, sounded to him like an invitation to say something very harsh—harsh as Proust was capable of being in those last months—and inescapable. By way of a pretext, Proust chose the preface he had agreed to write for a very sophisticated young writer friend, Paul Morand, and he wrote about something quite different: starting from France's errors, he linked them with the far more insinuating ones penned by Sainte-Beuve, whom he had felt the need to attack years before, as if in a theological prelude to the *Recherche*. Both ways of understanding literature were incompatible with his. So instead of discussing the qualities of the young writer, he decided to say something about the qualities he thought ought to be those of *every* writer.

"Since the end of the eighteenth century no one is capable of writing any more": this was one of France's apothegms in the *Revue de Paris* article. Proust does not dwell on the foolishness of the statement. All he had to do was turn it on its head. Not because the great classics were not masters of style. But because style, just when France thought it had been lost (with the first Romantics), had instead taken on a different character, not entirely implicit in preceding literature. And it was a characteristic that Proust recognized in himself. He did not wish to state this outright, but tried to describe it, outlining a theory that led up to an invitation to sabotage the intelligence. Finally, the chance had come to comment on and specify the opening sentence of *Contre Sainte-Beuve* (then unknown): "With every day that passes, I attribute less value to intelligence." And so he wrote a few stunning lines, which not only explain the remark but permeate, like a deep dye, the entire *Recherche* and

serve as the true passport to Baudelaire's Kamchatka, by now populated by the various solitary outposts of those who had followed him,
from Rimbaud to Mallarmé: "In all the arts, it seems that talent lies in
the artist's drawing nearer to the subject to be expressed. As long as
there is a gap, the task has not been carried out. A certain violinist plays
a phrase very well, but you see its effects, you applaud them, he is a virtuoso. But only when all this has disappeared, when the musical phrase
is no longer distinguishable from the artist entirely lost in it, will the
miracle come to pass. In past centuries, it seems that there has always
been a distance between the subject and the greatest minds that enter
into discourse with it. But in Flaubert, for example, the intelligence,
which perhaps was not one of the greatest, attempts to become the shud-
dering of a steamboat, the color of moss, an island in a bay. Then there
comes a moment in which the intelligence is no longer to be found (not
even Flaubert's average intelligence) and before us there is the boat that
proceeds encountering rows of trunks that set to swaying with the movement of the waves. That swaying is intelligence transformed, incorporated in matter. It even manages to penetrate the moorlands, the beech
trees, the silence and the light of the undergrowth. Might it not be perhaps that this transformation of the energy into which the thinker has
vanished and that drags things before us is the writer's first effort toward style?" If style must be this, the cautious Anatole France would
certainly not have liked it. And it certainly would have alarmed Sainte-
Beuve. But the same Sainte-Beuve, with his subtle use of two-edged
words, had talked of Baudelaire's *folie*, a place of fancies and sensuality
like every eighteenth-century *folie*, but also a sanctuary for people lost in
a desolate place where you can be either a shaman or an exile, or both.

Why would such a fierce attack on the intelligence come from
Proust, who exhibited it lavishly at every step? His was a strategic move:
it was a matter of definitively dismembering a certain image of the
psyche that had taken root in the epoch between Sainte-Beuve and
Taine. Formidable minds, both of them. But for this reason also perni-
cious, because they sought to reduce the economy of the psyche to the
task of sketching "the first outlines of a sort of literary botany." Proust's
plan—which showed through most clearly where all pretensions are
thwarted: in style—was, rather, to dethrone the sterile sovereignty of

bitter intelligence. To make himself understood, Proust seized on a faux pas by Anatole France, who had offered as an example of perfect French prose Racine's *Lettre à l'auteur des hérésies imaginaires*. "There is nothing so arid, so barren, so lacking in breath," Proust noted, before delivering the mortal blow: "It is not difficult to take a form that contains so little thought and make it diverting and pleasing." If Racine had done only this, we would soon have forgotten him. But luckily there was more to him: "In Racine there struggled a hysteric of genius, who, under the control of a superior intelligence, simulated for him in his tragedies, with a perfection that has never been matched, the ebb and flow, the manifold pitching and—that notwithstanding, completely rendered—of passion." This admirable definition can be applied, point by point, to Proust himself. In fact, that "manifold pitching" seems to refer more to his prose than to Racine's verse, except that in Proust it wasn't mere passion but an amorphous cloud of unknowing that deserved the restitution of the "supreme crown." But this would have been consigned by intelligence itself, because among all the powers it is "the only one that may confer it." A metaphysical *chassé-croisé*: this was what Proust was proposing.

In a similar way, in the distant past, the Vedic seers used images to explain the doctrine of the primacy of *manas* over *vāc*, of Mind over the Word. Now, as the circle of the times was closing, that which had been (in *manas*) absolute knowledge became an absolute non-knowledge, which every so often, due to "mere chance," managed to break down the "shaken bulkheads of memory" and to give us back something of "pure life purely preserved." There was no more, there was nothing else to expect from literature. The same holds for thought, which Proust saw as absorbed by literature. When, in a state of fury and impatience, he dashed off a few notes about *Jean-Christophe*, by Romain Rolland—an author proudly unaware of all this—Proust noted in shorthand what thinking meant to him: "Basically, all my philosophy consists, as does every philosophy, in justifying, in reconstructing that which is." And in that "justifying" there resounded, without Proust's either knowing or caring, the "aesthetic *justification of existence*" about which Nietzsche had written. Hence Proust was aiming not at a hasty demotion of the intelligence, but at a reordering of the powers that sustain us, often misunderstood (the "hysteric of genius" within Racine was no more than possession, by then reduced to psychopathology) or overestimated (the intelligence as the guarantor of an inner police). Only in the meanders of *Albertine disparue* would this be formulated in the most felicitous and relaxed fashion, without the polemical spasms of *Contre Sainte-Beuve*: "But . . . the fact that the intelligence is not the subtlest, most powerful instrument, and the one best suited to capturing the truth, is only one more reason for starting with the intelligence and not with an intuitionism of the unconscious, with a ready-made faith in forebodings. It is life that, little by little, case by case, allows us to observe that what is most important for our heart or our mind is not taught us by reason, but by other powers. And so it is the intelligence itself that, realizing their superiority, abdicates before them by virtue of reasoning, and agrees to become their collaborator and servant. It is experimental faith." Proust's only ascertainable faith—and these lines are its confession.

Proust's "experimental faith" also implied its own catechism, whose articles are encountered, always by surprise, by those who plumb the depths of the *Recherche* and, if possible, lose themselves in them. A catechism of an unbridled polytheist—or rather of someone whom the ethnologists of his day would have defined as a fetishist, a person convinced that small, countless, hard-to-find objects contain countless hours of life, as if in tiny jewel caskets. But unexpected is the moment, unpredictable the reason why articles of faith are declared. The narrator has just abandoned himself, for more than forty pages, to the dizzying circumnavigation triggered in him by the princess Guermantes's *matinée*. And until shortly before, everything was flowing toward a discovery, expressed in a brief sentence, linear and transparent as are all the theorems and corollaries that Proust always hits on, after lengthy undulations, reprises, convolutions, digressions: "Real life, life finally revealed and illuminated, and consequently the only life fully lived, is literature." After which the "manifold pitching" picks up again, because now it is a matter of ascertaining which task is necessary, and on what subject, if one yields to the "great temptation to re-create true life." And it is here that, after further swirling undulations, we come across one of those *theologoumena* that stun us with their suddenness and severity. All is now expressed in the indicative: "Every person who makes us suffer can be associated by us with a divinity of which he or she is no more than a fragmentary reflection and the last step, a divinity (Idea) the contemplation of which instantly gives us joy instead of the suffering we felt. The entire art of living lies in not making use of the persons who make us suffer if not as a step that permits access to their divine form and hence to populate joyously our life with divinities." Who is speaking here? Plotinus? Or Damascius, or Iamblichus? It is an Egyptian theurgy, of an extreme Neoplatonist, which presents itself here as the "art of living," indeed as the only possible art of living. One is enthralled by the *sprezzatura*, the tranquillity with which the judgments are pronounced, commingled with accidental observations—for example, regarding the slight smirk that always accompanied Sainte-Beuve's "spoken phrase." Now in order to call up swarms of divinities it is no longer necessary to assume a pagan or Parnassian pose before the names of a remote past. There is no longer any need for Flaubert's incondite impulse toward the sonority of the Carthaginians. One's own past is enough, the narrator has us understand. The matter is more than suitable—and sufficient. In the meantime, like hierodules and initiators, the shades of Gilbertine and Albertine file past.

Lautréamont and Laforgue appeared as agents of a celestial conspiracy. They took on the delicate mission of picking up parody from the irresponsible regime of the operetta and installing it at the point closest to the dark heart of literature. They acted in parallel, without one knowing anything of the other, sent by the same mother company. They worked in different registers. Lautréamont: stinging, livid, and cosmic. Laforgue: frivolous and desolate. But both were aiming at the same target: to demolish all obligatory respect for stories and forms ancient and modern.

They were both born in Montevideo, fourteen years apart. As boys, both crossed the ocean on sailing ships to attend school in France. Both went to the same high school in Tarbes, the place of origin of both families, and they shared a certain number of teachers. Both published at their own expense and both died before thirty. Both of them could have said, like a character from *La Vie parisienne*, "I am Uruguayan, I have gold, I come from Montevideo."

In Montevideo, in a square behind the Solís theater, on the corner between calle Reconquista and calle Juncal, a bronze caravel ("which today stands above rancid water of an extraordinary stench, collected in a basin") reunites the names of Isidore Ducasse and Jules Laforgue in the same monument to their "genio renovador."

More than Rimbaud, more than Mallarmé, more than Verlaine, Laforgue was the reader most congenial to Baudelaire's physiology. He described it, broke it down, and put it back together in fragments of notes that say things about *Les Fleurs du mal* that whole shelves of subsequent commentary do not say. He wanted to fix in words, forms, and procedures the nature of that "new thrill" noticed by Hugo, an old fox in the business. Generally speaking, Baudelaire abhorred the *new* that the world was throwing up in abundance all around him, yet the *new* was both the host and demon indispensable to what he wrote. Intolerant of every school, he could not help becoming an originator. And with him there was no getting away from the game that has people saying: *He was the first to* . . . Laforgue knew how to play that game, with infallible shrewdness: "*He was the first* to tell his tale in the moderate tones of the confessional and without assuming an inspired air"; "The first to speak of Paris like an everyday damned soul of the capital"; "The first who was not triumphant but accused himself, exposed his afflictions, his idleness, his bored uselessness in the heart of this industrious and bigoted century"; "The first to introduce to our literature the boredom of sensuality and its bizarre scenario: the sad bedroom"; "He was the first to find, after all the audacities of Romanticism, those coarse comparisons, which suddenly, in the middle of the harmony of a sentence, emerge bluntly—(and not for the whim of the moment)—palpable comparisons, too much in the foreground; in sort, American, one would say—palisander, disconcerting and refreshing junk"; "The first poet to have made a church—a sect. A single book—a single note—dogma and liturgy. Scenario—and consequent devotion of the faithful. And outside here there is no salvation"; "He was the first to break with the public— Poets addressed the public—human repertoire—he was the first to say to himself: poetry shall be something for initiates. The public think I am damned—Very well—The public will not enter here"; "The first to create immense comparisons":

Et dormir dans l'oubli comme un requin dans l'onde
—Je suis un cimitière abhorré de la lune
un vieux boudoir
Ses yeux polis sont faits de minéraux charmants.

And again: "In him the angel always looks a bailiff." Or: "He has dramatized and enhanced the bedroom" (if we think of the insipidity of the beds of the Romantics).

All of Laforgue's observations are indisputable. What he is talking about was happening *for the first time*, as if Baudelaire couldn't escape what Bazlen called "firstimeness." Yet without undermining prosody or syntax, as avant-garde movements were later to demand. Nothing was further from Baudelaire's inclinations. All his poetry seems *translated from Latin*. Or sometimes a variation on a draft by Racine.

Some characteristics of Baudelaire that Laforgue identified, and after him passed unnoticed, were: "cat, Hindu, Yankee, Episcopal alchemist." This is a line from his notes: a peremptory, stenographic definition, where the most puzzling term is *Yankee*. In what sense could Baudelaire have been a Yankee? In his writings on Poe, he sketched out a somewhat banal and stereotyped image of America, as the geometrical locus of utilitarianism and vulgar modernity, a kind of elephantine and stultifying Belgium—and to think that those were the years of Melville, Hawthorne, and Emily Dickinson . . . So what could Baudelaire's "Americanism" consist of? Well, in a certain exacerbation, in a deliberate grating, in the disproportion of images: when Baudelaire describes the body and the gestures of his beloved, "It is Americanism applied to the similes of *The Song of Songs*." And here Laforgue displays foresight: the excessiveness that is ingrained in America, and that was to make America the promised land of the cinema, would have been introduced to European literature through Baudelaire. You can understand his images better through the cinema. Through Max Ophuls, or even von Stroheim. Or any anonymous movie in black and white.

But Laforgue goes further; he probes the texture of the poem: he considers the use of the superlative in Baudelaire as a mannered distortion, which would have shocked Lamartine and which not even Hugo would have dared employ: "His use of *très* before an adjective is Yan-kee." The same epithet applies to his "irritating landscapes" or to certain comparisons where "you can see the wires and the tricks." Everything conspires to empty the verse of its oratorical poses. The ultimate goal? "To make brief, detached verses *without a theme worthy of note* (unlike the others, who wrote sonnets to recount something poetically, to support an argument, and so on), but vague and unmotivated as the wafting of a fan, ephemeral and ambiguous as a made-up face, which has the bour-geois who reads them say 'So what?'" *Americanism* could also serve this purpose, which is an extreme and radical description of what Baude-laire's poetry sought to be—and to which *Les Fleurs du mal* corresponds only in part. But still it's the hidden target of the book.

No matter what the dictionaries say, *décadence* is a German term—or at least one that takes on its full significance when transplanted into Ger-man prose. This happened when Nietzsche came across it, in 1883, on reading Paul Bourget's essay on Baudelaire. In those pages, he found the definition of what is "decadent style," lines that were to have a great future, even after Bourget had been forgotten or was spoken of only as a novelist for ladies: "Decadent style is one in which the unity of the book is broken down to make way for the independence of the page, in which the page is broken down to make way for the independence of the sen-tence, and the sentence to make way for the independence of the word." Since then, Nietzsche tended to prefer *décadence* to the German *Verfall*, to such a point that he obsessively changed the word in the supreme prose of *Ecce homo*. But already in 1886, in a letter to Fuchs, Nietzsche wrote, "This is *décadence*: a word that, among people like us, obviously, is not a condemnation, but a definition."

A singular shift: Bourget had defined the "decadent style" thinking of Baudelaire, but Nietzsche saw those words as applicable above all to Wagner. Baudelaire, in his turn, struck him as the only mind capable of understanding Wagner completely: "Has there ever been someone as modern, morbid, multifarious and contorted enough to be considered equal to the problem of Wagner? At best in France: Charles Baudelaire, for example." In the meantime, however, Bourget's words were applied directly to Wagner: "The *style* of *decadence* in Wagner: the single phrase becomes *sovereign*, subordination and order become fortuitous. Bourget p. 25" (and in fact page 25 of Bourget's *Essais de psychologie contemporaine* contains the passage about "decadent style"). But it is in the letter to Fuchs that the sense of "decadent style" in relation to Wagner is given the most extensive treatment: "The Wagnerian concept of 'endless melody' expresses in the most agreeable way the danger, the corruption of the instincts, good faith, and good conscience in the midst of such corruption. The rhythmic ambiguity, by virtue of which we no longer know, we *must* no longer know whether something is head or tail, is without any doubt a trick thanks to which one can obtain marvelous effects—*Tristan* is full of them: but as a symptom of the totality of an art it is, and remains, the mark of dissolution. The part rules over the whole, the phrase over melody, the moment over time (musical tempo too), pathos over ethos (whether you call it character or style), and finally the spirit over the 'sense.'" With those words, Nietzsche anticipated a decisive point in *The Case of Wagner*, perhaps the most important one if we wish to understand Wagner and not condemn him: "Wagner is worthy of admiration and love only by virtue of his inventiveness in small things, in his poetic elaboration of detail—we are entirely right if in this we hail him as a master of the first order, as our greatest *miniaturist* in music, who can concentrate in the smallest space an infinity of meaning and sweetness." Here Nietzsche admits that, despite the employment of the *"style of decadence* [*Verfall*]," in Wagner there existed "an infinity of meaning."

When, in 1881, Bourget published his essay on Baudelaire, the word *décadence* had yet to become a byword of the period. Bourget stressed this in a note, as soon as the essay came out in book form: "Written in 1881, before this theory of *décadence* became the watchword of a school." Certainly there was little theory in those pages, except for the paragraph on the emancipation of the parts from the whole. Only with Nietzsche would *décadence* be grafted onto a grandiose structure of thought.

Yet Bourget touched on a most delicate point. Baudelaire was a *décadent* who had no objections to being one: "He realized that he had arrived late in a culture grown old and, instead of deploring this late arrival, like La Bruyère or Musset, he was glad about it, I was about to say honored." While he recognized guilt all around, Baudelaire did not feel guilty about recognizing himself as a *décadent*. It was a fact of his sensibility. To be *"décadent* and *beginning* at the same time," this "dual descent, as from the highest and the lowest step on the scale of life" would have been Nietzsche's insignia, not his. Baudelaire was content to be *décadent*. Considering himself a *"beginning"* was too much for him, in a life dominated by anxiety. But what allows us to recognize a *décadent*? Here Bourget may serve us again. If we purify the word of all its distressing implications of biological degeneration—implications so dear in those years and in some way hovering even over Nietzsche—decadents can present themselves as oddities who cut all ties with society as a whole, refusing to serve any function within it. These refractory citizens, "unfit for private or public action," were that way precisely because they were "too skilled at solitary thinking." And so there appeared certain " 'cases' of an impressive singularity." Baudelaire chose to be one of these: "He had the courage to adopt that attitude from his youth and the boldness to keep it up right to the end." The *décadent* is similar to the fetishist: he celebrates the triumph of the idiosyncratic; he opposes the notion that his singularity might be reabsorbed into a whole. In this, Baudelaire is comparable only with Max Stirner.

The man of *décadence* described by Bourget, taking Baudelaire as an example, is above all *he who proceeds alone*. The more this new man was content with his "singularities of ideal and form," the more he risked "imprisoning himself in a solitude without visitors," an expression applicable to Baudelaire in the desolation of Brussels. But the one who put two and two together, yet again, was Nietzsche, in a fragment dated November 1887: "We must want nothing from ourselves that we cannot do. We wonder: do we wish to *go ahead*? Or do we wish *to go ahead alone*? In the first case, at most, we become a shepherd, that's to say we satisfy the needs of the flock. In the other case it's necessary to be able to do something else—to *know* how to go ahead alone, to *know* how to move in another way and in another direction. In both cases we need to know and, if we know one of the two things, we cannot want the other." A description and diagnosis of perfect lucidity. But in the following thirteen months, Nietzsche was not to take his own advice: he would go farther than he had ever gone before in this *"go[ing] ahead alone"* (*Ecce homo* was to be the culmination of this path); and at the same time he would disseminate proclamations throughout Europe, using the mail as well as writing *The Antichrist* and the *Twilight of the Idols*, like an invisible "shepherd" goading an apathetic and reluctant flock.

In a list of *"décadent* types," written early in his last year (1888), Nietzsche included "the *brutalists"* and the *refined,"* without providing any further explanation. Perhaps Baudelaire belonged to both types, he was *obliged* to belong to them, to be a blend of them. He was certainly not one of the *"Romantics,"* who appear in the list as the first of the *"décadent* types." Because these last resemble George Sand and consequently, Nietzsche insinuated with formidable intuition, they are "cold like Victor Hugo, like Balzac," cold "like all true Romantics." And this could not be said of Baudelaire, whose only concern was to camouflage his immense reserve of pathos in the urban landscape. On reading Baudelaire one understands why, for Nietzsche, the nerve center of *décadence* lay in Paris and in no other place, to the point that he adopted the French word. When moved to another metropolis, *décadence* became diminished and euphemized. One need only compare the poetic style of the 1890s in England with the poetry of Baudelaire or Mallarmé (or even Verlaine) to measure the abyss that separated them. It suffices to see how Arthur Symons translated "L'invitation au voyage" into vapid, woolly language:

> Là, tout n'est qu'ordre et beauté,
> Luxe, calme et volupté.

became:

> There all is beauty, ardency
> Passion, rest and luxury.

Here every syllable jars. Rightly, T. S. Eliot remarked, with cold scorn, "Among these words the only correct one is 'beauty.'" In the London of those years, the only one impeccably cut out for *décadence* was Oscar Wilde. And he ended up exiled in Paris.

Modern—new—décadence: three words that radiate from Baudelaire's every sentence, every breath. To separate them would be to bleed them white. Exactly as happened with *modernité*, the word *décadence* cautiously made its way, almost apologetically, into the lexicon used by writers to describe themselves. Preceding Bourget by a few years, Gautier blazed the trail: "The poet of *Les Fleurs du mal* loved what improperly became known as the decadent style, which is nothing more than art arrived at that point of extreme maturity produced by aging civilizations when their sun begins to set: an ingenious style, complicated, skillful, full of nuances and refinements, that constantly extends the confines of language, that borrows words from all technical lexicons, colors from all palettes, notes from all keyboards, that strives to render thought in all its most ineffable forms and form in its vaguest and elusive contours, that listens in order to translate the subtle confidences of neurosis, the confessions of passion that, in aging, becomes depraved and the bizarre hallucinations of the idée fixe that becomes madness. This style of decadence is the last word of the Word, which is enjoined to express everything and is pushed to absolute excess." This passage could hold for all the art that, for at least a century, would dare to define itself as *new*. But that *décadence* and *modernité* were intertwined and kin right from the beginning is shown by Gautier a little further on, when he touches on Guys, the lighthearted, frivolous, and night-loving herald of modernity. Why did Baudelaire, Gautier wonders, have such an inflexible preference for Guys? For what reason had he placed that illustrator before all rigorous and solemn artists? This was how he replied: "What [Baudelaire] loved in those drawings was the complete absence of antiquity, that is to say the classical tradition, and the profound sentiment of what we shall call *decadence*, for lack of a better word to describe our idea; but we know what Baudelaire meant by decadence." And if someone did not know this, Gautier is ready to explain, employing a device that reveals the deeply felt congeniality that led Baudelaire to dedicate *Les Fleurs du mal* to him. Baudelaire's choice of an anticlassical style had been his riskiest move on the literary chessboard. To make this understood, Gautier does not refer to some thesis on poetics regarding Raphael, the Greeks, or Homer, but quotes a passage in which Baudelaire talks about *two kinds of women*. This is the Parisian cheek that Nietzsche would have liked to possess—but never attained. All must be inferred from these words of Baudelaire: "It's as if I were introduced to two women: one is a coarse matron, repugnant in health and virtue, without style and without expression, in short, *a woman who owes everything to simple nature*; the other, one of those beauties who dominate and oppress the memory, whose deep and original allure is united with all the eloquence of her dress, sovereign in her gait, aware, and the queen of herself—with a voice that speaks like a well-tuned instrument, and looks that are laden with thought but let transpire only what she wishes. There would be no doubt about my choice, and yet there would be certain ideological sphinxes who would rebuke me for a lack of respect toward classical honor."

When the Nazi regime organized the exhibition "Degenerate Art," not only did it invent nothing, but it picked up on themes widely discussed for decades by well-educated Europeans. In 1892, one of the most widely read essayists of the end of the century, Max Nordau, had published in Berlin two hefty tomes with the title *Entartung* (Degeneration), whose primary aim was to show how the coming *fin de siècle* was threatened by the rampantly unhealthy state of the arts and culture in general, which was to be considered a symptom of *degeneration*. Hence, even more than a *fin de siècle* one should have spoken of a *fin de race*. Others would soon put two and two together.

As Nordau declared in the preface to the work, the term (*degeneration*) derived from that which, with unwavering credulity, was held to be science—particularly by Cesare Lombroso, who is accorded the merit for having "brilliantly worked out the concept of degeneration." Nordau's task was to apply it, well beyond the world of criminals and prostitutes, to culture in general. The list of suspects and proven guilty parties is extremely long and coincides to a great extent with the one that, a few decades later, was drawn up by György Lukács in his *The Destruction of Reason*. Only the arguments vary: in Nordau they were based on psychiatry; in Lukács, on the class struggle. Another similarity was their white-hot indignation. In Nordau's view, the forerunner of all degeneration was Baudelaire. All the others—such as Villiers de l'Isle-Adam and Barbey d'Aurevilly—were instantly recognized by a certain "family resemblance" to him. These were the numerous insidious and indomitable crests of the *Baudelaire wave*.

•

A short newspaper article erroneously announced Baudelaire's death fifteen months in advance. He wasn't dead, but aphasic. The news did not seem to shake Paris. But after reading the article in the bleak depths of the provinces, in Tournon, a young English teacher, Stéphane Mallarmé, spent two days in disconsolate sadness. ("Ah! what a couple of days!" he wrote to Cazalis.)

Mallarmé, hieratic even in frivolity. Baudelaire, frivolous even in solemnity. Both accustomed to the shocks of life, but Baudelaire to countless, irregular, and exasperating stab wounds. Mallarmé oppressed by a constant weight, threatened with suffocation. Both were able to capture metaphysical hints, unlike their predecessors Gautier and Hugo. But only Baudelaire had access to a region of the purest pathos, unscathed by any sentimentality, that of "Les petites vieilles" and "À une passante."

Already stricken by paralysis, and reduced to writing "in an indecipherable way," Baudelaire dictated to Gustave Millot a letter in which he indicated a final modification to a poem. In "Bien loin d'ici," one of his lightest lyrics, pervaded by and glittering with eroticism in every syllable, he wanted the final verse to be preceded by a dash, "to give it a kind of isolation, of distraction." So it had to be: "—Des fleurs se pâment dans un coin."

Requests for money (innumerable), declarations of unhappiness ever more embittered, furtive encounters, occasional insults: for Caroline this had been her son Charles for more than twenty years. And how many bad things were said about him by certain artillery officers, friends of the deceased General Aupick, who frequented her in Honfleur.

But after Charles's death there came about, within her, a sudden change of course. This happened when she received a letter of condolence from Sainte-Beuve. That letter "bowled her over," wrote Asselineau to Poulet-Malassis. With his insinuating and penetrating tone, a whispered "brief low Mass," Sainte-Beuve—the critic whose articles came out every Monday, the academician, the senator—testified beyond any doubt that her son Charles had existed. Caroline found herself thinking only of him. She was surrounded by a circle of women who chatted about the usual everyday things, in stock phrases, as Caroline herself had done for years. But now the best she could do was pretend to be listening. Writing to Asselineau, her son's old and faithful friend, she recognized this openly, with the words of an abandoned lover: "Nothing interests me except things connected with his memory. It sometimes happens, to avoid making myself intolerable to the people I see, that I must make unprecedented efforts to seem as if I'm listening to them and am interested in what they say, while deep in my heart I remain with him and am entirely his."

The successive thump of logs on the paving of the courtyards. They were unloaded from carts, house by house, as the cold weather loomed. The wood fell on the ground and announced winter. Baudelaire stayed awake. There was no need of anything else but that sound—dull, repetitive. The sun already knows that soon it will be imprisoned "in its polar inferno." It is as if auscultating labored breathing: "Trembling, I listen to every log that falls."

Anatole France, with the amiable skepticism that sometimes prevented him from understanding, recounted that one day a sailor showed Baudelaire an African fetish, "a monstrous little head carved out of a piece of wood by a poor negro. It's really ugly, said the sailor. And he threw it away in scorn. "Watch out!" said Baudelaire anxiously. "It might be the one true god!" It was his firmest declaration of faith.

SOURCES

The first number refers to the page, the second to the line of text where the quotation ends.

I. THE NATURAL OBSCURITY OF THINGS

3, 4: Letter from Ch. Baudelaire to C. Aupick dated December 16, 1847, in *Correspondance*, edited by C. Pichois, with the collaboration of J. Ziegler, Paris: Gallimard, 1973 (hereafter *Correspondance*, 1973), 1:148.

3, 23: A. Gide, "Théophile Gautier et Charles Baudelaire," in *Essais critiques*, edited by P. Masson, Paris: Gallimard, 1999, p. 1144; op. cit. in W. Benjamin, "Das Passagen-Werk," in *Gesammelte Schriften*, with the collaboration of Th. W. Adorno and G. Scholem, edited by R. Tiedemann and H. Schweppenhäuser, Frankfurt a. M.: Suhrkamp, vol. 5, tome 1, 1982, p. 328.

4, 3: M. Barrès, *La Folie de Charles Baudelaire*, Paris: Les Écrivains Réunis, 1926, p. 20.

4, 6: Ch. Baudelaire, "À une heure du matin," in *Le Spleen de Paris*, in *Œuvres complètes*, edited by C. Pichois, Paris: Gallimard, 1975, 1:287.

4, 7: J. Rivière, "Baudelaire," in *Études (1909–1924)*, edited by A. Rivière, Paris: Gallimard, new edition, 1999, p. 460.

4, 30: Ch. Baudelaire, "Le Voyage," verse 144, in *Les Fleurs du mal*, in Pichois, ed., *Œuvres complètes*, 1:134.

4, 32–5, 5: Ch. Baudelaire, *Salon de 1859*, ibid., 1976, 2:661.

5, 20: Ch. Baudelaire, "Théophile Gautier [I]," ibid., 2:124.

6, 10: Letter from D. Diderot to S. Volland, dated September 6, 1774, in *Œuvres*, vol. 5, *Correspondance*, edited by L. Versini, Paris: Robert Laffont, 1997 (hereafter *Correspondence*, 1997), p. 1255.

6, 16: D. Diderot, *Salon de 1767*, in *Salons*, vol. 3, 1963, edited by J. Seznec and J. Adhémar, Oxford: Clarendon Press, p. 206.

6, 21: D. Diderot, *Salon de 1765*, in *Salons*, vol. 2, 1960, p. 57.

6, 29: Letter from Ch. Baudelaire to Champfleury in the second half of May 1845, in Pichois, ed., *Correspondance*, 1:123.

6, 32: Champfleury, in "Le Corsaire-Satan," May 27, 1845; op. cit. in C. Pichois, "Notes et variantes," in Pichois, ed., *Œuvres complètes*, 2:1265.

6, 34: Ch. Baudelaire, "'Prométhée delivré' par L. Ménard," in Pichois, ed., *Œuvres complètes*, 2:11.

7, 2: Letter from Ch. Baudelaire to H. Hostein, dated November 8, 1854, in Pichois, ed., *Correspondance*, 1:299.

7, 5: Letter from D. Diderot to S. Volland, dated October 28, 1760, in *Œuvres, Correspondance*, 1:287.

7, 14: Ch. Baudelaire, *Salon de 1846*, in Pichois, ed., *Œuvres complètes*, 2:475.

8, 5: Ibid., p. 459.

8, 17: Ch. Baudelaire, *Le Peintre de la vie moderne*, in Pichois, ed., *Œuvres complètes*, 2:686.

8, 30: Stendhal, "Rome, Naples et Florence," in *Voyages en Italie*, edited by V. Del Litto, Paris: Gallimard, 1973, pp. 310–11.

9, 16: Th. Gautier, Introduction, in *L'Artiste*, 27 vol. 3 (December 1856–January-February-March 1857): 4.

9, 19: Ch. Baudelaire, *Salon de 1859*, 2:624.

9, 21: Ch. Baudelaire, *Notes diverses sur "L'Art philosophique,"* in Pichois, ed., *Œuvres complètes*, 2:607.

9, 25: Ch. Baudelaire, *Le Peintre de la vie moderne*, 2:722.

9, 33–10, 2: Ibid., 2:723.

10, 6: Ch. Baudelaire, *Mon cœur mis à nu*, in *Journaux intimes*, in Pichois, ed., *Œuvres complètes*, 1:701.

10, 19: Ch. Baudelaire, *Salon de 1859*, 2:642.

10, 21: Ibid., 2:644.

10, 25–11, 1: Ibid., 2:644–45.

11, 24: Ibid., 2:645.

11, 26: Ibid.

11, 31: Ibid.

11, 34: Ibid., 2:620.

11, 36–12, 1: Letter from Ch. Baudelaire to A. Toussenel, dated January 21, 1856, in Pichois, ed., *Correspondance*, 1:336.

12, 21: Ch. Baudelaire, *Réflexions sur quelques-uns de mes contemporains: Victor Hugo*, in Pichois, ed., *Œuvres complètes*, 2:132.

12, 27: Ibid., 2:133.

12, 31: Ch. Baudelaire, "Le Poème du hachisch," in *Les Paradis artificiels*, in Pichois, ed., *Œuvres complètes*, 1:430.

13, 3: Ch. Baudelaire, "Richard Wagner et 'Tannhäuser' à Paris," in Pichois, ed., *Œuvres complètes*, 2:784.

13, 10: Ch. Baudelaire, *Exposition universelle, 1855, Beaux-arts*, in Pichois, ed., *Œuvres complètes*, 2:580.

13, 11: F. Hölderlin, "Anmerkungen zum Oedipus," in *Sämtliche Werke*, edited by F. Beissner, Frankfurt a. M.: Insel, 1961, p. 1184.

13, 15: S. Mallarmé, *Divagations*, in *Œuvres complètes*, edited by B. Marchal, Paris: Gallimard, 2003, 2:86.

13, 37–14, 1: Ch. Baudelaire, *Fusées*, in *Journaux intimes*, 1:661.

14, 8: Ch. Baudelaire, *Exposition universelle, 1855*, 2:578.

14, 28: F. Nietzsche, "Nachgelassene Fragmente 1884–1885," in *Sämtliche Werke: Kritische Studienausgabe*, edited by G. Colli and M. Montinari, Berlin-München: dtv-de Gruyter, reviewed 2nd ed., 1988, 11:428, fragment 34[21].

15, 1: Ch. Baudelaire, *Exposition universelle, 1855*, 2:578.

15, 11: Ibid., 2:577.

15, 30: J. W. Goethe, *Maximen und Reflexionen*, in *Gedenkausgabe der Werke, Briefe und Gespräche*, vol. 9, edited by E. Beutler, Zürich-Stuttgart: Artemis, 1949, p. 571.

16, 12: Ch. Baudelaire, "Le Poème du hachisch," 1:401.

16, 15: Ch. Baudelaire, *Fusées*, 1:658.

16, 20: Ch. Baudelaire, "Le Poème du hachisch," 1:401.

16, 21: Ch. Baudelaire, *Edgar Poe, sa vie et ses œuvres*, in Pichois, ed., *Œuvres complètes*, 2:318.

16, 22: Ch. Baudelaire, "Le Poème du hachisch," 1:430.

16, 23: Vauvenargues, *Réflexions et maximes*, in *Œuvres morales*, vol. 3, Paris: Plon, 1874, p. 90, n. 367.

16, 26: Ch. Baudelaire, "L'Invitation au voyage," in *Le Spleen de Paris*, 1:303.

16, 29: Ch. Baudelaire, "Le Poème du hachisch," 1:430–31.

17, 2: Ch. Baudelaire, *Fusées*, 1:664, 667; "Le Poème du hachisch," 1:432.

17, 5: Ibid.

17, 6: Ibid.

17, 11: Letter from Ch. Baudelaire to C. Aupick, dated December 31, 1853, in Pichois, ed., *Correspondance*, 1:245.

17, 12: Letter from Ch. Baudelaire to F. Desnoyers, in late 1853–early 1854, ibid., 1:248.

17, 21: Ibid.

17, 26: Ibid.

17, 34: Ibid.

18, 9: Ibid.

18, 25: G. Benn, *Briefe an F. W. Oelze, 1932–1945*, Wiesbaden-München: Limes, 1977, pp. 92–93.

18, 26: Ch. Baudelaire, "Correspondances," verse 1, in *Les Fleurs du mal*, 1:11.

18, 31: Ch. Baudelaire, *Le Peintre de la vie moderne*, 2:715.

18, 32: Ibid.

18, 37: Th. W. Adorno, *Versuch über Wagner*, Berlin-Frankfurt a. M.: Suhrkamp, 1952, p. 180.

19, 8: W. Benjamin, "Das Passagen-Werk," 5:570–71.

19, 11: Ibid., 5:571.

19, 13: Ch. Baudelaire, "Correspondances," verse 3, 1:11.

19, 18: Letter from Ch. Baudelaire to A. Toussenel, dated January 21, 1856, in Pichois, ed., *Correspondance*, 1:335.

19, 20: Ibid.

19, 30: Letter from Ch. Baudelaire to A. Poulet-Malassis, dated May 14, 1857, ibid., 1:399.

19, 32: Ibid.

20, 7: Ch. Baudelaire, "À une passante," verse 8, in *Les Fleurs du mal*, 1:92.

20, 12: E. M. Cioran, *Solitude et destin*, French translation by A. Paruit, Paris: Gallimard, 2004, p. 391.

20, 19: M. Barrès, *La Folie de Charles Baudelaire*, p. 62.

20, 21: J. Renard, *Journal*, edited by L. Guichard and G. Sigaux, Paris: Gallimard, 1965, p. 1.

20, 33: J. Gracq, *En lisant en écrivant*, in *Œuvres complètes*, edited by B. Boie, Paris: Gallimard, with the collaboration of C. Dourguin, vol. 2, 1995, 2:664.

21, 12: J. Renard, *Journal*, p. 112.

21, 13: Ch. Baudelaire, "La Destruction," verse 14, in *Les Fleurs du mal*, 1:111.

21, 16: Ibid., verses 2–3.

21, 19: Ch. Baudelaire, "Au Lecteur," verses 23–24, in *Les Fleurs du mal*, 1:5.

21, 26: J. Renard, *Journal*, p. 112.

21, 29: F.-R. de Chateaubriand, *René*, in *Œuvres romanesques et voyages*, edited by M. Regard, Paris: Gallimard, 1969, 1:127.

21, 31: Ch. Baudelaire, "Le Poème du hachisch," 1:431; *Fusées*, 1:658; *Théophile Gautier [I]*, 2:118; *Exposition universelle, 1855*, 2:580.

21, 36: M. Proust, *Contre Sainte-Beuve*, edited by P. Clarac, with the collaboration of Y. Sandre, Paris: Gallimard, 1971, p. 260.

22, 4: Ibid., p. 252.

22, 5: Ibid., p. 259.

22, 6: Ibid.

22, 13: Ibid.

22, 30: Ch. Baudelaire, *Le Peintre de la vie moderne*, 2:696.

23, 1: Ch. Baudelaire, *Edgar Poe, sa vie et ses œuvres*, 2:316.

23, 4: Ch. Baudelaire, *Théophile Gautier [I]*, 2:122.

23, 9: Ch. Baudelaire, *Salon de 1846*, 2:429.

23, 10: Ch. Baudelaire, "Un mangeur d'opium," in *Les Paradis artificiels*, 1:497.

23, 11: Ch. Baudelaire, *Fusées*, 1:661.

23, 12: Ch. Baudelaire, "Au Lecteur," verse 22, 1:5.

23, 14: Ch. Baudelaire, "Spleen ('Quand le ciel bas et lourd . . .')," verses 11–12, in *Les Fleurs du mal*, 1:75.

23, 15: E. Dickinson, *Poems*, vol. 1, edited by Th. H. Johnson, Cambridge, Mass.: The Belknap Press of Harvard University Press, 1955, p. 199, n. 280.

23, 18: Ch. Baudelaire, "Un mangeur d'opium," 1:498.

23, 34: Ch. Baudelaire, *Le Peintre de la vie moderne*, 2:700.

24, 3: Ibid., 2:704.

24, 3: Ch. Baudelaire, *Salon de 1846*, 2:422.

24, 7: Ch. Baudelaire, *Théophile Gautier [I]*, 2:117.

24, 9: Ch. Baudelaire, *Fusées*, 1:650.

24, 30: Letter from G. Flaubert to E. Chevalier, prior to January 1, 1831, in *Correspondance*, edited by J. Bruneau, Paris: Gallimard, 1973, 1:4.

25, 5: Letter from Ch. Baudelaire to A. Baudelaire, dated February 1, 1832, in Pichois, ed. *Correspondance*, 1:3–4.

25, 16: Ibid., 1:4.

25, 21: Ibid.

25, 22: Ibid.

25, 23: Ibid.

25, 30: Ibid.

25, 34: Letter from Ch. Baudelaire to C. Aupick, dated February 6, 1834, ibid., 1:23–24.

26, 14: Letter from Ch. Baudelaire to C. Aupick, dated March 3, 1844, in ibid., 1:105.

26, 15: Ibid., 1:106.

26, 20: Molière, *Les Précieuses ridicules*, scene iv.

27, 12: Ch. Baudelaire, "'Prométhée delivré' par L. Ménard," 2:11.

27, 14: Letter from G. Flaubert to L. Colet, dated June 27, 1852, in Bruneau, ed., *Correspondance*, 1980, 2:119.

27, 24: Ch. Baudelaire, "Choix de maximes consolantes sur l'amour," in Pichois, ed., *Œuvres complètes*, 1:549.

27, 27: Ibid.

27, 30: Mme de Staël, *De l'Allemagne*, vol. 1, edited by S. Balayé, Paris: Garnier-Flammarion, 1968, p. 100.

27, 35: Letter from Ch. Baudelaire to J. Soulary, dated February 23, 1860, in Pichois, ed., *Correspondance*, 1:679.

28, 3: Letter from Ch. Baudelaire to A. Baudelaire, dated August 23, 1839, ibid., 1:78.

28, 4: Letter from C. Aupick to Ch. Asselineau, dated 1868, in E. Crépet, *Charles Baudelaire*, Paris: Léon Vanier, 1906, p. 255.

28, 8: Letter from Ch. Baudelaire to C. Aupick, dated August 3, 1838, in Pichois, ed., *Correspondance*, 1:61.

28, 9: Ibid.

28, 15: Ch.-A. Sainte-Beuve, *Volupté*, Paris: Charpentier, 10th ed. reviewed and corrected, 1881, p. 389.

28, 20: Ch. Baudelaire, "[À Sainte-Beuve]," verse 51, in Pichois, ed., *Œuvres complètes*, 1:207.

28, 22: Ibid., verse 49.

28, 24: M. Fumaroli, *Rhétorique de la décadence: l'"À rebours" de Joris-Karl Huysmans*, in *Exercices de lecture*, Paris: Gallimard, 2006, p. 721.

28, 32: Ch.-A. Sainte-Beuve, *Volupté*, p. 1.

28, 37–29, 3: Ibid.

29, 9: Ibid.

29, 20: Ibid., p. 2.

29, 24: Ibid.

29, 32: Letter from Ch. Baudelaire to Ch.-A. Sainte-Beuve, from late 1844–early 1845, in Pichois, ed., *Correspondance*, 1:116.

30, 8: Ibid., 1:116–18.

30, 12: Ibid., 1:116.

30, 18: Ch. Baudelaire, *Edgar Allan Poe, sa vie et ses ouvrages*, 2:257.

30, 21: Ibid.

30, 26: Ch. Baudelaire, "[À Sainte-Beuve]," verse 32, 1:207.

31, 8: C. Pichois, J.-P. Avice, *Dictionnaire Baudelaire*, Tusson: Du Lérot, 2002, p. 360.

31, 11: Th. de Banville, *Mes souvenirs*, Paris: Charpentier, 1882, p. 79.

31, 20: Ch. Asselineau, *Charles Baudelaire: Sa vie et son œuvre*, in *Baudelaire et Asselineau*, edited by J. Crépet and C. Pichois, Paris: Nizet, 1953, p. 67.

31, 22: Th. Gautier, "Le Club des Hachichins," in *Revue des Deux Mondes* n.s., 16 no. 13 (January–February 1846): 520.

32, 2: R. de Beauvoir, *Les Mystères de l'île Saint-Louis. Chroniques de l'hôtel Pimodan*, vol. 1, Paris: Calmann-Lévy, 1877, p. 8.

32, 15: Th. Gautier, "Le Club des Hachichins," p. 522.

32, 18: Ibid.

33, 8: Ch. Baudelaire, "Le Poème du hachisch," p. 421.

33, 23: Ibid., p. 422.

33, 29: Ibid.

33, 31: Ibid., p. 421.

34, 4: Letter from Ch. Baudelaire to N. Ancelle, dated June 30, 1845, in Pichois, ed., *Correspondance*, 1:124.

34, 5: Ibid.

34, 6: Ibid., 1:125.

34, 8: Ibid.

34, 27: Ph. Berthelot, "Louis Ménard," in *Baudelaire devant ses contemporains*, edited by W. T. Bandy and C. Pichois, Monaco: Éditions du Rocher, 1957, p. 74.

34, 35: Th. Gautier, "Charles Baudelaire," in *Portraits littéraires*, Paris: Aubry, 1943, p. 191.

35, 2: Ibid., p. 192.

35, 6: Letter from C. Aupick to Ch. Asselineau, dated 1868, in Crépet, *Charles Baudelaire*, pp. 254–55.

35, 17: Letter from Ch. Baudelaire to Champfleury, dated March 15, 1853, in Pichois, ed., *Correspondance*, 1:209.

35, 22: Letter from Ch. Baudelaire to Champfleury, dated March 4, 1863, ibid., 2:292.

35, 23: Letter from Ch. Baudelaire to Champfleury, dated March 6, 1863, ibid., 2:293.

35, 26: Ibid.

36, 10: M. Du Camp, *Souvenirs littéraires*, Paris: Hachette, 1962, p. 205.

36, 13: Ibid.

36, 16: Ibid., p. 204.

36, 21: Ch. Baudelaire, *Fusées*, 1:660.

37, 6: E. Marsan, *Les Cannes de M. Paul Bourget et Le Bon Choix de Philinte*, Paris: Le Divan, 1924, p. 210.

37, 12: Ibid., p. 216.

38, 11: Ch. Baudelaire, *Edgar Poe, sa vie et ses œuvres*, in Pichois, ed., *Œuvres complètes*, 2:306.

39, 16: Nadar, *Quand j'étais photographe*, Paris: Flammarion, n.d., p. 309.

39, 24: Letter from H. de Balzac to *La Presse*, dated August 17, 1839, in *La Presse*, August 18, 1839.

39, 32: A. Cassagne, *La Théorie de l'art pour l'art en France*, Lucien: Dorbon, Paris, 1959, p. 29.

39, 36: Ch. Baudelaire, "Je n'ai pas pour maîtresse une lionne illustre," verse 8, in Pichois, *Œuvres complètes*, 1:203.

40, 3: C. Pichois and J.-P. Avice, *Dictionnaire Baudelaire*, p. 381.

40, 11: Ch. Baudelaire, dedication in *Les Fleurs du mal*, 1:3.

40, 17: Ch. Baudelaire, *L'Œuvre et la vie d'Eugène Delacroix*, in Pichois, ed., *Œuvres complètes*, 2:765.

40, 20: Ch. Baudelaire, "Enivrez-vous," in *Le Spleen de Paris*, 1:337.

40, 26: Ibid.

40, 26: Ibid.

40, 30: Ibid.

41, 1: Letter from Ch. Baudelaire to G. Flaubert, dated June 26, 1860, in Pichois, ed., *Correspondance*, 2:54.

41, 4: Ibid.

41, 12: Letter from Ch. Baudelaire to C. Aupick, dated September 11, 1856, ibid., 1:356.

41, 13: Ibid.

41, 17: Ibid.

41, 29: Letter from G. Courbet to Champfleury, dated January 1855, in *L'Intermédiaire des chercheurs et curieux*, 58, no. 85 (first semester 1922): col. 19.

43, 3: Letter from J. Buisson to E. Crépet, dated February 1882, in C. Pichois, *Baudelaire: Études et témoignages*, Neuchâtel: La Baconnière, 1967, p. 41.

43, 11: Letter from Ch. Baudelaire to C. Aupick, dated December 31, 1853, in Pichois, ed., *Correspondance*, 1:244.

43, 14: Letter from Ch. Baudelaire to C. Aupick, dated March 9, 1858, ibid., 1:489.

43, 14: Letter from Ch. Baudelaire to C. Aupick, dated May 24, 1862, ibid., 2:246.

43, 27: Letter from Ch. Baudelaire to C. Aupick, dated May 21, 1861, ibid., 2:164.

44, 6: Ibid., 2:163.

44, 12: Letter from Ch. Baudelaire to C. Aupick, dated May 31, 1862, ibid., 2:248.

44, 24: Letter from Ch. Baudelaire to C. Aupick, dated June 6, 1862, ibid., 2:250.

44, 34: M. Du Camp, *Souvenirs littéraires*, p. 199.

45, 4: Ibid.

45, 8: Ibid.

45, 15: Letter from Ch. Baudelaire to C. Aupick, dated March 26, 1853, in Pichois, ed., *Correspondance*, 1:210.

45, 16: Ibid.

45, 17: Ibid.

45, 23: Letter from Ch. Baudelaire to C. Aupick, dated December 26, 1853, ibid., 1:242.

45, 25: Ibid.

45, 26: Ibid.

45, 28: Letter from Ch. Baudelaire to C. Aupick, dated March 26, 1853, ibid., 1:216.

45, 33: Letter from Ch. Baudelaire to C. Aupick, dated December 26, 1853, ibid., 1:242.

46, 10: A. Thibaudet, *Intérieurs*, Paris: Plon, 1924, p. 18.

46, 33: Ch. Baudelaire, "Le Cadre," verses 3–4, in "Un fantôme," in *Les Fleurs du mal*, 1:39.

47, 8: Ch. Baudelaire, "Le Cygne," verse 7, in *Les Fleurs du mal*, 1:85.

47, 12: Ibid., verse 5.

47, 12: Ibid., verse 6.

47, 17: Ibid., verses 41–44, p. 87.

47, 30: Ibid., verse 1, p. 85.

47, 35: Ibid., verse 38, p. 86.

47, 36: Ibid., verse 37.

48, 17: Th. Gautier, "Le Nouveau Paris," in A. Dumas et al., *Paris et les Parisiens au dix-neuvième siècle: Mœurs, arts et monuments*, Paris: Morizot, 1856, pp. 50–51; op. cit. in K. Stierle, *Der Mythos von Paris*, München-Wien: Hanser, 1993, p. 948.

48, 29: A. Delvau, *Les Dessous de Paris*, Paris: Poulet-Malassis et de Broise, 1860, pp. 258–60.

49, 10: G. de Nerval, *La Bohême galante*, in *Œuvres complètes*, edited by J. Guillaume and C. Pichois, Paris: Gallimard, 1993, 3:237.

49, 15: Ibid., 3:236.

49, 21: Ibid., 3:237.

49, 24: Ibid.

49, 30: Ibid., 3:238.

50, 3: H. de Balzac, *La Cousine Bette*, in *La Comédie Humaine*, vol. 6, edited by M. Bouteron, Paris: Gallimard, 1950, p. 178.

50, 11: Ibid.

50, 14: Ibid., p. 179.

50, 19: Ch. Baudelaire, "Le Cygne," verse 35, 1:86.

50, 24: Ibid., verse 20.

50, 24: Ibid., verse 22.

50, 32: J. de Gaulle, "Le Louvre," in A. Audiganne et al., *Paris dans sa splendeur: Monuments, vues, scènes historiques, descriptions et histoire*, vol. 1, Paris: Charpentier, 1861, p. 1.

50, 34: Ch. Baudelaire, "Le Cygne," verse 19, 1:86.

51, 11: Ibid., verse 45, p. 87.

51, 13: Ibid., verse 51.

51, 13: Ibid., verse 52.

51, 17: Ibid.

51, 22: Vergil, *Aeneid*, III:302.

51, 24: Ch. Baudelaire, *Théophile Gautier [I]*, 2:125.

51, 25: Ch. Baudelaire, "L'Esprit et le style de M. Villemain," in Pichois, ed., *Œuvres complètes*, 2:194.

51, 26: Ibid., 2:195.

51, 27: Letter from Ch. Baudelaire to A. de Calonne, dated December 3, 1860, in Pichois, ed., *Correspondance*, 2:108.

51, 33: F.-R. de Chateaubriand, "Génie du christianisme," in *Essai sur les révolutions—Génie du christianisme*, edited by M. Regard, Paris: Gallimard, 1978, p. 599.

52, 4: Ibid., p. 595.

52, 9: Ch. Baudelaire, "Le Cygne," verse 9, 1:86.

52, 11: Ibid., verse 22.

52, 12: Ibid., verse 41, p. 87.

52, 13: Ibid., verse 43.

52, 14: Ibid., verse 46.

52, 15: Ibid.

52, 15: Ibid., verse 48.

52, 16: Ibid., verse 51.

52, 16: Ibid., verse 52.

52, 16: Ibid.

52, 24: Ibid., verse 43.

52, 24: Ibid., verse 44.

53, 1: Letter from Ch. Baudelaire to C. Aupick, dated March 26, 1853, in Pichois, ed., *Correspondance*, 1:213.

53, 5: C. Pichois and J. Ziegler, *Baudelaire*, Paris: Julliard, 1987, p. 324.

53, 6: Ibid.

53, 7: Ibid.

53, 9: Ibid.

53, 10: Ibid.

53, 11: Ibid.

53, 13: Ibid.

53, 20: Ibid.

53, 26: Ibid., p. 325.

53, 29: Letter from Ch. Baudelaire to A. Sabatier, dated May 1853, in Pichois, ed., *Correspondance*, 1:224.

54, 1: R. W. Griswold, *Memoir of the Author*, introduction to E. A. Poe, *The Works of the Late Edgar Allan Poe*, vol. 3, New York: Redfield, 1850; op. cit. in C. Pichois, "Notes et variantes," in Baudelaire, *Correspondance*, 1:828.

54, 3: Ch. Baudelaire, "L'Aube spirituelle," verse 3, in *Les Fleurs du mal*, 1:46.

54, 4: J. de Maistre, *Les Soirées de Saint-Pétersbourg*, Paris: Librairie Grecque, Latine et Française, 1821, 2:280.

54, 5: Ibid.

54, 6: Ibid., p. 283.

54, 9: Ibid., pp. 253–54.

54, 14: Ibid., p. 255.

54, 21: Ch. Baudelaire, "Réversibilité," verse 1, in *Les Fleurs du mal*, 1:44.

54, 23: Ibid., verses 1–3.

54, 25: Ibid., verse 24, p. 45.

54, 36: J. de Maistre, *Les Soirées de Saint-Pétersbourg*, 2:281–82.

55, 2: Ch. Baudelaire, "À celle qui est trop gaie," verse 32, in *Les Épaves*, in Pichois, ed., *Œuvres complètes*, 1:157.

55, 3: Ibid., verse 36.

55, 7: Ibid., p. 157, note.

55, 8: Ibid.

55, 31: J. Gautier, *Le Collier des jours: Le second rang du collier: souvenirs littéraires*, Paris: F. Juven, n.d., pp. 182–83.

56, 6: Letter from Ch. Baudelaire to A. Sabatier, dated February 7, 1854, in Pichois, ed., *Correspondance*, 1:266.

56, 12: Letter from Ch. Baudelaire to C. Aupick, dated July 27, 1857, ibid., 1:418.

56, 17: E. and J. de Goncourt, *Journal*, edited by R. Ricatte, Paris: Robert Laffont, 1989, 1:1066.

56, 26: Letter from Ch. Baudelaire to A. Sabatier, dated August 18, 1857, in Pichois, ed., *Correspondance*, 1:421.

56, 29: Ibid., p. 422.

56, 30: Ibid., p. 423.

56, 35: Ibid.

57, 1: J. Brodsky, *On Grief and Reason*, New York: Farrar, Straus and Giroux, 1995, p. 84.

57, 4: Ibid., p. 88.

57, 13: Letter from Ch. Baudelaire to A. Sabatier, dated August 18, 1857, in Pichois, ed., *Correspondance*, p. 1:422.

57, 14: Ibid.

57, 19: Ibid.

58, 2: Ibid.

58, 6: Ibid.

58, 8: Ibid.

58, 16: Ch. Baudelaire, "À celle qui est trop gaie," 1:156.

58, 20: Ibid., verse 24, 1:157.

58, 35: Ch. Baudelaire, "Que diras-tu ce soir . . . ," verse 7, in *Les Fleurs du mal*, 1:43.

59, 9: J. Prévost, *Baudelaire*, Paris: Mercure de France, 1964, p. 186.

59, 16: Ch. Baudelaire, "Confession," verses 29–32, in *Les Fleurs du mal*, 1:46.

59, 23: Ibid., verses 39–40.

60, 9: Letter from A. Sabatier to Ch. Baudelaire, dated September [?]13, 1857, in *Lettres à Charles Baudelaire*, edited by C. Pichois, with the collaboration of V. Pichois, Neuchâtel: La Baconnière, 1973, p. 323.

60, 14: Ibid.

60, 16: Letter from Ch. Baudelaire to A. Sabatier, dated August 31, 1857, in Pichois, ed., *Correspondance*, 1:425.

60, 18: Ibid.

60, 21: Ibid., 1:426.

60, 22: Letter from Ch. Baudelaire to A. Sabatier, dated May 9, 1853, ibid., 1:225.

60, 30: Ch. Baudelaire, "Un mangeur d'opium," 1:499.

60, 33: Ibid.

61, 1: Ibid.

61, 4: Letter from Ch. Baudelaire to A. Poulet-Malassis, dated April 23, 1860, in Pichois, ed., *Correspondance*, 2:30.

61, 6: Ch. Baudelaire, "Un mangeur d'opium," 1:499.

61, 18: Ch. Baudelaire, "La Beauté," verse 6, in *Les Fleurs du mal*, 1:21.

61, 19: Ibid., verse 9.

61, 20: Ibid., verse 10.

61, 27: Ch. Baudelaire, "L'Amour du mensonge," verse 20, in *Les Fleurs du mal*, 1:99.

61, 33: Ibid., verses 1–4, p. 98.

62, 1: Ibid., verse 2.

62, 5: C. Pichois, "Notes et variantes," in Pichois, ed., *Œuvres complètes*, 1:1034.

62, 8: Ch. Baudelaire, "L'Amour du mensonge," verse 10, 1:99.

62, 8: Ibid.

62, 12: Ch. Baudelaire, "La Beauté," verse 6, 1:21.

62, 13: Ch. Baudelaire, "L'Amour du mensonge," verse 11, 1:99.

62, 17: Ibid., verse 19.

62, 19: Ibid., verse 22.

62, 22: F. Nietzsche, "Nachgelassene Fragmente 1887–1889," in *Sämtliche Werke*, 13:500, fragment 16[40].

63, 2: Ch. Baudelaire, *Fusées*, 1:664.

63, 5: Letter from Ch. Baudelaire to C. Aupick, dated February 19, 1858, in Pichois, ed., *Correspondance*, 1:451.

63, 7: Ibid.

63, 10: Ch. Baudelaire, "Un mangeur d'opium," 1:490.

63, 10: Ibid.

63, 11: Ibid.

63, 13: Ibid.

63, 22: Ch. Baudelaire, "Le Poème du hachisch," 1:433.

63, 24: Ibid., pp. 433–34.

63, 28: Ibid., p. 434.

63, 28: Ibid.

63, 35: J. Ziegler and C. Pichois, note in *Carnet*, in Pichois, ed., *Œuvres complètes*, 1:1515–16.

64, 4: J. Ziegler, "Répertoire des personnes et des lieux cités dans le 'Carnet,'" ibid., 1:1568.

64, 5: Ch. Baudelaire, *Mon cœur mis à nu*, 1:707.

64, 8: Ibid.

64, 15: Letter from Ch. Baudelaire to C. Aupick, dated July 9, 1857, in Pichois, ed., *Correspondance*, 1:410.

64, 20: Ibid.

64, 25: Ibid., pp. 410–11.

64, 29: Letter from Ch. Baudelaire to C. Aupick, dated June 3, 1857, ibid., 1:403.

64, 30: Ibid.

64, 32: Ibid.

65, 3: Ibid.

65, 4: Ibid.

65, 7: Ibid.

65, 25: Letter from Ch. Baudelaire to C. Aupick, dated May 6, 1861, ibid., 2:153.

65, 34: Letter from Ch. Baudelaire to C. Aupick, dated August 10, 1862, ibid., 2:254.

66, 1: Letter from Ch. Baudelaire to A. Poulet-Malassis, dated November 3, 1858, ibid., 1:521.

66, 2: Ibid.

66, 8: Letter from Ch. Baudelaire to C. Aupick, dated December 13, 1862, ibid., 2:273.

66, 16: Letter from Ch. Baudelaire to A. Poulet-Malassis, dated February 16, 1859, ibid., 1:551.

66, 31: Letter from Ch. Baudelaire to Ch. Asselineau, dated February 20, 1859, ibid., 1:552.

66, 33: Ibid., 1:553.

66, 34: Letter from Ch. Baudelaire to C. Aupick, dated May 6, 1861, ibid., 2:151.

66, 35: Letter from Ch. Baudelaire to C. Aupick, dated February–March 1861, ibid., 2:141.

67, 1: Ibid.

67, 2: Letter from Ch. Baudelaire to A. de Calonne, dated February 24, 1859, ibid., 1:556.

67, 19: Letter from Ch. Baudelaire to N. Ancelle, dated February 12, 1865, ibid., 2:460.

67, 28: Letter from Ch. Baudelaire to C. Aupick, dated August 10, 1862, ibid., 2:254.

67, 29: Letter from Ch. Baudelaire to C. Aupick, dated January 3, 1863, ibid., 2:285.

67, 32: Ibid.

68, 2: Letter from Ch. Baudelaire to A. Poulet-Malassis, dated February 4, 1859, ibid., 1:546.

68, 4: Ibid.

68, 9: Letter from Ch. Baudelaire to A. Poulet-Malassis, dated April 29, 1859, ibid., 1:568.

68, 14: Ch. Baudelaire, "Au Lecteur," verse 37, 1:6.

68, 17: W. Jesse, *The Life of Beau Brummell*, vol. 2, London: The Navarre Society, new edition, 1927, p. 212.

68, 21: Letter from Ch. Baudelaire to H. Lejosne, dated November 16, 1865, in Pichois, ed., *Correspondance*, 2:546.

68, 22: Letter from Ch. Baudelaire to Ch.-A. Sainte-Beuve, dated January 15–February 5, 1866, ibid., 2:585.

68, 28: Ibid., 2:584.

69, 1: Ch. Baudelaire, *Pauvre Belgique!*, in Pichois, ed., *Œuvres complètes*, 2:952.

69, 6: Ibid.

69, 7: Ibid.

69, 10: Ibid., 2:951.

69, 14: Letter from Ch. Baudelaire to C. Aupick, dated June 6, 1862, in Pichois, ed., *Correspondance*, 2:249.

69, 17: Letter from Ch. Baudelaire to N. Ancelle, dated February 18, 1866, ibid., 2:611.

69, 23: Ibid.

69, 33: E. M. Cioran, *Cahiers, 1957–1972*, Paris: Gallimard, 1997, p. 684.

II. INGRES THE MONOMANIAC

73, 5: Ch. Baudelaire, *Exposition universelle, 1855*, 2:588.

73, 12: Th. Silvestre, *Histoire des artistes vivants français et étrangers*, Paris: E. Blanchard, [1856], p. 33.

73, 22: S. Mallarmé, "Las de l'amer repos . . . ," verse 15, in *Poésies*, in Marchal, ed., *Œuvres complètes*, 1:12.

74, 10: R. de La Sizeranne, "L'œil et la main de M. Ingres," in *Revue des Deux Mondes*, 81, 3 (May–June 1911): 417.

74, 14: Ibid.

74, 23: P. Valéry, *Degas Danse Dessin*, in *Œuvres*, vol. 2, edited by J. Hytier, Paris: Gallimard, 1960, pp. 1188–89.

74, 32: Letter from Ch. Baudelaire to N. Ancelle, dated February 12, 1865, in Pichois, ed., *Correspondance*, 2:459.

75, 2: Ibid.

75, 7: Th. Thoré, *Salon de 1846*, in *Salons 1844, 1845, 1846, 1847, 1848*, Paris: Jules Renouard, 1870, p. 207.

75, 23: Ibid., p. 240.

76, 11: W. Bürger, preface, ibid., p. vi.

76, 21: Th. Thoré, *Salon de 1846*, p. 241.

76, 36: Ibid., p. 245.

77, 3: J.-A.-D. Ingres, *Notes et pensées*, in H. Delaborde, *Ingres. Sa vie, ses travaux, sa doctrine*, Paris: Henri Plon, 1870, p. 107.

78, 6: Th. Silvestre, *Histoire des artistes vivants français et étrangers*, pp. 3–4.

78, 18: Ibid., pp. 12–13.

78, 26: Ibid., p. 12.

78, 28: Ibid.

78, 37: Ibid.

79, 6: Ch. Blanc, *Ingres: Sa vie et ses ouvrages*, Paris: Jules Renouard, 1870, p. 118.

79, 15: Ch.-A. Sainte-Beuve, *Causeries du Lundi*, vol. 11, Paris: Garnier Frères, n.d., p. 495.

79, 20: J.-A.-D. Ingres, *Notes et pensées*, p. 123.

80, 10: H. Lapauze, *Le Roman d'amour de M. Ingres*, Paris: Pierre Lafitte & Cie, 1910, p. 21.

80, 26: Ch. Blanc, *Ingres*, pp. 160–61.

80, 36: Ibid., p. 161.

81, 2: E.-E. Amaury-Duval, *L'Atelier d'Ingres*, edited by D. Ternois, Paris: Arthena, 1993, p. 113.

81, 5: Ibid.

81, 7: Ibid., p. 99.

81, 13: J.-A.-D. Ingres, *Notes et pensées*, p. 119.

81, 15: Ibid.

81, 17: Ibid., p. 123.

81, 21: Letter from J.-A.-D. Ingres to Ch. Marcotte, dated December 21, 1834, in N. Schlenoff, *Ingres: Ses sources littéraires*, Paris: Presses Universitaires de France, 1956, p. 226.

81, 25: Stendhal, "Rome, Naples et Florence," p. 519.

81, 30: Ch. Blanc, *Ingres*, p. 10.

81, 35: J. W. Goethe, "Epirrhema," verse 6, in *Gedenkausgabe der Werke, Briefe und Gespräche*, vol. 9, p. 519.

82, 2: E.-E. Amaury-Duval, *L'Atelier d'Ingres*, p. 171.

82, 7: Ibid.

82, 20: Th. Silvestre, *Histoire des artistes vivants français et étrangers*, p. 33.

83, 8: Ch. Blanc, *Ingres*, pp. 25–26.

83, 14: Ch. Baudelaire, *Exposition universelle, 1855*, 2:589.

83, 27: Ch. Blanc, *Ingres*, p. 173, note.

83, 29: Ch. Baudelaire, *Exposition universelle, 1855*, 2:589.

84, 7: Ch. Baudelaire, *Le Musée classique du Bazar Bonne-Nouvelle*, in Pichois, ed., *Œuvres complètes*, 2:413.

84, 14: Ibid.

84, 16: Ch. Baudelaire, *Le Peintre de la vie moderne*, 2:713.

84, 18: Ibid.

84, 22: Ibid., p. 714.

85, 5: Ibid., p. 713.

85, 7: Ibid., p. 714.

86, 9: Ch. Blanc, *Ingres*, p. 25.

87, 24: Letter from J.-A.-D. Ingres to the Forestier family, dated December 25, 1806, in H. Lapauze, *Le Roman d'amour de M. Ingres*, pp. 73–74.

87, 35: *Iliad*, I, verses 500–501.

88, 7: [Comte de Caylus], *Tableaux tirés de l' "Iliade," de l' "Odyssée" d'Homere et de l' "Eneide" de Virgile; avec des observations générales sur le Costume*, Paris: Tilliard, 1757, p. 18.

89, 17: Ch. Baudelaire, *Le Musée classique du Bazar Bonne-Nouvelle*, 2:412.

89, 20: H. Lapauze, *Ingres. Sa vie et son œuvre (1780–1867)*, Paris: Georges Petit, 1911, p. 100.

89, 31: Louis Gillet, "Visites aux musées de province, III, Aix en Provence," in *Revue des Deux Mondes*, 102, no. 11 (September 15, 1932): 340.

89, 35: Ibid., pp. 340–41.

90, 15: *Iliad*, I, verse 499.

90, 31: H. Lapauze, *Ingres: Sa vie et son œuvre*, p. 100.

91, 11: Pindar, *Isthmian Odes*, VIII, 69–70; Aeschylus, *Prometheus bound*, 762.

91, 25: H. Lapauze, *Ingres: Sa vie et son œuvre*, p. 99.

92, 21: Ch. Blanc, *Ingres*, pp. 26–27.

93, 22: Ibid., p. 27.

94, 37: H. Lapauze, *Ingres: Sa vie et son œuvre*, p. 519.

95, 7: J.-É. Blanche, "Quelques mots sur Ingres," in *Revue de Paris*, 18, no. 3 (May–June 1911): p. 416.

95, 8: Ibid.

95, 11: Ibid.

95, 15: Ibid.

95, 25: H. Lapauze, *Ingres: Sa vie et son œuvre*, p. 100.

97, 3: P.-J. Toulet, *Notes d'art*, Paris: Le Divan, 1924, p. 9.

97, 6: Ibid., p. 13.

98, 27: Th. Silvestre, *Histoire des artistes vivants français et étrangers*, p. 19.

98, 35: S. Aubenas, "Eugène Delacroix et la photographie," in *L'Art du nu au XIXᵉ siècle*, Paris: Hazan/Bibliothèque Nationale de France, 1997, p. 92.

101, 13: Ch. Baudelaire, *Exposition universelle, 1855*, 2:584.

101, 14: Ibid.

102, 1: Ibid.

102, 3: Ibid., 2:583.

102, 5: Ibid., 2:584.

102, 7: Ibid., 2:585.

102, 7: Ibid.

102, 9: Ibid.

102, 18: Ibid.

102, 22: Ibid.

102, 25: Ibid.

102, 28: Ibid., 2:576.

102, 32: Ibid., 2:585.

103, 1: Ibid., 2:586.

103, 7: Ibid.

103, 20: Ibid., 2:577.

103, 25: Ibid.

103, 27: Ibid., 2:578.

103, 33: Ibid., 2:577.

103, 36: Ibid., 2:580.

104, 1: Ibid., 2:582.

104, 14: J.-A.-D. Ingres, *Notes et pensées*, p. 123.

104, 26: R. de La Sizeranne, "L'œil et la main de M. Ingres," p. 420.

105, 4: Ch. Baudelaire, *Salon de 1846*, 2:459.

105, 16: Ibid., 2:460.

105, 26: P. Valéry, *Cahiers*, edited by J. Robinson, Paris: Gallimard, 2:950.

105, 30: J.-A.-D. Ingres, *Notes et pensées*, p. 123.

106, 19: W. Bürger, *Salon de 1866*, in *Salons, 1861 à 1868*, vol. 2, Paris: Jules Renouard, 1870, pp. 311–12.

106, 35: Ch. Baudelaire, *Exposition universelle, 1855*, 2:587–88.

106, 35: Letter from É. Manet to H. Fantin-Latour, dated 1865, in É. Moreau-Nélaton, *Manet raconté par lui-même*, vol. 1, Paris: Henri Laurens, 1926, p. 72.

107, 13: Ch. Blanc, *Ingres*, p. 8.

107, 15: Ibid.

107, 17: Ibid.

108, 16: J.-A.-D. Ingres, *Notes et pensées*, p. 107.

108, 17: Ch. Blanc, *Ingres*, p. 45.

109, 7: E.-E. Amaury-Duval, *L'Atelier d'Ingres*, p. 336.

109, 18: Ibid.

109, 27: Ibid., p. 117.

110, 3: H. Lapauze, *Ingres. Sa vie et son œuvre*, p. 506.

110, 11: Ibid., p. 554.

III. VISITING MADAME AZUR

113, 2: Ch. Baudelaire, *Exposition universelle, 1855*, 2:590.

113, 8: Ibid., p. 597.

113, 10: Ch. Baudelaire, *Quelques caricaturistes étrangers*, in Pichois, ed., *Œuvres complètes*, 2:573.

113, 14: Ch. Baudelaire, *Salon de 1846*, 2:436.

113, 20: Ch. Baudelaire, *Salon de 1859*, 2:619.

114, 5: Ch. Baudelaire, *L'Œuvre et la vie d'Eugène Delacroix*, p. 756.

114, 10: Ibid., p. 759.

114, 16: E. Marsan, *Les Cannes de M. Paul Bourget et Le Bon Choix de Philinte*, p. 215.

114, 18: Ibid.

114, 19: Ch. Baudelaire, *L'Œuvre et la vie d'Eugène Delacroix*, p. 760.

114, 21: Ibid., p. 761.

114, 22: Ibid.

114, 28: Ibid., p. 758.

114, 30: Ibid., p. 763.

114, 32: Ch. Baudelaire, "La servante au grand cœur . . . ," verse 1, in *Les Fleurs du mal*, 1:100.

115, 4: Ch. Baudelaire, *Salon de 1846*, 2:440.

115, 4: Pichois, ed., *Lettres à Charles Baudelaire*, p. 112.

115, 7: Ibid.

115, 16: Ch. Baudelaire, *L'Œuvre et la vie d'Eugène Delacroix*, p. 766.

116, 2: E. Delacroix, *Journal, vol. I: 1822–1852*, Paris: Plon, reviewed and extended edition, 1950, p. 108.

116, 4: Ibid.

116, 8: Ibid., p. 58.

116, 11: R. Escholier, *Delacroix et les femmes*, Paris: Fayard, 1963, p. 68.

117, 10: O. Redon, *À soi-même*, Paris: José Corti, 1961, p. 180.

117, 11: Ibid.

117, 22: Ibid.

117, 23: Ch. Baudelaire, "Richard Wagner et 'Tannhäuser' à Paris," 2:800.

117, 30: Ibid.

118, 7: Ch. Baudelaire, *Pauvre Belgique!*, 2:874.

118, 10: Ch. Baudelaire, "Richard Wagner et 'Tannhäuser' à Paris," 2:807.

118, 13: Ibid., p. 792.

118, 20: Ibid., p. 801.

118, 26: E. Delacroix, *Journal, vol. 3: 1857–1863*, 317.

118, 31: Letter from E. Delacroix to G. Sand, dated January 12, 1861, in R. Escholier, *Delacroix*, Paris: H. Floury, 1927, 2:163.

119, 5: O. Redon, *À soi-même*, p. 181.

119, 6: Ibid.

119, 11: Ch. Baudelaire, *L'Œuvre et la vie d'Eugène Delacroix*, p. 757.

119, 17: Ibid.

119, 24: R. Escholier, *Delacroix et les femmes*, p. 72.

120, 12: E. Delacroix, *Journal, vol. 2: 1853–1856*, 116–18.

120, 14: Ch. Baudelaire, "Les Phares," verse 29, in *Les Fleurs du mal*, 1:14.

120, 18: Ch. Baudelaire, *Exposition universelle, 1855*, 2:595.

121, 13: Ch. Baudelaire, *Exposition Martinet*, in Pichois, ed., *Œuvres complètes*, 2:734.

121, 15: Ch. Baudelaire, *Salon de 1859*, 2:622.

121, 18: Ch. Baudelaire, *Exposition Martinet*, 2:733–34.

121, 25: Ch. Baudelaire, *L'Œuvre et la vie d'Eugène Delacroix*, p. 760.

121, 28: Ch. Baudelaire, *Salon de 1846*, 2:444.

122, 12: Ch. Baudelaire, *Exposition Martinet*, 2:734.

122, 12: Ch. Baudelaire, *Exposition universelle, 1855*, 2:593.

122, 13: Ch. Baudelaire, *Exposition Martinet*, 2:734.

123, 1: G. Sand, *Impressions et souvenirs*, 3rd ed., Paris: Michel Lévy Frères, 1873, p. 80.

123, 5: Ibid., p. 81.

123, 7: Ibid.

123, 8: Ibid.

123, 10: Ibid.

123, 14: Letter from G. Sand to J. Lamber, dated April 20, 1868, in *Nouvelles lettres d'un voyageur*, Paris: Calmann-Lévy, 1877, p. 78.

123, 20: Letter from E. Delacroix to J.-B. Pierret, dated June 7, 1842, in *Lettres de Eugène Delacroix, 1815–1863*, edited by Ph. Burty, Paris: Quantin, 1878, p. 161.

124, 12: E. Delacroix, *Journal*, 1:288.

124, 19: C. Jaubert, *Souvenirs de Madame C. Jaubert*, Paris: Hetzel, n.d. [1881], p. 44.

124, 26: Ibid.

125, 2: E. Delacroix, *Journal*, 1:283.

125, 12: Ibid., p. 284.

125, 30: Ibid., pp. 283–84.

125, 34: Ch. Baudelaire, *Edgar Poe, sa vie et ses ouvrages*, p. 283.

125, 36: Ibid.

126, 5: Ch. Baudelaire, *L'Œuvre et la vie d'Eugène Delacroix*, 2:761.

IV. THE DREAM OF THE BROTHEL-MUSEUM

129, 10: Letter from Ch. Baudelaire to Ch. Asselineau, dated March 13, 1856, in Pichois, ed., *Correspondance*, 1:338.

130, 13: Ch. Baudelaire, "'La Double Vie' par Charles Asselineau," in Pichois, ed., *Œuvres complètes*, 2:90.

130, 16: C. Pichois and J.-P. Avice, *Dictionnaire Baudelaire*, p. 88.

130, 27: Ch. Baudelaire, *Mon cœur mis à nu*, 1:680.

131, 18: Ch. Baudelaire, "'La Double Vie' par Charles Asselineau," 2:90.

131, 19: Ibid.

131, 22: Letter from Ch. Baudelaire to Ch. Asselineau, dated March 13, 1856, in Pichois, ed., *Correspondance*, 1:338.

131, 23: Ibid.

131, 24: Ch. Baudelaire, "Correspondances," verse 2, p. 11.

131, 26: Ibid., verse 4.

131, 31: Ch. Baudelaire, *Salon de 1859*, 2:645.

131, 34: Ch. Baudelaire, "L'Irrémédiable," verse 40, in *Les Fleurs du mal*, 1:80.

134, 21: Letter from Ch. Baudelaire to Ch. Asselineau, dated March 13, 1856, in Pichois, ed., *Correspondance*, 1:338–41.

134, 29: Ibid., 1:338.

135, 4: Ch. Baudelaire, "'La Double Vie' par Charles Asselineau," 2:89.

135, 6: Letter from Ch. Baudelaire to Ch. Asselineau, dated March 13, 1856, in Pichois, ed., *Correspondance*, 1:338.

135, 8: Letter from Ch. Baudelaire to C. Aupick, dated December 4, 1854, ibid., 1:300–301.

135, 13: Letter from Ch. Baudelaire to Ch. Asselineau, dated March 13, 1856, ibid., 1:339.

135, 15: Ibid., 1:338.

136, 1: Letter from Ch. Baudelaire to C. Aupick, dated October 4, 1855, ibid., 1:324.

136, 6: Ibid.

136, 11: Letter from Ch. Baudelaire to Ch. Asselineau, dated March 13, 1856, ibid., 1:338.

136, 25: Ibid.

136, 32: Ibid.

136, 33: Ibid.

137, 4: Ibid.

137, 6: Ibid.

137, 10: Ibid.

137, 28: Ibid., 1:339.

137, 31: Ibid.

138, 1: Ibid.

138, 2: Ibid.

138, 11: Ibid.

138, 13: Ibid.

138, 38: Festus, *De verborum significatione*, p. 218, 16 (Lindsay).

139, 7: Letter from Ch. Baudelaire to Ch. Asselineau, dated March 13, 1856, in Pichois, ed., *Correspondance*, 1:339.

139, 11: Ibid.

139, 18: Ibid.

139, 23: Ch. Baudelaire, "Le 'Confiteor' de l'artiste," in *Le Spleen de Paris*, 1:278.

139, 25: Ch. Baudelaire, *Salon de 1859*, 2:653.

139, 31: Letter from Ch. Baudelaire to Ch. Asselineau, dated March 13, 1856, in Pichois, ed., *Correspondance*, 1:338.

140, 16: Ibid., 1:340.

140, 23: Ibid., 1:338.

140, 24: Ibid.

140, 28: Ibid.

141, 9: Ibid.

141, 18: Ibid., 1:340.

141, 33: Letter from Ch. Baudelaire to N. Ancelle, dated February 18, 1866, ibid., 2:611.

141, 35: Ibid.

142, 9: Ch. Baudelaire, *Salon de 1859*, 2:653.

142, 12: Ibid.

142, 13: Ch. Baudelaire, "'Les Martyrs ridicules' par Léon Cladel," in Pichois, ed., *Œuvres complètes*, 2:182.

142, 19: Ibid., 2:182–83.

142, 33: Letter from Ch. Baudelaire to Ch. Asselineau, dated March 13, 1856, in Pichois, ed., *Correspondance*, 1:339.

143, 5: Ibid.

143, 11: Ch. Baudelaire, *Salon de 1846*, 2:443.

143, 18: Ibid.

143, 20: Ibid.

143, 35: Ibid.

144, 10: Letter from Ch. Baudelaire to Ch. Asselineau, dated March 13, 1856, in Pichois, ed., *Correspondance*, 1:339.

144, 13: Ibid., 1:340.

144, 18: Ibid.

144, 22: Ibid.

144, 24: Ibid.

144, 32: Ch. Baudelaire, "'Les Martyrs ridicules' par Léon Cladel," 2:183.

145, 3: Letter from Ch. Baudelaire to Ch. Asselineau, dated March 13, 1856, in Pichois, ed., *Correspondance*, 1:340.

145, 6: Ibid., 1:339.

145, 7: Ibid., 1:340.

145, 10: Ibid.

145, 33: W. Benjamin, "Das Paris des Second Empire bei Baudelaire," in *Gesammelte Schriften*, 1:538.

145, 35: Ibid., p. 539.

146, 2: Ibid.

146, 8: Letter from Ch. Baudelaire to Ch. Asselineau, dated March 13, 1856, in Pichois, ed., *Correspondance*, 1:339.

146, 19: Ibid.

146, 20: P. Valéry, *Degas Danse Dessin*, 2:1187.

146, 23: Ibid.

146, 26: Ch. Baudelaire, *Mon cœur mis à nu*, 1:701.

146, 27: Letter from Ch. Baudelaire to Ch. Asselineau, dated March 13, 1856, in Pichois, ed., *Correspondance*, 1:339.

146, 29: Ibid.

147, 2: Ibid., 1:338.

147, 5: Ibid., 1:339.

147, 10: Ibid.

147, 19: Ibid.

147, 33: Ibid., 1:340.

148, 10: Ibid.

148, 27: Ibid.

148, 30: Ibid.

149, 5: Ibid.

149, 9: Ibid.

149, 19: Ibid., 1:338.

149, 28: Ch. Baudelaire, "'La Double Vie' par Charles Asselineau," 2:90.

150, 4: Letter from Ch. Baudelaire to Ch. Asselineau, dated March 13, 1856, in Pichois, ed., *Correspondance*, 1:339.

150, 7: Ibid., 1:340.

150, 17: Ibid.

150, 31: Ibid.

150, 33: Ch. Baudelaire, "Le Crépuscule du matin," verse 26, in *Les Fleurs du mal*, 1:104.

150, 37: Letter from Ch. Baudelaire to Ch. Asselineau, dated March 13, 1856, in Pichois, ed., *Correspondance*, 1:340.

151, 4: Ibid.

152, 1: Ibid.

152, 4: Ibid.

152, 13: Ibid.

152, 14: Ibid.

152, 17: Ibid.

153, 11: Ibid.

154, 5: Ibid., 1:341.

154, 6: Ibid.

154, 10: Ibid., 1:340.

V. THE FLEETING SENSE OF MODERNITY

157, 11: Ch. Baudelaire, *Le Peintre de la vie moderne*, 2:683.

157, 25: Ibid., 2:684.

158, 2: Ibid., 2:683.

159, 8: K. Clark, "Ingres: Peintre de la vie moderne," in *Apollo* 93 (1971): 357.

159, 18: Letter from Ch. Baudelaire to É. Manet, dated May 11, 1865, in Pichois, ed., *Correspondance*, 2:497.

159, 21: Letter from Ch. Baudelaire to F. Desnoyers in late 1853–early 1854, ibid., 1:248.

159, 32: Letter from Ch. Baudelaire to A. Poulet-Malassis, dated December 13, 1859, ibid., 1:627.

160, 10: F.-R. de Chateaubriand, *Mémoires d'outre-tombe*, vol. 4, edited by J.-C. Berchet, Paris: Garnier, 1998, p. 221.

160, 21: Th. Gautier, *Les Beaux-Arts en Europe, 1855*, vol. 1, Paris: Michel Lévy Frères, 1857, p. 19.

160, 23: Ch. Baudelaire, *Le Peintre de la vie moderne*, 2:694.

160, 28: A. Stevens, *De la modernité dans l'art: Lettre à M. Jean Rousseau*, Bruxelles: Office de Publicité, et chez J. Rozez et fils, 1868; in C. Pichois, *Œuvres complètes*, 2:1420.

161, 18: W. Benjamin, "Das Passagen-Werk," 5:286.

161, 34: Ch. Baudelaire, *Théophile Gautier [I]*, 2:123.

161, 36: Ch. Baudelaire, *Le Peintre de la vie moderne*, 2:694.

162, 3: Ibid.

162, 10: Ibid., 2:695.

162, 12: Ibid., 2:694.

162, 16: Ibid.

162, 22: Ibid., 2:696.

162, 23: Ibid.

162, 33: Th. Gautier, *Les Beaux-Arts en Europe, 1855*, 1:7.

163, 3: Ch. Baudelaire, *Le Peintre de la vie moderne*, 2:698.

163, 6: Ibid., 2:698–99.

163, 9: Ch. Baudelaire, "Comment on paie ses dettes quand on a du génie," in Pichois, ed., *Œuvres complètes*, 2:6.

163, 12: Ch. Baudelaire, *Théophile Gautier [I]*, 2:120.

163, 13: Ibid.

163, 15: Ibid.

163, 17: Ibid.

163, 19: Ibid.

163, 21: Ibid.

163, 31: Ch. Baudelaire, *Le Peintre de la vie moderne*, 2:698.

163, 34: A. Rimbaud, *Une Saison en enfer*, in *Œuvres complètes*, edited by A. Adam, Paris: Gallimard, 1972, p. 116.

164, 10: Ch. Baudelaire, *Mon cœur mis à nu*, 1:690.

164, 11: Ibid., 1:691.

164, 15: Ibid., 1:698.

164, 16: Ibid., 1:691.

164, 17: Ibid.

164, 20: Ibid.

164, 31: E. Dacier, *Gabriel de Saint-Aubin, peintre, dessinateur et graveur (1724–1780)*, Paris-Bruxelles: G. Van Oest, 1929, 1:14.

165, 2: H. Focillon, preface to *Le Dessin français dans les collections du dix-huitième siècle*, Paris: Les Beaux-Arts, 1935, pp. 2–3; op. cit. in P. Rosenberg, "Boucher and Eighteenth-Century French Drawing," in *The Drawings of François Boucher*, edited by A. Laing, New York/London: American Federation of Arts-Scala, 2003, p. 17.

166, 4: Ch. Baudelaire, *Le Peintre de la vie moderne*, 2:684.

166, 11: E. and J. de Goncourt, *Journal*, 1:345.

166, 21: Ibid., 1:345–46.

166, 23: Ch. Baudelaire, *Le Peintre de la vie moderne*, 2:683.

166, 23: Ibid., 2:720.

166, 35: E. and J. de Goncourt, *Journal*, 1:347.

168, 9: Ch. Baudelaire, *Le Peintre de la vie moderne*, 2:719–20.

168, 17: Ibid., p. 721.

170, 12: Ibid., p. 686.

170, 14: Ibid.

171, 6: Letter from E. Degas to A. Bartholomé, dated January 17, 1886, in *Lettres*, edited by M. Guérin, preface by D. Halévy, Paris: Grasset, reviewed and extended edition, 1945, p. 118.

171, 7: G. Moore, "Memories of Degas," in *The Burlington Magazine* 32, (first semester 1918): 29.

171, 34: Letter from E. Degas to H. Rouart, dated 1886, in *Lettres*, 119.

172, 3: A. Vollard, *En écoutant Cézanne, Degas, Renoir,* Paris: Bernard Grasset, 1938, p. 103.

172, 10: Ibid., p. 118.

172, 13: Ibid.

172, 15: D. Halévy, *Degas parle,* Paris: Éditions de Fallois, 1995, p. 199.

172, 15: Ibid.

173, 8: Ibid., p. 108.

173, 16: G. Moore, "Memories of Degas," p. 28.

173, 20: A. Michel, "Degas et son Modèle," in *Mercure de France,* 30, no. 131 (January–February 1919): 624.

173, 26: P. Valéry, *Degas Danse Dessin,* 2:1205.

173, 29: Ibid., 2:1204.

173, 32: Ibid., 2:1205.

173, 33: P. Valéry, *Cahiers, 1894–1914,* edited by N. Celeyrette-Pietri and R. Pickering, vol. 10: *1910–1911,* Paris: Gallimard, 2006, p. 23.

174, 3: P. Valéry, *Degas Danse Dessin,* 2:1205.

174, 9: Ibid., 2:1227.

174, 9: Ibid.

174, 10: Ibid.

174, 16: Ibid., 2:1224.

174, 20: Letter from B. Varchi to Bronzino and to the Tribolo, dated May 1539, Biblioteca Nazionale di Firenze, Magliabechiano, cod. VII, 730, f. 15–16*v*.

174, 31: P. Valéry, *Degas Danse Dessin,* 2:1237.

174, 33: Ibid., 2:1238.

174, 34: Ibid.

175, 4: Ibid., 2:1240.

175, 7: Letter from E. Rouart to P. Valéry, dated September 27, 1896, in J. Hytier, "Notes," in P. Valéry, *Œuvres,* p. 1386.

175, 15: E. Jaloux, "Valéry romancier," in *Le Divan* 14 (1922): 214.

175, 17: P. Valéry, *Degas Danse Dessin,* 2:1167.

175, 18: Ibid., 2:1168.

175, 20: Letter from P. Valéry to A. Gide, dated February 7, 1896, in A. Gide and P. Valéry, *Correspondance 1890–1942,* edited by R. Mallet, Paris: Gallimard, 1955, p. 260.

181, 4: D. Halévy, *Degas parle,* p. 201.

186, 16: *The Notebooks of Edgar Degas,* edited by Th. Reff, Oxford: Clarendon Press, 1976, 1:109.

187, 9: Ibid.

187, 12: Ibid.

188, 4: W. Sickert, "Degas," in *The Burlington Magazine* 31 (November 1917): 185.

188, 25: Letter from P. Poujaud to M. Guérin, dated July 11, 1936, in E. Degas, *Lettres,* 255.

190, 26: Ch. Baudelaire, "Lola de Valence," verse 4, in *Les Épaves*, 1:168.

190, 28: *The Notebooks of Edgar Degas*, 1:109.

190, 31: Letter from P. Poujaud to M. Guérin, dated July 11, 1936, in E. Degas, *Lettres*, p. 255.

191, 8: Ibid.

191, 22: S. Mallarmé, *Les Impressionnistes et Édouard Manet*, in Marchal, ed., *Œuvres complètes*, 2:464.

191, 26: Ibid.

191, 26: Ibid.

191, 30: Ibid.

192, 7: F. Fénéon, *Au-delà de l'impressionnisme*, edited by F. Cachin, Paris: Hermann, 1966, p. 104.

192, 21: D. Halévy, *Degas parle*, p. 116.

192, 28: Letter from B. Morisot to E. Morisot, dated May 23, 1869, in *Correspondance*, edited by D. Rouart, Paris: Quatre Chemins-Éditart, 1950, p. 31.

193, 15: D. Halévy, *Degas parle*, p. 120.

193, 17: Ibid.

193, 24: Letter from E. Degas to E. Dobigny, dated 1869, in "Some Unpublished Letters of Degas," edited by Th. Reff, in *The Art Bulletin*, 50 (1968): 91.

193, 30: L. Halévy, *La Famille Cardinal*, Paris: Calmann Lévy, 1883, p. 36.

193, 32: Ibid., p. 69.

194, 16: Ibid., p. 188.

194, 29: L. Halévy, *Carnets*, Paris: Calmann-Lévy, 1935, 2:128.

195, 9: L. Halévy, annotation dated January 1, 1882, in *Mes carnets, vol. 3: 1881–1882*, in *Revue des Deux Mondes*, 108, no. 43 (January–February 1938): 399.

195, 19: Ibid.

195, 35: F. Sévin, "Répertoire des mots de Degas," in "Degas à travers ses mots," in *Gazette des Beaux-Arts*, 117, no. 86 (July–August 1975): 45.

196, 12: L. Halévy, *Carnets*, 1:213.

196, 21: Ibid., 1:212.

197, 11: Ibid., 1:80.

197, 17: Ibid., 1:167.

197, 19: Ibid.

197, 20: Ibid.

197, 23: Ibid., 1:120.

197, 29: Ibid., 1:99.

197, 32: Ibid., 1:98.

197, 34: J.-K. Huysmans, "Degas," in *Certains*, Paris: Tresse and Stock, 1889, p. 23.

198, 2: Ibid.

198, 4: Ibid.

198, 6: Ibid., p. 24.

198, 12: F. Fénéon, *Les Impressionnistes en 1886*, in *Œuvres plus que complètes*, edited by J. U. Halperin, Genève: Droz, 1970, 1:30.

198, 21: P. Valéry, *Cahiers, 1894–1914*, 10:23.

199, 11: D. Halévy, *Degas parle*, p. 179.

199, 20: Ibid., p. 140.

199, 21: Ibid.

199, 22: Ibid.

199, 23: A. Vollard, *En écoutant Cézanne, Degas, Renoir*, p. 114.

199, 25: D. Halévy, *Degas parle*, p. 180.

199, 31: Ibid., p. 149.

199, 32: Ibid.

200, 2: Ibid., p. 150.

201, 6: A. Vollard, *En écoutant Cézanne, Degas, Renoir*, p. 121.

202, 15: D. Halévy, *Degas parle*, p. 243.

202, 20: Ibid., p. 222.

202, 27: K. Kraus, *Beim Wort genommen*, München: Kösel, 1965, p. 341.

203, 2: É. Moreau-Nélaton, *Manet raconté par lui-même*, 1:71.

203, 5: Letter from É. Manet to H. Fantin-Latour, dated 1865, ibid.

203, 6: Ibid., 1:72.

203, 11: Ibid.

203, 15: Ibid.

203, 21: Th. Duret, *Histoire d'Édouard Manet et de son œuvre*, Paris: Floury, 1902, p. 36.

203, 28: G. Moore, *Confessions d'un Jeune Anglais*, Paris: Albert Savine, 1889, p. 110.

203, 33: Letter from É. Manet to H. Fantin-Latour, dated 1865, in É. Moreau-Nélaton, *Manet raconté par lui-même*, 1:72.

203, 34: E. and J. de Goncourt, *Journal*, 2:570.

204, 13: Letter from G. T. Robinson to S. Mallarmé, dated July 19, 1876, in *Documents Stéphane Mallarmé*, edited by C. P. Barbier, Paris: Nizet, 1968, 1:65.

204, 15: A. Vollard, *En écoutant Cézanne, Degas, Renoir*, p. 283.

204, 20: Letter from S. Mallarmé to A. O'Shaughnessy, dated October 19, 1876, in *Correspondance*, edited by H. Mondor and L. J. Austin, Paris: Gallimard, 1965, 2:130.

204, 24: S. Mallarmé, *Les Impressionnistes et Édouard Manet*, 2:444.

204, 25: Ibid.

204, 27: Ibid., 2:445.

204, 28: Ibid.

204, 29: Ibid.

204, 30: Ibid.

204, 31: Ibid., 2:446.

205, 2: Ibid., 2:460.

205, 4: Ibid., 2:452.

205, 7: Ibid., 2:454.

205, 12: F. Carco, *Le Nu dans la peinture moderne*, Paris: Crès, 1924, p. 33.

205, 14: G. Duthuit, *Renoir*, Paris: Stock, 1923, p. 29.

205, 19: A. Vollard, *En écoutant Cézanne, Degas, Renoir*, p. 291.

205, 21: J. Renoir, *Pierre-Auguste Renoir, mon père*, Paris: Gallimard, 1981, p. 220.

205, 24: S. Mallarmé, *Les Impressionnistes et Édouard Manet*, 2:454.

205, 30: A. Vollard, *En écoutant Cézanne, Degas, Renoir*, p. 105.

207, 8: F. Fénéon, *Œuvres*, Paris: Gallimard, 1948, p. 60.

209, 12: S. Mallarmé, *Les Impressionnistes et Édouard Manet*, 2:468.

209, 17: Ibid., 2:463.

209, 19: Ibid., 2:461.

209, 23: Ibid., 2:462.

210, 14: P. de Saint-Victor, "Salon de 1865," in *La Presse*, May 28, 1865, p. 3.

210, 23: Th. Gautier, "Salon de 1865," in *Le Moniteur Universel*, June 24, 1865, p. 3.

210, 24: Ibid.

210, 32: W. Bürger, *Salon de 1865*, in *Salons, 1861 à 1868*, 2:221.

210, 37: D. Halévy, *Degas parle*, p. 159.

211, 13: A.-J.-B. Parent-Duchâtelet, *De la prostitution dans la ville de Paris*, Bruxelles: Hauman, Cattoir et C.ie, 1836, p. 85.

211, 33: Ibid.; P. Valéry, "Triomphe de Manet," in *Œuvres*, p. 1329.

211, 35: Letter from G. Flaubert to L. Colet, dated January 23, 1854, in Bruneau, ed., *Correspondance*, 2:514.

212, 31: Ch. Baudelaire, "À celle qui est trop gaie," 1:156.

213, 6: É. Zola, "Édouard Manet," in *Mon Salon—Manet—Écrits sur l'art*, Paris: Garnier-Flammarion, 1970, p. 95.

213, 9: S. Mallarmé, *Les Impressionnistes et Édouard Manet*, 2:453.

213, 16: S. Mallarmé, *Le Jury de peinture pour 1874 et M. Manet*, in *Œuvres complètes*, 2:412.

214, 2: E. Texier, *Tableau de Paris*, Paris: Paulin et Le Chevalier, 1852, 1:47.

214, 7: S. Mallarmé, *Le Jury de peinture pour 1874 et M. Manet*, 2:411.

214, 8: Ibid.

214, 10: Ibid., 2:412.

214, 12: Ibid.

214, 13: Ibid.

214, 16: Ibid.

214, 17: Ibid.

215, 8: Ibid., 2:411.

215, 14: Th. de Banville, "Édouard Manet," verses 1–4, in *Nous Tous*, in *Œuvres poétiques complètes*, edited by P. J. Edwards, Paris: Champion, 1997, 7:81.

215, 18: Letter from B. Morisot to E. Morisot, dated May 2, 1869, in Rouart, ed., *Correspondance*, p. 26.

217, 8: Letter from M.-J.-C. Morisot to B. Morisot, dated 1869, ibid., p. 32.

217, 27: Letter from B. Morisot to E. Morisot, ibid., p. 73.

218, 17: P. Valéry, "Triomphe de Manet," in *Œuvres*, p. 1332.

218, 17: Ibid., p. 1333.

218, 19: Ibid.

218, 21: Ibid.

218, 22: P. Valéry, "Berthe Morisot," ibid., p. 1302.

218, 27: Letter from É. Manet to H. Fantin-Latour, dated August 26, 1868, in É. Moreau-Nélaton, *Manet raconté par lui-même*, 1:102.

218, 29: Ibid., 1:103.

218, 31: Ibid.

219, 9: Letter from Léon Koëlla-Leenhoff to A. Tabarant, dated December 6, 1920, in N. Locke, *Manet and the Family Romance*, Princeton, N.J./Oxford: Princeton University Press, 2001, p. 191.

219, 10: Ibid.

220, 7: Ibid.

220, 10: Ibid.

220, 24: Letter from M.-J.-C. Morisot to B. Morisot in the summer of 1871, in A. Higonnet, *Berthe Morisot, une biographie*, Paris: Adam Biro, 1989, p. 93.

222, 4: É. Zola, "Édouard Manet," p. 362.

222, 23: Letter from B. Morisot to E. Morisot, dated March 1869, in Rouart, ed., *Correspondance*, p. 25.

222, 30: F. Fénéon, *Les Impressionnistes en 1886*, 1:29.

222, 33: H. Perruchot, *La Vie de Manet*, Paris: Hachette, 1959, p. 231.

223, 5: Letter from Ch. Baudelaire to C. Aupick, dated October 11, 1860, in Pichois, ed., *Correspondance*, 2:97.

223, 7: F. Fénéon, "Calendrier de Mars," in *La Revue indépendante*, April 1888, in Halperin, ed., *Œuvres plus que complètes*, 1:102.

223, 13: Ch. Baudelaire, "Le Monstre," verse 6, in *Les Épaves*, 1:164.

223, 13: Ibid., verse 7.

223, 15: F. Fénéon, "Calendrier de Mars," 1:102.

225, 9: J.-K. Huysmans, *L'Art moderne*, Paris: Charpentier, 1883, p. 157.

227, 3: Letter from B. Morisot to E. Morisot, dated April 30, 1883, in Rouart, ed., *Correspondance*, p. 114.

227, 4: Ibid.

227, 5: F. Sévin, "Répertoire des mots de Degas," p. 31.

228, 3: Letter from Ch. Baudelaire to Th. Thoré, dated June 20, 1864 [circa], in Pichois, ed., *Correspondance*, 2:386.

228, 23: M. Angoulvent, *Berthe Morisot*, Paris: Albert Morancé, 1933, pp. 156–57.

228, 31: S. Mallarmé, *Divagations*, 2:147.

228, 33: Ibid., 2:148.

229, 3: Letter from B. Morisot to J. Manet, dated March 1, 1895, in Rouart, ed., *Correspondance*, p. 184.

229, 4: Ibid., p. 185.

229, 13: D. Halévy, *Degas parle*, pp. 43–44.

229, 16: Ibid., p. 44.

229, 20: P. Valéry, *Cahiers*, 2:1046.

229, 28: Note by Ch. Collé dated December 1763, in *Journal et mémoires (1748–1772)*, edited by H. Bonhomme, Paris: Firmin Didot, extended edition, 1868, 2:325.

229, 29: Ibid.

229, 30: Ibid.

230, 3: M. Proust, *Du côté de chez Swann*, in *À la recherche du temps perdu*, edited by J.-Y. Tadié, Paris: Gallimard, 1987, 1:328.

230, 4: M. Proust, *Le Côté de Guermantes*, ibid., 1988, 2:342.

230, 5: Ibid., 2:505.

230, 7: Ibid.

230, 10: Ibid.

231, 7: A. Michel, "Degas et son Modèle," p. 463.

231, 10: Ibid.

231, 18: A. Vollard, *En écoutant Cézanne, Degas, Renoir*, p. 135.

232, 1: H. Loyrette, *Degas*, Paris: Fayard, 1991, p. 447.

232, 14: Ibid., p. 498.

232, 16: Ibid.

232, 18: D. Halévy, *Degas parle*, pp. 152–53.

232, 20: P. Valéry, *Degas Danse Dessin*, p. 1176.

232, 30: P.-A. Lemoisne, *Degas et son œuvre*, Paris: Plon, 1954, p. 9.

232, 33: D. Halévy, *Degas parle*, p. 197.

233, 5: Ibid., p. 189.

233, 6: Ibid.

233, 14: A. Vollard, *En écoutant Cézanne, Degas, Renoir*, p. 136.

233, 21: Ibid.

233, 23: D. Halévy, *Degas parle*, p. 192.

233, 25: Ibid.

233, 29: Ibid., p. 191.

233, 35: Ibid., pp. 192–93.

234, 5: Ibid., p. 196.

234, 9: Ibid., p. 200.

234, 11: Ibid., p. 159.

234, 12: Ibid.

234, 19: Ibid., p. 199.

234, 20: Ibid., p. 202.

234, 31: Ibid., p. 199.

VI. THE VIOLENCE OF CHILDHOOD

237, 9: C. Milosz, *Milosz's ABC's*, English translation by M. G. Levine, New York: Farrar, Straus and Giroux, 2001, p. 56.

237, 15: Letter from Ch. Baudelaire to G. Charpentier, dated June 20, 1863, in Pichois, ed., *Correspondance*, 2:307.

237, 18: Letter from A. Rimbaud to P. Demeny, dated May 15, 1871, in *Correspondance*, in Adam, ed., *Œuvres complètes*, p. 253.

237, 22: Ibid., pp. 253–54.

237, 23: Ibid., p. 254.

238, 10: J. Laforgue, "Baudelaire," in *Œuvres complètes*, edited by J.-L. Debauve, M. Dottin-Orsini, D. Grojnowski, and P.-O. Walzer, Lausanne: L'Age d'Homme, 2000, 3:165.

238, 24: A. de Musset, "Rolla," verses 1–4, in *Poésies complètes*, edited by M. Allem, Paris: Gallimard, 1957, p. 273.

238, 27: Ch. Baudelaire, "J'aime le souvenir de ces époques nues," verse 1, in *Les Fleurs du mal*, 1:11.

238, 29: Letter from A. Rimbaud to P. Demeny, dated May 15, 1871, in Adam, ed., *Correspondance*, p. 253.

238, 31: A. de Musset, "Rolla," verse 3, p. 273.

239, 6: J. Racine, *Phèdre*, act I, scene i.

239, 9: Letter from A. Rimbaud to G. Izambard, dated August 25, 1870, in Adam, ed., *Correspondance*, p. 238.

239, 16: Letter from A. Rimbaud to Th. de Banville, dated May 24, 1870, ibid., p. 236.

239, 18: Ibid., pp. 236–37.

239, 22: Ibid., p. 236.

239, 30: Ibid.

239, 35: Ibid.

239, 36: Ibid.

240, 7: A. Rimbaud, "Sensation," verses 1–4, in *Poésies*, in Adam, ed., *Œuvres complètes*, p. 6.
240, 8: Ibid., verse 5.
240, 10: Ibid., verse 6.
240, 14: Ibid., verse 7.
240, 32: A.-M. de Chénier, *Poésies*, edited by H. de Latouche, Paris: Charpentier, 1840, p. 194.
240, 33: A. Rimbaud, "Soleil et chair," verse 4, in *Poésies*, p. 6.
241, 2: Ibid., verses 10–11, p. 7.
241, 9: Ibid., verses 12–13.
241, 16: Ibid., verse 29.
241, 20: Ibid., verse 35.
241, 21: Ibid., verse 36.
241, 22: Ibid., verse 34.
241, 23: Ibid., verse 36.
241, 29: Ibid., verse 48, p. 8.
242, 5: Ibid., verse 61.
242, 8: Ibid., verse 65.
242, 8: Ibid., verse 66.
242, 10: Ibid., verse 42.
242, 10: Ibid., verse 74, p. 9.
242, 14: Ibid., verse 80.
242, 21: Ibid., verses 85–86.
242, 29: Ibid., verses 92–93.
243, 13: Ibid., verses 158–59, p. 11.
243, 27: Ibid., verse 160.
243, 29: Ibid., verse 161.
244, 3: Ibid., verses 162–64.
244, 8: Ibid., verse 73, p. 9.
244, 16: S. Solmi, *Saggio su Rimbaud*, Torino: Einaudi, 1974, p. 11.
244, 18: Ibid.
244, 21: Ibid., p. 5.
244, 22: Ibid., p. 7.
244, 26: A. Rimbaud, "Les Poètes de sept ans," in *Poésies*, p. 43.
244, 31: Ibid., verse 4.
244, 32: Ibid., verse 15, p. 44.
244, 34: Ibid., verse 26.
244, 34: Ibid., verse 31.
245, 2: Ibid., verses 31–33.
245, 8: Ibid., verse 61, p. 45.
245, 11: Ibid., verse 36, p. 44.
245, 12: Ibid., verse 38.
245, 13: Ibid., verse 37.
245, 15: Ibid., verses 40–41.
245, 16: Ibid., verse 42.
245, 18: Ibid., verse 43.
245, 26: S. Solmi, *Saggio su Rimbaud*, p. 15.

245, 28: Ibid.

246, 5: Ibid.

246, 8: Ibid.

246, 9: Ibid.

246, 12: Ibid.

246, 20: J. Rivière, *Rimbaud*, Paris: Kra, 1930, pp. 32–33.

246, 27: A. Rimbaud, "Les Pauvres à l'église," verse 36, in *Poésies*, p. 46.

246, 27: Ibid., verse 13, p. 45.

246, 28: Ibid.

246, 29: A. Rimbaud, "Les Premières communions," verse 2, in *Poésies*, p. 60.

246, 32: A. Rimbaud, "Les Chercheuses de poux," verse 8, in *Poésies*, p. 65.

246, 33: Ibid., verse 7.

247, 1: Ch. Baudelaire, "Le Voyage," verse 144, p. 134.

247, 11: A. Rimbaud, "Le Bateau ivre," verses 93–94, in *Poésies*, p. 69.

247, 12: Ibid., verse 95.

247, 16: F. Dostoevsky, *Ricordi dal sottosuolo*, Italian translation by T. Landolfi, Milano: Adelphi, 1995, p. 13.

247, 21: Ibid., p. 63.

247, 22: A. Rimbaud, *Une Saison en enfer*, p. 93.

247, 23: Ibid., p. 97.

247, 27: F. Dostoevsky, *Ricordi dal sottosuolo*, p. 18.

247, 33: A. Rimbaud, *Une Saison en enfer*, p. 94.

248, 3: Letter from A. Rimbaud to his family, dated September 28, 1885, in Adam, ed., *Correspondance*, 402.

248, 5: Ibid.

248, 8: Letter from A. Rimbaud to his family, dated November 16, 1882, ibid., p. 353.

248, 14: Letter from A. Rimbaud to his family, dated September 10, 1884, ibid., p. 391.

249, 2: Letter from A. Rimbaud to M. Bautin, dated January 30, 1881, ibid., p. 324.

249, 5: Letter from A. Rimbaud to his mother [V. Cuif], dated December 8, 1882, ibid., p. 356.

249, 8: Letter from A. Rimbaud to his family, dated April 14, 1885, ibid., p. 398.

249, 17: Ibid., p. 399.

250, 2: Letter from A. Rimbaud to Ilg, dated June 25, 1888, ibid., p. 496.

250, 9: Ibid.

250, 11: Letter from the French consul in Massaua [A. Merciniez] to the consul in Aden [É. de Gaspary], dated August 5, 1887, ibid., p. 429.

250, 13: Ibid.

250, 16: Letter from the French consul in Massaua [A. Merciniez] to the marquis Grimaldi-Régusse, ibid.

250, 18: Letter from A. Rimbaud to his family, dated August 23, 1887, ibid., p. 441.

250, 27: Letter from A. Rimbaud to his sister [I. Rimbaud], dated June 24, 1891, ibid., p. 672.

251, 1: Letter from A. Rimbaud to Ras Mekonen, dated May 30, 1891, ibid., p. 668.

251, 4: Letter from A. Rimbaud to his sister [I. Rimbaud], dated July 10, 1891, ibid., p. 681.

251, 10: Letter from A. Rimbaud to his sister [I. Rimbaud], dated June 24, 1891, ibid., p. 673.

251, 13: Letter from I. Rimbaud to her brother [A. Rimbaud], dated June 30, 1891, ibid., p. 676.

251, 18: Letter from I. Rimbaud to her mother [V. Cuif], dated October 28, 1891, ibid., p. 704.

251, 25: Ibid., p. 705.

252, 13: Letter from A. Rimbaud to his mother [V. Cuif] and his sister [I. Rimbaud], dated May 18, 1889, ibid., p. 543.

VII. KAMCHATKA

255, 3: Letter from Ch. Baudelaire to Ch. Asselineau, dated February 24, 1859, in Pichois, ed., *Correspondance*, 1:555.

256, 27: Letter from Ch. Baudelaire to Ch.-A. Sainte-Beuve, dated July 1, 1860, ibid., 2:56.

256, 12: Ibid.

257, 8: Ch.-A. Sainte-Beuve, *Nouveaux Lundis*, Paris: Michel Lévy Frères, 1863, 1:384.

257, 17: Ibid., 1:390.

257, 18: Ibid., p. 1:388.

257, 20: Ibid., p. 1:391.

257, 24: Ibid.

257, 33: Ibid.

257, 34: Ibid., 1:392.

258, 6: Ibid.

258, 12: Ibid.

258, 15: Ibid., p. 403.

258, 20: Ibid., p. 395.

258, 23: Ibid.

258, 29: Ibid., p. 391.

258, 31: Th. Gautier, "Charles Baudelaire," p. 197.

259, 5: Ch.-A. Sainte-Beuve, *Nouveaux Lundis*, 1:397.

259, 13: Ibid., 1:397–98.

259, 23: Ibid., 1:398.

259, 30: Ibid.

260, 14: Ibid.

260, 31: Ibid.

260, 35: Ibid.

261, 5: Ibid., 1:391.

261, 25: Ibid., 1:398.

261, 36: Ibid., 1:398–99.

262, 16: G. de Nerval, "Aurélia," in Guillaume and Pichois, eds., *Œuvres complètes*, cit. pp. 743–44.

262, 21: Ch.-A. Sainte-Beuve, *Nouveaux Lundis*, 1:398.

262, 29: Letter from Ch. Baudelaire to A. Poulet-Malassis, dated October 1, 1865, in Pichois, ed., *Correspondance*, 2:532.

262, 30: Ibid.

262, 31: Ibid.

263, 4: Letter from Ch. Baudelaire to Ch.-A. Sainte-Beuve, dated September 3, 1865, ibid., p. 529.

263, 17: G. Flaubert, *Salammbô*, in *Œuvres*, edited by A. Thibaudet and R. Dumesnil, Paris: Gallimard, 1951, 1:718.

263, 19: Ch.-A. Sainte-Beuve, *Nouveaux Lundis*, Paris: Calmann Lévy, 1885, 4:45.

263, 26: G. Flaubert, *Salammbô*, 1:718.

263, 32: Ch.-A. Sainte-Beuve, *Nouveaux Lundis*, 4:45–46.

263, 35: G. Flaubert, *Salammbô*, 1:718.

264, 9: Ch. Baudelaire, *"Madame Bovary" par Gustave Flaubert*, in Pichois, ed., *Œuvres complètes*, 2:80.

264, 11: Ch.-A. Sainte-Beuve, *Nouveaux Lundis*, 4:93.

264, 29: Polybius, *Histories*, I, 88.

264, 30: Ch.-A. Sainte-Beuve, *Nouveaux Lundis*, 4:35.

264, 31: Ibid., p. 34.

265, 1: Letter from G. Flaubert to J. Duplan, dated March 29, 1863, in Bruneau, ed., *Correspondance*, 1991, 3:314.

265, 4: G. Flaubert, *Salammbô*, 1:829.

265, 7: Letter from Ch. Baudelaire to Ch.-A. Sainte-Beuve, dated September 3, 1865, in Pichois, ed., *Correspondance*, 2:529.

265, 19: G. Flaubert, *Madame Bovary*, in Thibaudet and Dumesnil, eds., *Œuvres*, 1:349.

265, 27: G. Flaubert, *Salammbô*, 1:869–70.

265, 33: Ch. Baudelaire, *"Madame Bovary" par Gustave Flaubert*, 2:83.

265, 35: Ibid.

265, 36: Ibid., 2:84.

266, 6: Letter from G. Flaubert to Ch.-A. Sainte-Beuve, dated December 23–24, 1862, in Bruneau, ed., *Correspondance*, 3:284.

266, 7: Ibid., p. 277.

266, 9: Ibid.

266, 13: Ibid.

266, 14: Ch.-A. Sainte-Beuve, *Nouveaux Lundis*, 4:72.

266, 27: G. Flaubert, *Salammbô*, 1:881–82.

266, 37: Ch.-A. Sainte-Beuve, *Nouveaux Lundis*, 4:71.

267, 9: Letter from G. Flaubert to Ch.-A. Sainte-Beuve, dated December 23–24, 1862, in Bruneau, ed., *Correspondance*, 3:285.

267, 16: Ch.-A. Sainte-Beuve, *"'Madame Bovary' par Gustave Flaubert,"* in *Causeries du Lundi*, n.d., 13:362.

267, 17: Ibid.

267, 20: Ch.-A. Sainte-Beuve, *"M. de Stendhal,"* ibid., 9:335.

267, 33: Ibid.

268, 21: Ch.-A. Sainte-Beuve, *"'Madame Bovary' par Gustave Flaubert,"* 13:362.

269, 12: Ch.-A. Sainte-Beuve, *"M. de Stendhal,"* 9:314–15.

269, 26: E. M. Cioran, *"Joseph De Maistre,"* in *Exercices d'admiration*, Paris: Gallimard, 1986, p. 13.

269, 30: Ibid., p. 68.

269, 35: Ibid., p. 67.

270, 24: Note by Ch.-A. Sainte-Beuve to the cabinet of Napoleon III, dated March 31, 1856, in *Papiers secrets et correspondance du Second Empire*, edited by A. Poulet-Malassis, Paris: Auguste Ghio, 3rd ed., 1873, pp. 418–19.

270, 28: A. Cassagne, *La théorie de l'art pour l'art en France*, p. 94.

271, 1: Letter from G. Flaubert to M. Du Camp, dated October 13, 1869, in Bruneau, ed., *Correspondance*, 1998, 4:111.

271, 4: Letter from Ch. Baudelaire to Ch. Asselineau, dated February 24, 1859, in Pichois, ed., *Correspondance*, 1:554.

271, 11: J.-A. Barbey d'Aurevilly, *Les Quarante médaillons de l'Académie*, Paris: Dentu, 1864, p. 9.

271, 21: Ibid., p. 127.

271, 29: Ibid., p. 130.

271, 31: M. Proust, "Préface de 'Tendres Stocks,'" in *Contre Sainte-Beuve*, p. 607.

272, 5: Dedication by M. Proust to A. France, dated mid-November 1913, in M. Proust, *Correspondance*, vol. 13: *1913*, edited by Ph. Kolb, Paris: Plon, 1984, p. 316.

272, 6: M. Proust, "Préface de 'Tendres Stocks,'" p. 606.

272, 8: Ibid.

272, 24: Ibid., p. 612.

272, 35: M. Proust, *Contre Sainte-Beuve*, p. 211.

273, 22: M. Proust, "Préface de 'Tendres Stocks,'" p. 612.

273, 34: M. Proust, *Contre Sainte-Beuve*, p. 221.

274, 4: M. Proust, "Préface de 'Tendres Stocks,'" p. 613.

274, 6: Ibid.

274, 12: Ibid., p. 614.

274, 13: Ibid.

274, 16: M. Proust, *Contre Sainte-Beuve*, p. 216.

274, 18: Ibid.

274, 24: Ibid., p. 211.

274, 25: Ibid., p. 212.

274, 26: Ibid.

274, 32: Ibid., p. 309.

274, 34: F. Nietzsche, "Nachgelassene Fragmente 1882–1884," in *Sämtliche Werke*, 10:238, fragment 7[7].

275, 7: M. Proust, "Préface de 'Tendres Stocks,'" p. 614.

275, 14: M. Proust, *Albertine disparue*, in *À la recherche du temps perdu*, 4:7.

275, 30: M. Proust, *Le Temps retrouvé*, ibid., p. 474.

275, 31: M. Proust, "Préface de 'Tendres Stocks,'" p. 614.

275, 33: M. Proust, *Le Temps retrouvé*, 4:475.

276, 6: Ibid., 4:477.

276, 12: Ibid., 4:476.

277, 3: J.-J. Lefrère, *Isidore Ducasse*, Paris: Fayard, 1998, p. 635.

277, 4: Ibid.

277, 10: Letter from V. Hugo to Ch. Baudelaire, dated October 6, 1859, in Pichois, ed., *Lettres à Charles Baudelaire*, p. 188.

277, 11: Ch. Baudelaire, "Le Voyage," verse 144, 1:134.

277, 18: J. Laforgue, "Baudelaire," 3:161.

277, 19: Ibid.
277, 22: Ibid., p. 162.
277, 24: Ibid.
277, 29: Ibid., p. 164.
277, 32: Ibid., p. 168.
277, 36: Ibid., p. 171.
278, 4: Ibid., pp. 173–74.
278, 5: Ibid., p. 180.
278, 6: Ibid., p. 166.
278, 10: R. Bazlen, "Note senza testo," in *Scritti*, edited by R. Calasso, Milano: Adelphi, 1984, p. 230.
278, 16: J. Laforgue, "Baudelaire," 3:178.
278, 23: Ibid., 3:165.
278, 26: Ibid.
279, 2: Ibid., 3:178.
279, 2: Ibid.
279, 3: Ibid., 3:179.
279, 9: Ibid., 3:172.
279, 17: P. Bourget, *Essais de psychologie contemporaine*, Paris: Plon, definitive edition with the addition of appendices, 1901, 1:20.
279, 22: Ibid.
279, 27: Letter from F. Nietzsche to C. Fuchs [probably mid-April 1886], in *Sämtliche Briefe: Kritische Studienausgabe*, edited by G. Colli and M. Montinari, Berlin-München, Berlin-New York: dtv-de Gruyter, 1986, 7:177.
279, 28: P. Bourget, *Essais de psychologie contemporaine*, 1:20.
279, 34: F. Nietzsche, "Nachgelassene Fragmente 1887–1889," 13:404, fragment 15[6].
280, 3: F. Nietzsche, "Nachgelassene Fragmente 1882–1884," 10:646, fragment 24[6].
280, 4: P. Bourget, *Essais de psychologie contemporaine*, Paris: Lemerre, 1883, p. 25.
280, 5: Letter from F. Nietzsche to C. Fuchs [probably mid-April 1886], in *Sämtliche Briefe*, 7:177.
280, 22: F. Nietzsche, "Der Fall Wagner," in *Sämtliche Werke*, 6:28.
280, 23: F. Nietzsche, "Nachgelassene Fragmente 1882–1884," 10:646, fragment 24[6].
280, 24: F. Nietzsche, "Der Fall Wagner," p. 28.
280, 28: P. Bourget, *Essais de psychologie contemporaine* (1901), p. 19.
280, 36: Ibid.
281, 2: F. Nietzsche, *Ecce homo*, in *Sämtliche Werke*, 6:264.
281, 3: Ibid.
281, 12: P. Bourget, *Essais de psychologie contemporaine* (1901), p. 22.
281, 13: Ibid.
281, 14: Ibid., p. 21.
281, 16: Ibid., p. 24.
281, 22: Ibid., p. 23.
281, 23: Ibid.
281, 32: F. Nietzsche, "Nachgelassene Fragmente 1887–1889," 13:9, fragment 11[1].
282, 4: Ibid., 13:12, fragment 11[10].
282, 5: Ibid., 13:13, fragment 11[10].

282, 8: Ibid., 13:12, fragment 11[10].

282, 11: Ibid., 13:44, fragment 11[24].

282, 22: Ch. Baudelaire, "L'Invitation au voyage," verses 13–14, in *Les Fleurs du mal*, 1:53.

282, 27: T. S. Eliot, *Essays Ancient and Modern*, London: Faber and Faber, 1936, p. 71.

283, 16: Th. Gautier, *Baudelaire*, edited by J.-L. Steinmetz, Le Castor Astral, Pantin, 1991, pp. 45–46.

283, 27: Th. Gautier, *Charles Baudelaire*, p. 241.

284, 8: Ch. Baudelaire, "Notes nouvelles sur Edgar Poe," in Pichois, ed., *Œuvres complètes*, 2:319.

284, 22: M. Nordau, *Entartung*, Berlin: Carl Duncker, 1892, 1:vii.

284, 32: Ibid., 1893, 2:88.

285, 6: Letter from S. Mallarmé to H. Cazalis, dated April 28, 1866, in Marchal, ed., *Œuvres complètes*, 1:697.

285, 16: Letter from Ch. Baudelaire to C. Mendès, dated March 29, 1866, in Pichois, ed., *Correspondance*, 2:630.

285, 20: Ibid.

285, 21: Ch. Baudelaire, "Bien loin d'ici," verse 14, in *Les Fleurs du mal*, 1:145.

285, 29: Letter from Ch. Asselineau to A. Poulet-Malassis, dated September 6 or 7, 1867, in E. Crépet, *Charles Baudelaire*, p. 276.

285, 31: F. Porché, *Baudelaire: Histoire d'une âme*, Paris: Flammarion, 1944, p. 484.

286, 8: Letter from C. Aupick to Ch. Asselineau, dated June 10, 1869, ibid., p. 485.

286, 14: Ch. Baudelaire, "Chant d'automne," verse 7, in *Les Fleurs du mal*, 1:57.

286, 15: Ibid., verse 9.

286, 22: A. France, "Charles Baudelaire," in *La Vie littéraire*, Paris: Calmann-Lévy, 1891, 3:23.

IMAGES

p. 121: Eugène Delacroix, *Study for "The Death of Sardanapalus,"* pastel, lead pencil, sanguine, black pencil, white chalk on beige paper, 1826–1827. Musée National Eugène Delacroix, Paris.

p. 122: Eugène Delacroix, *Study for Sardanapalus,* brown ink, black ink, lead pencil, pen (drawing), watercolor highlights. Musée du Louvre, Paris.

p. 151: *Phanes,* marble statue from the temple of Mithras in Mérida, second century A.D. Museo Nacional de Arte Romano, Mérida.

p. 153: *Agathodaimon,* black granite, third–first century B.C. The Maritime Museum, Alexandria.

p. 159: Édouard Manet, *Music in the Tuileries,* detail, oil on canvas, 1862. National Gallery, London.

p. 165: François Boucher, *Head of Girl with Her Hair Up, Seen from Behind,* red, black, and white chalk on yellow paper, c. 1740–1741. Private collection, Switzerland.

p. 167: Jean-Auguste-Dominique Ingres, *Lady Harriet Mary Montagu and Lady Catherine Caroline Montagu,* pencil on paper, 1815. Private collection.

p. 168: Constantin Guys, *Threshold of a Brothel,* ink and watercolor, c. 1865–1867. Musée Carnavalet, Paris.

p. 169: Constantin Guys, *Study of a Woman Standing,* watercolor, pencil and ink on flimsy paper, c. 1860–1864. Musée Carnavalet, Paris.

p. 176: Edgar Degas, *The Bellelli Family,* oil on canvas, 1858–1869. Musée d'Orsay, Paris.

p. 177: Edgar Degas, *The Bellelli Sisters (Giovanna and Giulia Bellelli),* oil on canvas, 1865–1866. Los Angeles County Museum of Art, Los Angeles.

p. 179: Edgar Degas, *Medieval War Scene,* oil on paper, 1865. Musée d'Orsay, Paris.

p. 180: Jacques-Louis David, *The Death of Joseph Bara,* oil on canvas, 1794. Musée Calvet, Avignon.

p. 183: Edgar Degas, *Portrait of Mlle E.F.: Apropos of the Ballet "La Source,"* oil on canvas, 1867–1868. Brooklyn Museum of Art, New York.

p. 185 (top): Edgar Degas, *Ballerinas* (fan), gouache, oil, pastel on silk, c. 1879. Tacoma Art Museum, Tacoma.

p. 185: Edgar Degas, *Ballerinas and a Stage Set* (fan), gouache with gilded highlights on silk, mounted on paper, c. 1878–1880. Private collection, Switzerland.

p. 186: Edgar Degas, *Ballerinas,* drawing for a fan, gouache (or tempera) with gold and charcoal on silk, c. 1879. Baltimore Museum of Art, Baltimore.

p. 188: Edgar Degas, *Interior (The Rape),* oil on canvas, 1868 or 1869. Philadelphia Museum of Art, Philadelphia.

p. 199: Edgar Degas, *Portrait of Pierre-Auguste Renoir, seated, and Stéphane Mallarmé, standing,* photograph, 1895. Museum of Modern Art, New York.

p. 200: Edgar Degas, *Self-portrait with Bartholomé's "Young Girl Weeping,"* photograph, 1895. Musée d'Orsay, Paris.

p. 205: Édouard Manet, *La Viennese,* pastel on cardboard, c. 1880. Musée du Louvre, Paris.

p. 206: Tintoretto, *Portrait of a Woman Revealing Her Breasts,* oil on canvas, c. 1570. Museo del Prado, Madrid.

p. 207: Édouard Manet, *Blonde Woman with Bare Breasts,* oil on canvas, 1878? Musée d'Orsay, Paris.

p. 212: Édouard Manet, *The Masked Ball at the Opéra*, oil on canvas, 1873–1874. National Gallery of Art, Washington, D.C.

p. 214: Édouard Manet, *The Bar at the Folies-Bergère*, oil on canvas, 1881–1882. Courtauld Institute Galleries, London.

p. 216: Édouard Manet, *Berthe Morisot with a Bouquet of Violets*, oil on canvas, 1872. Musée d'Orsay, Paris.

p. 217: Édouard Manet, *Berthe Morisot with a Fan*, oil on canvas, 1872. Musée d'Orsay, Paris.

p. 220: Édouard Manet, *The Balcony*, oil on canvas, 1868–1869. Musée d'Orsay, Paris.

p. 222: Édouard Manet, *Baudelaire's Mistress*, oil on canvas, 1862. Szépművészeti Múzeum, Budapest.

p. 223: Édouard Manet, *Repose*, oil on canvas, 1870. Museum of Art, Providence, RI.

p. 224 (top): Édouard Manet, *The Bouquet of Violets*, oil on canvas, 1872. Private collection.

p. 224: Édouard Manet, *Berthe Morisot with Fan*, watercolor, 1874. The Art Institute of Chicago, Chicago.

p. 225: Édouard Manet, *Portrait of Berthe Morisot in Mourning with Hat*, oil on canvas, 1874. Private collection, Zürich.

p. 248: Aden, the jetty and the signal station at Steamer Point around 1880. In *Rimbaud à Aden*, photographs by J.-H. Berrou, texts by J.-J. Lefrère and P. Leroy, Paris: Fayard, 2001, p. 24.

ACKNOWLEDGMENTS

Right from the start, this book, as was the case with *Tiepolo Pink*, was accompanied by the illuminating observations of Claudio Rugafiori. Federica Ragni took it from manuscript to proofs. Maddalena Buri contributed to the final touches with an eagle eye. Ena Marchi and Giorgio Pinotti ably checked out the French texts. Paolo Rossetti looked after the various phases of make-up. My gratitude to them all.

INDEX

Page numbers in *italics* refer to illustrations.

A NOTE ABOUT THE AUTHOR

Roberto Calasso, publisher of Adelphi in Milan, is the author of many books, among them *The Ruin of Kasch*, *The Marriage of Cadmus and Harmony*, *Ka*, *K.*, and *Tiepolo Pink*, all parts of a work in progress of which *La Folie Baudelaire* is the sixth panel.